PATRICIA ROBERTS STYLE

PHOTOGRAPHS BY JAMES WEDGE

W H ALLEN

PLANET

Copyright © 1988 by Patricia Roberts

First published in 1988 by Planet Books, a division of W.H. Allen & Co. Plc.

Printed and bound in Singapore
for the publishers W. H. Allen & Co. Plc,
44 Hill Street, London W1X 8LB.

ISBN 1-85227-075-6

Sections of this work have appeared previously in other forms.

Acknowledgements

Photographs: James Wedge

Stylist: Caroline Baker

Illustrator: Connie Jude

Cover design: Osborn & Stephens

British Library Cataloguing in Publication Data
Roberts, Patricia
    Patricia Roberts style: design-award
    knitting
    1. Knitting — Patterns
    I. Title
    476.43'2041   TT820

    ISBN 1-85227-075-6

CONTENTS

PATRICIA ROBERTS

Patricia Roberts Sweaters are collectors' items, prized not only by enthusiastic knitters but also by textile museums such as London's Victoria and Albert Museum. Their unique stitchcraft and fashionable styling, combined with inventive colouring, make it easy to understand why these designs sell in the most exclusive stores.

The sweaters can be bought ready-made or you can knit them yourself. Using the *Patricia Roberts* brand of hand knitting yarn. These yarns are spun from the highest quality natural fibres in exciting colours and the range includes pure cashmere, angora and wonderful chunky Shetland Tweeds or, for summer, beautiful cottons and chenilles. The yarns are available through a world-wide mail order service. If you would like further details of this write to one of the addresses opposite or visit one of the *Patricia Roberts Shops*. In Covent Garden you will be dazzled by the array of colours set off against the bright modern interior. Here you can buy the garments ready-made or choose your own colours to knit the design yourself. If you like a quiet browse, go to the original yarn shop at 60, Kinnerton Street, which has its own calm, old-world charm. For style, Patricia Roberts latest shop in the fashionable Brompton Road, offers you her latest designs, teamed with some of the best European Designer labels.

If you have any queries concerning the knitting patterns or would like a mail order price list for the yarns or knitting kits; please write , enclosing a stamped self-addressed envelope, to one fo the following Patricia Roberts Shops:

Mail-order Yarn Enquiries:
60, Kinnerton Street, London S.W.1.
31, James Street, Covent Garden, London W.C.2.

Made-up Sweaters:
236, Brompton Road, London S.W.3.
31, James Street, Covent Garden, London W.C.2.

Over the past decade or so, Patricia Roberts has changed the face of hand knitting, transforming it from cheap utility clothing into high fashion. Realising the fashion potential of hand knitting, on graduating from Art College she gained practical experience working for a group of women's magazines. Her first designs appeared in young fashion magazines of the day, such as *19* and *Honey*. In those early days, she was invited by the Shetland Education Authorities to teach knitwear design to the Shetlanders, but in return she herself learnt so much about thier traditional skills, that these have influenced her work ever since. When a freelance career became viable, Patricia set up her own knitwear design studio. Her ready-made hand knits were an immediate success with buyers from London boutiques and stores in the USA and since then she has designed two collections each year of her couture hand knits to exhibit at international designer shows in London, Paris and Milan.

In the mid-seventies her first pattern book was published. Entitled *20 Patricia Roberts' Knitting Patterns* (Queen Anne Press, 1975), its publication caused quite a shock to the then old-fashioned image of hand knitting. At the same time she introduced a selection of knitting kits containing patterns and special yarns. A whole series of stylish pattern books followed. Of particular note are *Patricia Roberts' Knitting* Book (W.H. Allen, 1981), *Patricia Roberts' Second Knitting* Book (W.H. Allen, 1983), and *Patricia Roberts' Collection* (W.H. Allen, 1985).

1976 saw the opening of the first Patricia Roberts' shop in London. There are now three shops in London, as well as franchise shops in other countries. The Covent Garden shop with its clean modern design philosophy is the model upon which the franchise shops are based. Design is all important – even the carrier bags have attained cult status.

In recognition of her outstanding achievements as a designer, Patricia Roberts' was awarded the 1986 *Duke of Edinburgh Design Award*. This, the supreme accolade for design in British industry, is all the more notable since it has never before been awarded to a fashion designer. This book includeds many of the designs for which the prize was awarded.

HOW TO KNIT

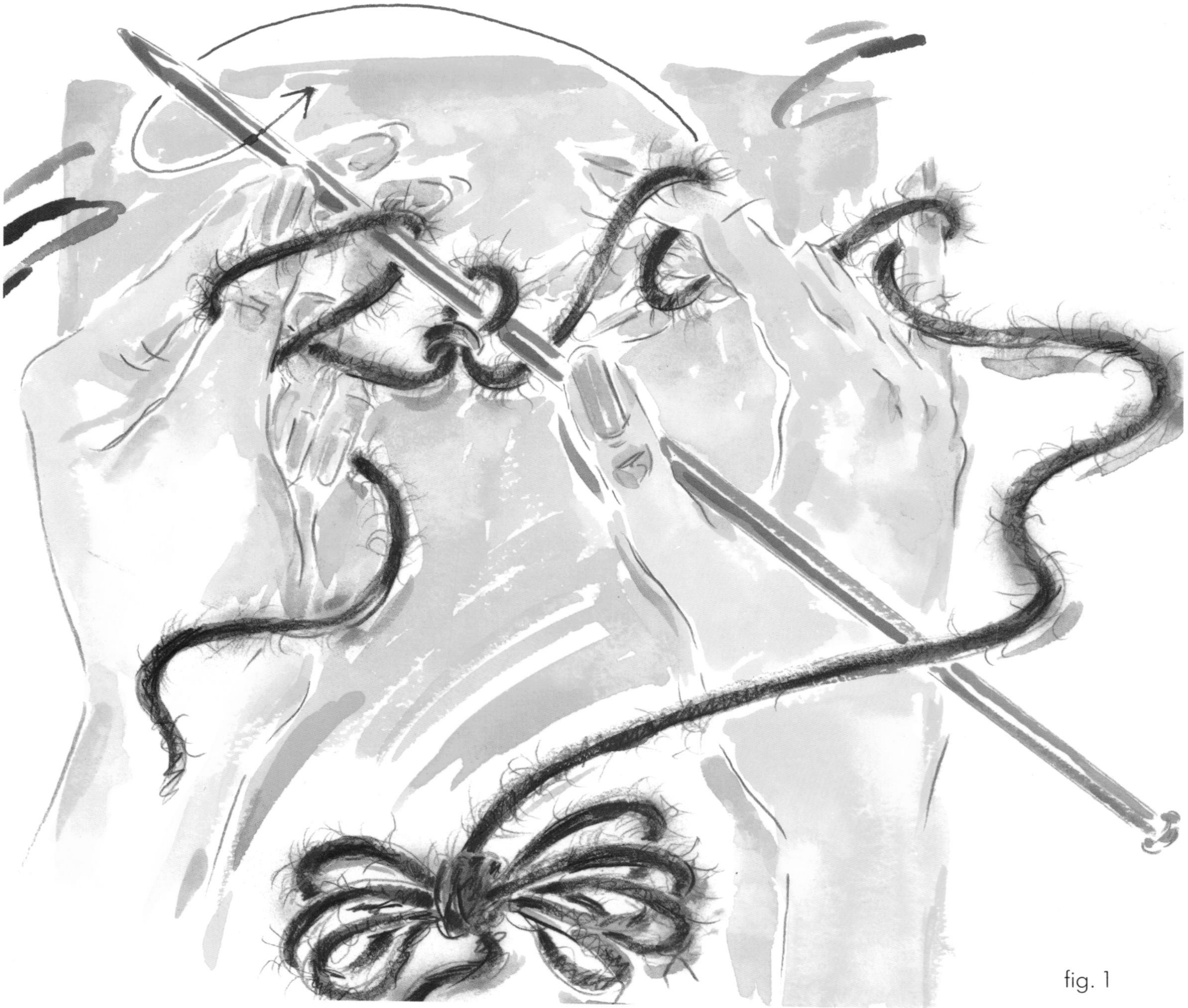

fig. 1

CASTING ON This is the first process in knitting and forms the first row of stitches. There are several methods of casting on.

SLIP KNOT For any of the methods used at the start of the work, first make a slip knot (figs 2 and 3). Make a loop, insert needle and draw a loop through, pulling yarn firmly to tighten the knot.

THUMB METHOD This is the best method to use at the start of the work. The edge formed by this method is both firm and elastic. Leaving a sufficiently long end of yarn – about 1 metre for the back of a sweater – make a slip-knot. With the needle holding the slip-knot in the right hand, place the yarn from the ball around the fingers (fig. 1). Now take the loose end in the left hand and form a loop on the left thumb. Insert the point of the needle into the loop on the thumb. Wrap the yarn around the point of the needle. With the needle draw the loop through the one on the thumb, to make a stitch. At the same time slip the loop from the thumb and pull the yarn in the left hand firmly. Repeat this action for the required number of stitches (fig. 1).

THROUGH STITCH-METHOD This cast-on method is usually used for casting on groups of stitches once work has commenced, such as at the beginning of a row. Insert the point of the right-hand needle into the front of the first stitch on the left-hand needle. With the right hand, wrap the yarn around the point of the right-hand needle. Draw the loop through the stitch on the left-hand needle and slip it onto the left-hand needle. Work into the stitch just made to form the next stitch and so on until the required number of stitches has been cast on (figs 4 and 5).

BETWEEN STITCH METHOD This forms a strong decorative cast-on edge, particularly suited to ribbed bands, ribbed sock tops and buttonholes. At the start of the work, make a slip-knot, slip it onto the left-hand needle and work 1 stitch by the through stitch method. Insert the point of the right-hand needle between the 2 stitches. With the right hand, wrap the yarn round the point of the right-hand needle and draw the loop through to form a stitch. Slip it onto the left-hand needle (figs 6 and 7).

fig. 2

fig. 3

fig. 4

fig. 5

fig. 6

fig. 7

fig. 8

fig. 9

KNIT STITCHES This is the stitch, upon which the principle of knitting is based. It is always worked with the yarn to the back of the work. With the needle containing the stitches in the left hand, insert the point of the right-hand needle into the front of the first stitch on the left-hand needle. The point of the right-hand needle will now pass towards the back of the work, beneath the left-hand needle. With the right hand, wrap the yarn round the point of the right-hand needle. With this needle draw the loop through the stitch, dropping the stitch off the left-hand needle at the same time (figs 8, 9 and 10).

PURL STITCHES With the yarn to the front of the work, insert the right-hand needle into the front of the first stitch on the left-hand needle, so that the point of the right-hand needle passes towards the front of the work, beneath the left-hand needle. With the right hand, wrap the yarn round the point of the right-hand needle. With this needle, draw the loop through the stitch on the left-hand needle, dropping the loop from the left-hand needle at the same time (figs 11 and 12).

fig. 10

fig. 11

fig. 12

fig. 13

fig. 14

fig. 15

INCREASE This is worked by knitting or purling into the back and the front of the same stitch as follows. Insert the right-hand needle into the back of the first stitch on the left-hand needle, wrap the yarn round the point of the right-hand needle and draw the loop through, then insert the needle into the front of the same stitch, wrap the yarn round the point of the right-hand needle and draw the loop through, dropping the stitch from the left-hand needle in the usual way (figs 13 and 14).

UP ONE This form of increase is usually worked when increasing across the work. Pick up the loop lying between the needles, slip it onto the left-hand needle and knit into the *back* of this loop in the usual way (fig. 15).

DECREASE This is worked by knitting or purling 2 stitches together as follows. Insert the point of the right-hand needle through the front of the first 2 sts. on the left-hand needle. Wrap the yarn round the point of the right-hand needle and draw 1 stitch through, dropping the 2 stitches from the right-hand needled (figs 16 and 17).

fig. 16

fig. 17

fig. 18

fig. 19

CASTING OFF This is used to finish a piece of knitting. Knit or purl 2 stitches. Then slip the point of the left-hand needle into the second stitch on the right-hand needle (the first stitch knitted) and pass this stitch over the first stitch on the right-hand needle. Knit or purl the next stitch on the left-hand needle and pass the second stitch on the right-hand needle over the stitch as before. Repeat this action until 1 stitch remains. Break off yarn. Thread the end of the yarn through the remaining stitch, draw up and fasten off. Care should be taken not to cast off too tightly (fig. 18).

CABLES Cables are easy to work. The principle of cabling is to place a number of stitches on a cable needle at the back or the front of the work, then to work the next group of stitches before working those from cable needle. For example, cable 4 front is worked as follows: slip the next 2 stitches onto a cable needle at the front of the work, knit 2 stitches, then knit the 2 stitches from the cable needle. Details of how to work the cables in a knitting pattern are usually given in the abbreviations column (fig. 19).

COLOUR MOTIFS Use separate small balls of the different colours for each section of a motif, so that the colours not in use are not taken across the back of the work. Where two colours join, twist the two around each other on the wrong side of the work to avoid holes appearing between the colours (fig. 20).

PICKING UP STITCHES This technique is used mainly for neckbands. With the right side of the work facing, rejoin the yarn to the work. Using one knitting needle, held in the right hand, insert the point of the needle into the appropriate edge, wrap the yarn round the needle and draw the loop through (fig. 21).

MAKING UP Follow the instructions given in the knitting pattern for which pieces to sew together.

PRESSING Hand knits usually rely on their textured stitches for effect and rarely need pressing. If, however, they do require pressing this should usually be done by placing a damp cloth over the garment pressing the garment lightly with an up-and-down movement rather than a side-to-side one. Always check the information on the yarn labels before ironing.

fig. 20

fig. 21

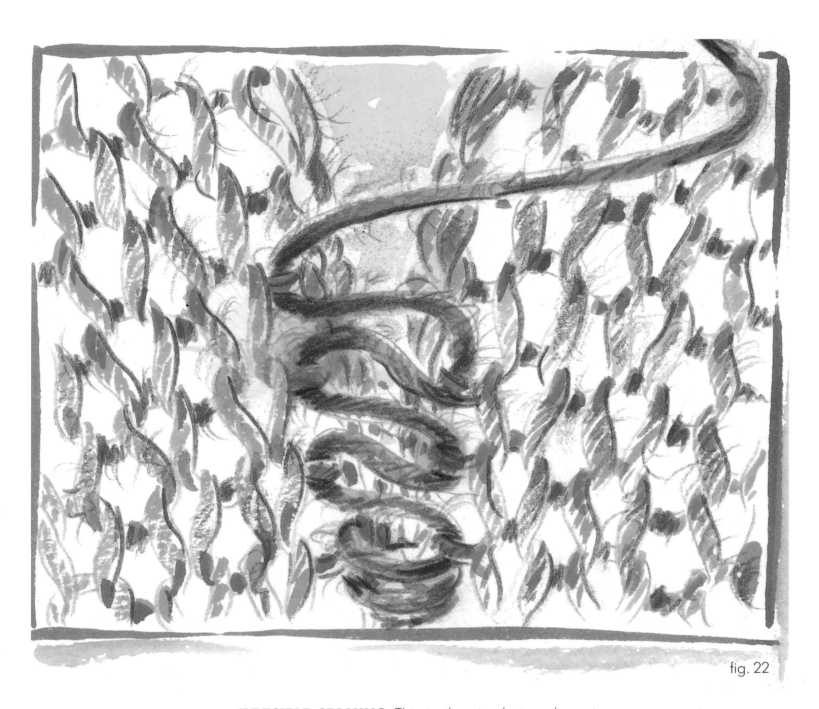

fig. 22

INVISIBLE SEAMING This is the simplest and most successful seaming method and has been used in the Shetland Islands for generations. It is worked with a bodkin a thick blunt-pointed needle made specially for making up knitwear. Place the first finger of the left hand between the two pieces of knitting to be joined, holding them edge to edge, with the right side of the work facing. Secure the thread at one edge, making sure that the bodkin is on the right side of the work. Taking the bodkin to the second edge, insert it under the thread which lies between the first and second stitches and draw the thread through. Take the needle back to the first edge, and insert it under the thread between the first and second stitches and draw the thread through. Take the yarn back to the second edge, inserting the bodkin under the thread above the one worked previously and draw the thread through. Return to the first edge and work in the same way. Continue until the seam is complete. It is not always necessary to use pins when working seams in this way as the number of rows on straight edges will match.

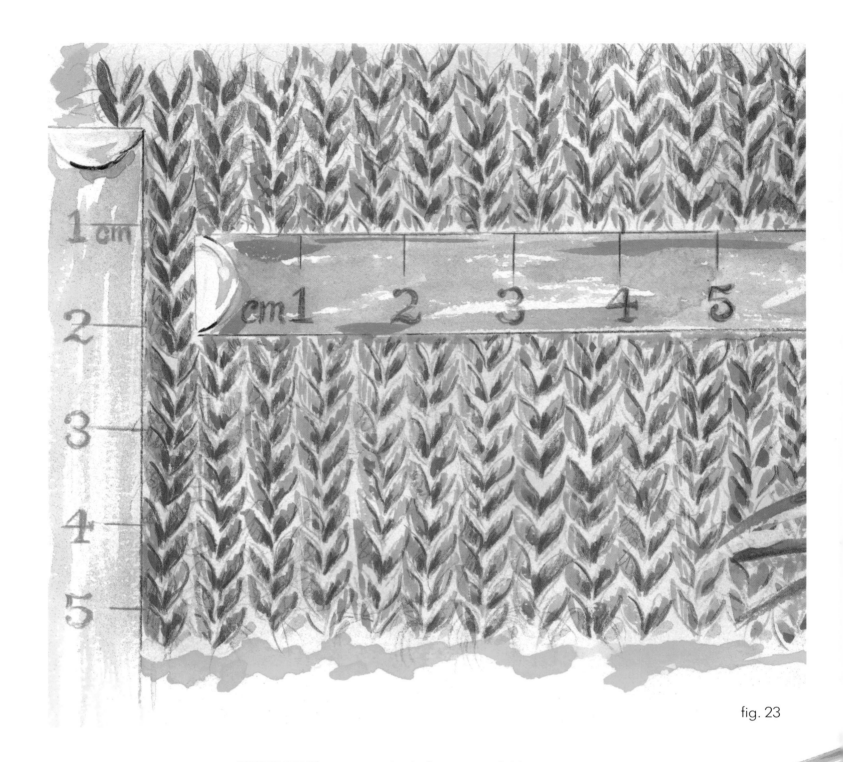

fig. 23

TENSION The essential rule for successful knitting is to work at the correct tension. This is given at the beginning of each knitting pattern. Every knitter's tension varies slightly; which is the reason it is so important to check your tension before commencing work. To do this, knit a small test piece in the pattern, over which the tension is given and using the size needles recommended. Measure the number of stitches and rows to the number of centimetres (inches) stated in the pattern. If your tension is too tight – too many stitches and rows to the measure – test it again using a size larger needles. If it is still too tight, test it yet again using even larger needles and so on until your tension is correct. If your tension is too loose – too few stitches and rows to the measure – test your tension again with smaller needles until it is correct. Only a garment knitted at the correct tension will have the measurements given in the knitting pattern (fig. 23).

WASHING There is no mystique about washing hand-knits. Just wash them by hand, making sure that the temperature of the water does not exceed that recommended on the yarn label. For the best result, spin without heat in a spin dryer or in the spin-only programme of a washing machine. If you do not have access to these machines, firmly roll the garment in a towel. Having removed the excess moisture by one of these methods, the garment will dry quickly. To dry, lay the garment flat on a towel away from direct heat or sunlight.

DRY CLEANING Most hand-knitting yarns are suitable for washing by hand. However certain yarns, such as silk, must be dry cleaned. Always check the yarn labels for details.

YARN Always use the yarn recommended in the knitting pattern. Different brands of yarn vary in thickness. This makes it difficult to obtain the correct tension and affects the amount of yarn required. Inferior yarns will produce inferior garments, regardless of the merits of the design. Natural fibre yarns are the most suitable for hand knitting.

ABBREVIATIONS At the beginning of each set of instructions there is a list of abbreviations for that particular pattern. Never assume that you understand how to work an abbreviation without first reading its explanation. There are many different ways to work certain stitches and therefore the explanations of how to work them will vary from pattern to pattern.

NEEDLE SIZES

Metric	U.S.A.	U.K. (old)	Metric	U.S.A.	U.K. (old)
2mm	0	14	5mm	8	6
2¼mm	1	13	5½mm	9	5
2¾mm	2	12	6mm	10	4
3mm		11	6½mm	10½	3
3¼mm	3	10	7mm		2
3½mm	4		7½mm		1
3¾mm	5	9	8mm	11	0
4mm	6	8	9mm	13	00
4½mm	7	7	10mm	15	000

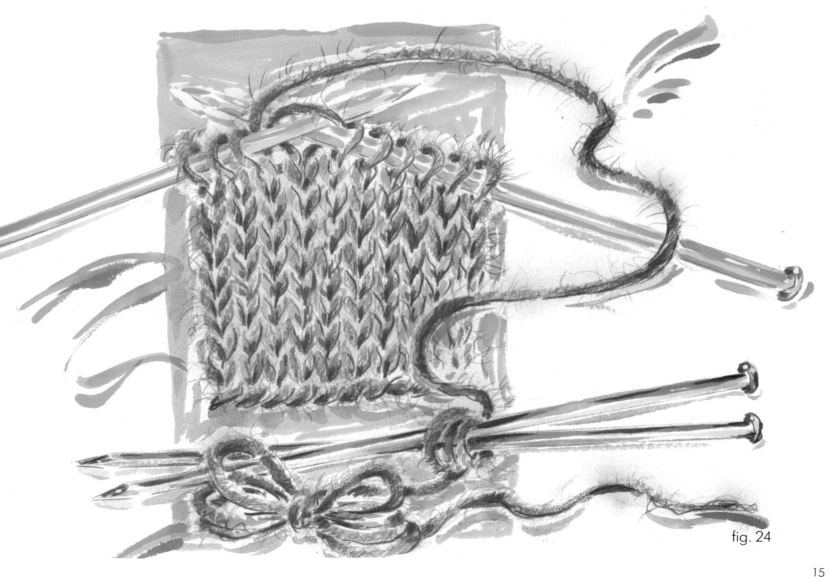

fig. 24

"Violet" chenille
cardigan and sweater,
worn with Georgina
von Etzdorf chiffons.

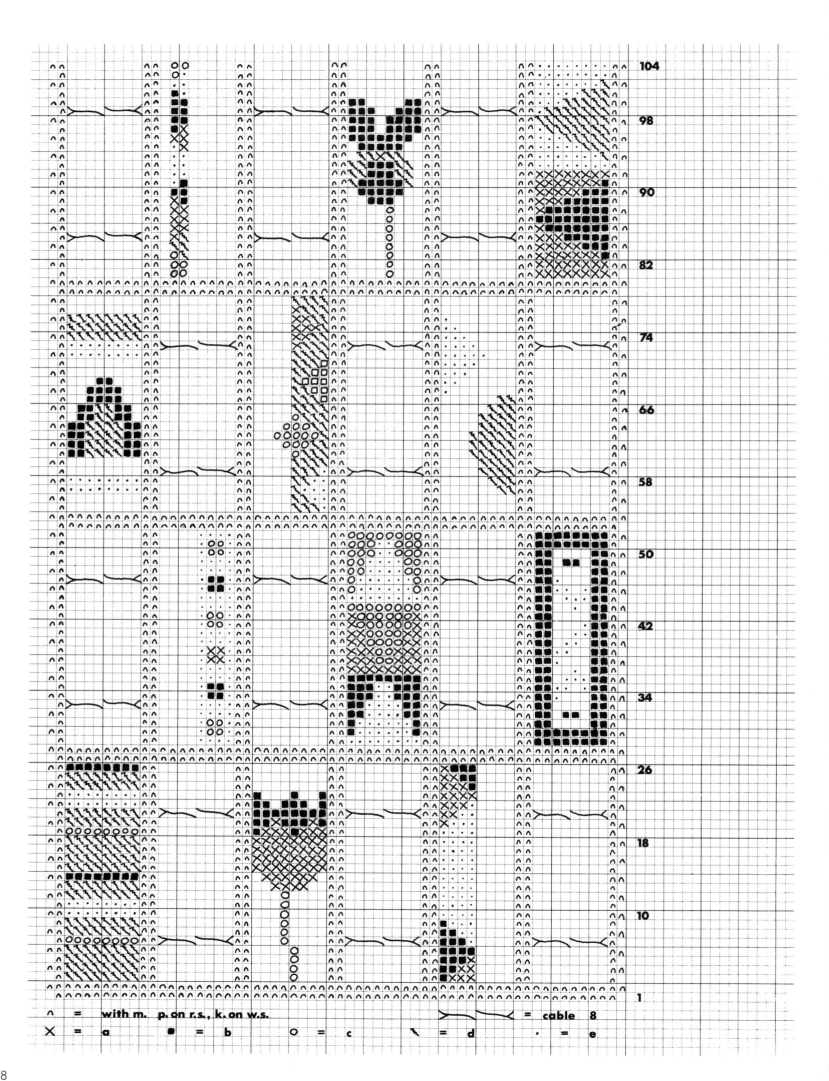

104

98

90

82

74

66

58

50

42

34

26

18

10

1

∩ = with m. p. on r.s., k. on w.s.   ⊃⊂ = cable 8

X = a   ■ = b   O = c   ⟍ = d   • = e

MATERIALS For either the cardigan or the sweater: 13 50 gram balls of "Patricia Roberts Chenille" in main colour 2 balls in contrasts b. and e. and 1 ball in each of contrasts a., c. and d● A pair each of size 2¾mm and 3¼mm Aero knitting needles, a medium sized cable needle●

TENSION 20 stitches – 1 repeat of the cable pattern to 9 centimetres (3½ inches) in width and 52 rows – 1 repeat of the 52 row cable pattern to 16 centimetres (6¼ inches) in depth, using size 3¼mm needles●

If you cannot obtain the correct tension using the size needles suggested, use larger or smaller ones accordingly●

ABBREVIATIONS K., knit● p., purl● st., stitch● tog., together● inc., increase (by working twice into same st.)● single rib is k.1 and p.1 alternately● cable 8, thus slip next 4 sts. onto cable needle at front of work, k.4., then k.4 from cable needle● garter stitch is k. plain on every row● m., main colour● a., first contrast● b., second contrast● c., third contrast● d., fourth contrast● e., fifth contrast● r.s., right side● w.s., wrong side●

MEASUREMENTS The measurements are given in centimetres followed by inches in brackets. The measurements for the cardigan and the sweater are alike●
Underarms 117 (45½)● Side seam 35 (13½)● Length 59 (23)● Sleeve seam 42.5 (16¾)●

NOTE Instructions in brackets are worked the number of times stated after the brackets●

CARDIGAN

BACK With size 2¾mm needles and m. loosely cast on 90 sts. and work 27 rows in single rib.

Now increase and divide the sts. for easier working as follows: Next row: (Inc., p.1) 20 times, inc. and leave these 62 sts. on a spare needle, until required for left half back, (inc., p.1) 4 times and leave these 12 sts. on a stitch-holder until required for centre panel, inc., (p.1, inc.) 20 times and continue on these 62 sts. for the right half back.

Right half back: Change to size 3¼mm needles and work in pattern as follows: Use separate small balls of colour for each motif, so that colours not in use are not taken across the back of the work.

1st row: With m. k.1, p. until 1 remains, k.1.
2nd row: With m. all k.
3rd row: With m. k.1, p.1, k.8, p.2, k.4, with a. k.3, with b. k.1, with m. p.2, k.8, p.2, k.3, with c. k.1, with m. k.4, p.2, k.8, p.2, with d. k.8, with m. p.1, k.1.
4th row: With m. k.2, with d. p.8, with m. k.2, p.8, k.2, p.4, with c. p.1, with m. p.3, k.2, p.8, k.2, with b. p.2, with a. p.2, with m. p.4, k.2, p.8, k.2.

The last 2 rows set the position of the pattern given in the chart. Work the 5th to 80th rows from the chart.

To shape the armholes: Continuing in pattern from chart as set, cast off 4 sts. at the beginning of the next row, then dec. 1 st. at the same edge on the 6 following alternate rows. –52 sts.

Work the 94th to 104th rows from the chart.***

Work the first 46 rows again.

To slope the shoulder: Cast off 9 sts. at the beginning of the next row and the 2 following alternate rows, then 8 sts. on the following alternate row. Work 1 row.

Cast off the remaining 17 sts.

Left half back: With right side of work facing, rejoin yarn to inner edge of 62 sts. left on spare needle and, using size 3¼mm needles, beginning with the 53rd pattern row, continue as follows:
53rd row: With m. k.1, p. until 1 remains, k.1

54th row: With m. all k.
55th row: With m. k.1, p.1, (k.8, p.2) 3 times, with e. k.1, with d. k.3, with m. k.4, (p.2, k.8) twice, p.1, k.1.
56th row: With m. k.2, (p.8, k.2) twice, p.4, with d. p.2, with e. p.2, with m. k.2, (p.8, k.2) 3 times.

The last 4 rows set the position of the pattern given in the chart. Now work the 57th to 104th rows, then the 1st to 29th rows.

To shape the armholes: Continuing in pattern from chart, cast off 4 sts. at the beginning of the next row, then dec. 1 st. at the beginning – same edge on the 6 following alternate rows.

On 52 sts. work the 43rd to 99th rows.

To slope the shoulder: Work as given for the right half back shoulder shaping to end.

Centre panel: With right side of work facing rejoin yarn to 12 sts. at centre back.

With size 3¼mm needles p.1 row and k. 1 row, then continue as follows:
1st row: k.1, p.1, k.8, p.1, k.1.
2nd row: k.2, p.8, k.2.
3rd and **4**th rows: As 1st and 2nd rows.
5th row: k.1, p.1, cable 8, p.1, k.1.
6th row: As 2nd row.
7th to **18**th rows: Repeat 1st and 2nd rows 6 times.
19th and **20**th rows: As 5th and 6th rows.
21st to **26**th rows: Repeat 1st and 2nd rows 3 times.

Repeat these 26 rows 4 times more, then work the first 24 rows again.

P.1 row and k.1 row, then cast off.

LEFT FRONT With size 2¾mm needles and m. cast on 41 sts. and work 27 rows in single rib.

Increase row: (Inc., p.1) 20 times, inc. – 62 sts.

Change to size 3¼mm needles and work as given for right half back until 68 rows have been worked in pattern.

**To slope the front edge; Continuing in pattern as set, dec. 1 st. at the end – front edge – on the next row and the 2 following 4th rows.

On 59 sts. work 3 rows.

To shape the armhole and continue to slope the front edge: While decreasing 1 st. at the front edge on every 4th row as before, cast off 4 sts. at the beginning of the next row then dec. 1 st. at the armhole edge on the 6 following alternate rows.

On 45 sts. pattern 3 rows.

To slope the front edge only: Dec. 1 st. at the end – front edge – on the next row and the 9 following 4th. rows.

On 35 sts. pattern 17 rows, marking the front edge with a coloured thread at the beginning of the last row.

To slope the shoulder: Cast off 9 sts. at the beginning of the next row and the 2 following alternate rows. On 8 sts. work 1 row, then cast off.

Left frontband and collar: With size 2¾mm needles and m. cast on 8 sts. and work 84 rows in single rib.

*Continuing in rib, inc. 1 st. at the beginning of the next row and the 16 following 4th rows.

On 25 sts. rib 3 rows.

Mark the end of the last row with a coloured thread.

Cast on 23 sts. at the beginning – shaped edge – of the next row.

On 48 sts. rib 11 rows, then cast off in rib.

RIGHT FRONT Front as given for left front until the increase row has been worked.

Change to size 3¼mm needles and work in pattern as given for left half back until 69 rows have been worked.

Now work as given for left front from ** to end.

Right frontband and collar: With size 2¾mm needles and m. cast on 8 sts. and work 4 rows in single rib.

1st Buttonhole row: Rib 3, cast off 2, rib to end.

2nd Buttonhole row: Rib 3, turn, cast on 2 over those cast off, turn rib to end.

Rib 24 rows.

Repeat the last 26 rows twice more, then work the 2 buttonhole rows again.

Rib 1 row, then work as given for left front band and collar from * to end.

SLEEVES Both alike: with size 2¾mm needles and m. cast on 41 sts. and work 27 rows in single rib.

Increase row: (Inc., p.1) 20 times, inc. – 62 sts.

Change to size 3¼mm needles and work 26 rows in pattern as given for right half back.

Continuing in pattern and working the extra sts. in garter st. as they occur, inc. 1 st. at each end of the next row and the 9 following 8th. rows.

On 82 sts. pattern 7 rows.

To shape the sleevetop: Cast off 4 sts. at the beginning of the next 2 rows. Then dec. 1 st. at each end of the next row and the 18 following alternate rows.

On 36 sts. work 1 row.

Cast off 3 sts. at the beginning of the next 4 rows, then 4 sts. at the beginning of the 4 following rows.

Cast off the remaining 8 sts.

MAKING UP Do not press. Join shoulder seams. Set in sleeves. Join sleeve and side seams. Join the 12 row end edges at the top of half collars. Matching the coloured threads on front edges with those on collar, neatly sew shaped edges of frontbands and collar in place, so that the first increases on frontbands are in line with the first front edge decreases. Sew on buttons.

SWEATER

BACK As given for cardigan.

FRONT Work as given for back until *** is reached on right half back. this will now be the left half front.

Left half front: On 52 sts. pattern 27 rows.

To shape the neck: Cast off 7 sts. at the beginning of the next row, then dec. 1 st. at the neck edge on each of the next 10 rows.

On 35 sts. pattern 8 rows.

To slope the shoulder: Cast off 9 sts. at the beginning of the next row and the 2 following alternate rows. On 8 sts. work 1 row, then cast off.

Right half front: With right side of work facing rejoin yarn to inner edge of the 62 sts. left on spare needle and using size 3¼mm needles work as given for left half back until the armhole shaping has been worked.

Pattern 38 rows.

To shape the neck: Work as given for left half front neck shaping to end.

Centre panel: Work as given for centre panel on back until the 26 cable rows have been worked 4 times, then work the first 24 rows again. P.1. row, then cast off.

Neckband: First sew cable panels at centre back and centre front in place, then join right shoulder seam.

Now with right side of work facing rejoin m. at left front shoulder and using size 2¾mm needles, pick up and k. 24 sts. from left front neck edge, 10 sts. from centre panel, 24 sts. from right front neck edge and 28 sts. from back neck edge.

On 86 sts. work 5 rows in single rib, then cast off loosely in rib.

SLEEVES Both alike: As given for cardigan.

MAKING UP Do not press. Join left shoulder seam. Set in sleeves. Join sleeve and side seams. ●

"Alice" cotton sweaters. The colour details are worked in chenille. Note that the pink sweater has ribbing and the white sweater is loose at the waist.

ALICE

PINK SWEATER

MATERIALS 14 25 gram balls of "Patricia Roberts Fine Cotton" in main colour and one ball in contrast colour e., plus 2 50 gram balls of "Patricia Roberts Chenille" in contrasts a., and b., and 1 ball in contrasts c., and d. ● A pair each of size 2¼mm and 2¾mm Aero knitting needles●

TENSION 16 stitches and 20 rows to 5 centimetres (2 inches) over the basket stitch using size 2¾mm needles●
If you cannot obtain the correct tension using the size needles suggested, use larger or smaller ones accordingly●

ABBREVIATIONS K., knit● p., purl● st., stitch● tog., together● dec., decrease by working 2 sts. tog.● inc., increase (by working twice into same st.)● k.1 or p.1b., k. or p.1 through back of stitch● twisted rib is k.1b. and p.1b alternately● m.k., make knot thus, on right side row k.1, slip st. just made onto left hand needle and p. this st., on wrong side rows, p.1. then slip this st. onto left hand needle and k. this st● up1, pick up the loop, which lies between the needles, slip it onto left hand needle and k. into back of it● m., main colour● a., first contrast● b., second contrast● c., third contrast● d., fourth contrast● e., fifth contrast – cotton●

MEASUREMENTS The measurements are given in centimetres followed by inches in brackets.
Underarms 97.5 (39)● Side seam 31 (12½)● Length 51 (20½)● Sleeve seam 13.5 (5½)●
NOTE Instructions in brackets are worked the number of times stated after the brackets●

BACK With size 2¼mm needles and m. cast on 138 sts. and work 35 rows in twisted rib.
Increase row: Rib 3, * up1, rib 7; repeat from * ending last repeat rib 2. – 158 sts.
Change to size 2¾mm needles and work in pattern as follows: Use separate small balls of contrast colours for each section of the motifs so that colours not in use are not taken across the back of the work.
1st. row: With m. k.1, * p.3, k.3; repeat from * ending last repeat k.1 more.
2nd. row: With m. k.1, * p.3, k.3; repeat from * ending last repeat k.1. more.
3rd. and **4**th. rows: As 1st. and 2nd. rows.
5th. row: With m. k.4, (p.3,k.3) 3 times, p.3, k.1, * with d. k.1, with m. k.1, (p.3.k.3) 6 times, p.1; repeat from * ending last repeat (p.3, k.3) twice; k.1 more.
Work the **6**th. to **20**th. rows from the chart.
21st. row: With m. k.1, work 19 sts. in basket st., * with a. m. k, with m. basket st. 43, with b. k.1, with m. basket st. 33; repeat from * ending last repeat basket st. 14, k.1 more.
The last 21 rows set the position of the pattern given in the chart. Work the 22nd. to 88th. rows from the chart, then work the first 8 rows again.
To shape the armholes: Continuing in pattern as set, cast off 3 sts. at the beginning of the next 2 rows, then dec. 1 st. at each end of the next row and 3 following alternate rows.
On 144 sts. pattern 63 rows.
To slope the shoulders: Cast off 10 sts. at the beginning of the next 6 rows then 12 sts. on the 2 following rows. – 60 sts.
Change to size 2¼mm needles and with m. work 12 rows in twisted rib. With b. k.1 row, then cast off loosely.

FRONT Work as given for back until the armhole shaping has been worked.
On 144 sts. pattern 38 rows.
Now divide the sts. for the neck: Next row: Pattern 62 and leave these sts. on a spare needle until required for right front shoulder, cast off 20 marking the centre of these sts. with a coloured thread, pattern to end and continue on these 62 sts. for the left front shoulder.

Left front shoulder: To shape the neck: Dec. 1 st. at the neck edge on each of the next 20 rows.
On 42 sts. pattern 4 rows.
To slope the shoulder: Cast off 10 sts. at the beginning of the next row and the 2 following alternate rows. On 12 sts. work 1 row, then cast off.
Right front shoulder: With right side of work facing, rejoin yarn to inner edge of sts., left on spare needle and work to end of row, then work as given for left front shoulder to end.
Front neckband: Left half: With right side of work facing rejoin m. and using size 2¼mm needles pick up and k. 34 sts. from left front neck edge, then 10 sts. up to marking thread.
On 44 sts. work 11 rows in twisted rib. Break off m., with b. k.1 row, then cast off k. wise loosely.
Right half: With right side of work facing rejoin m. at marking thread at centre front neck and using size 2¼mm needles pick up and k. 10 sts. from those cast off at centre and 34 sts. from right front neck edge.
On 44 sts. work as given for left front neckband.

SLEEVES Both alike: With size 2¼mm needles and m. cast on 80 sts. and work 23 rows in twisted rib.
Increase row: Rib 2, * up1, rib 2; repeat from * to end. – 119 sts.
Change to size 2¾mm needles and work as follows:
13th. row: With m. k.4, p.3, k.3, p.3, k.2, with d. k.1, with m. (p.3, k.3) 6 times, p.2, with d. k.1, with m. (k.3, p.3) 6 times, k.2, with d. k.1, with m. (p.3, k.3) 4 times, k.1.
14th. row to **20**th. rows: Work from chart as set.
21st. row: With m. k.1, basket st. 19, with a. m.k., with m. basket st. 43, with b. k.1, with m. basket st. 33, with a. m.k., with m. basket st. 19, k.1.
22nd. row: Work from chart as set.
Continuing in pattern from chart as set and working the extra sts. into the pattern as they occur, inc. 1 st. at each end of the next row and the 5 following 4th. rows.
On 131 sts. work 3 rows.
To shape the sleevetop: Cast off 3 sts. at the beginning of the next 2 rows, then dec. 1 st. at each end of the next 40 rows. – 45 sts.
Cast off 4 sts. at the beginning of the next 4 rows, 5 sts. on the 2 following rows and 6 sts. on the next 2 rows. Cast off the remaining 7 sts.

MAKING UP Do not press. Join shoulder seams. Set in sleeves. Join sleeve and side seams.●

WHITE SWEATER

MATERIALS As for main pattern but allow 13 balls of "Patricia Roberts Fine Cotton" in main colour.
TENSION and **ABBREVIATIONS** As for main pattern.
MEASUREMENTS Given in centimetres and inches.
Underarms 97.5 (39)● Side seam 25 (10)● Length 45 (18)● Sleeve seam 15 (6)●
BACK With size 2¾mm needles and m. cast on 158 sts. and work as follows: **1**st. row: With m. k.1, * k.3, p.3; repeat from * until 1 remains, k.1.
2nd. row: K.1, * k.3, p.3; repeat from * until 1 remains, k.1.
3rd. to **6**th. rows: Repeat the 1st. and 2nd. rows twice.
Now beginning with the first pattern row given in chart, work as given for main pattern to end.

FRONT Work as given for back until the armhole shaping has been worked, then work as given for front of main pattern to end.
SLEEVES As for main pattern.
MAKING UP As for main pattern.

22

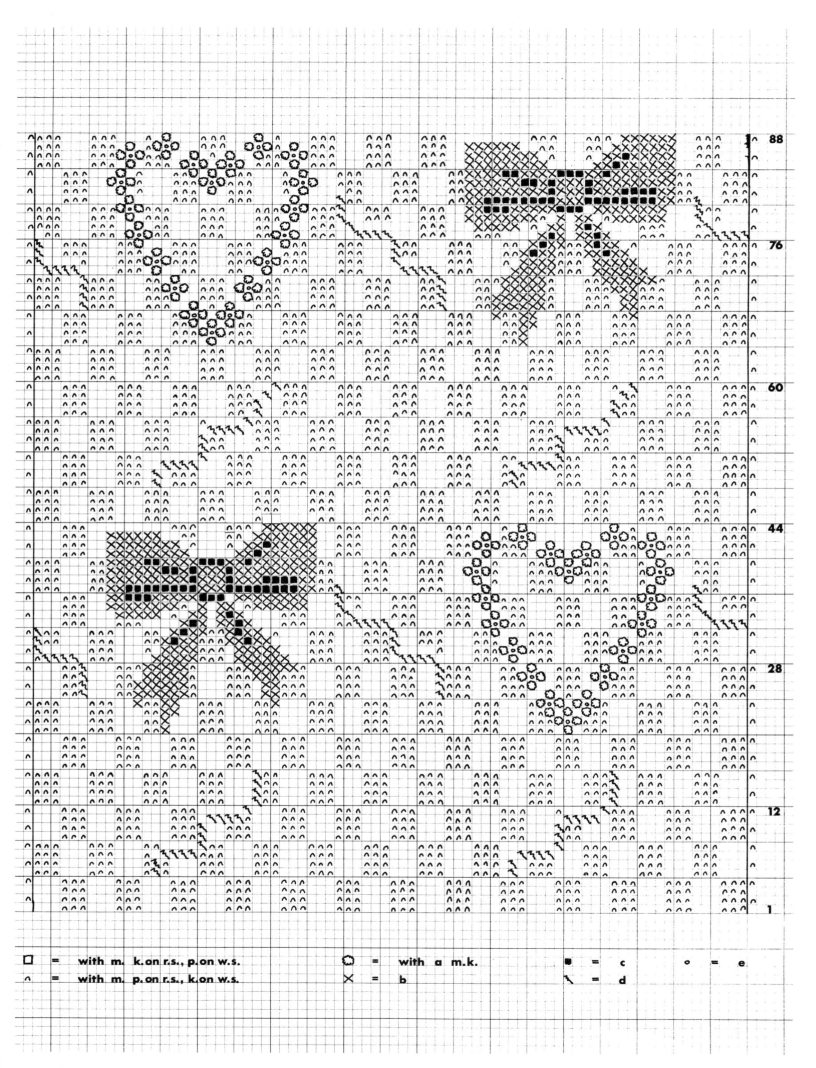

88

76

60

44

28

12

1

□ = with m. k.on r.s., p.on w.s.   ◯ = with a m.k.   ■ = c   o = e
∧ = with m. p.on r.s., k.on w.s.   ✕ = b   ⟍ = d

"Zelda" subtly depicts roses and bows in fine cotton lace.

Left: "Grace" knitted in
the longer length.
Right: "Mikado",
knitted in cotton with
short sleeves.

MATERIALS 22 25 gram balls of "Patricia Roberts Fine Cotton" ● a pair each of size 2¼mm and 2¾mm Aero knitting needles and a fine cable needle ●

TENSION 14 stitches and 24 rows to 5 centimetres (2 inches) over the lace pattern using size 2¾mm needles ●
If you cannot obtain the correct tension using the size needles suggested, use larger or smaller ones accordingly ●

ABBREVIATIONS K., knit ● p., purl ● st., stitch ● tog., together ● dec., decrease (by working 2 sts. tog.) ● inc. increase (by working twice into same st.) ● sl., slip ● p.s.s.o., pass sl. st. over ● y.r.n., yarn round needle ● r.s., right side ● w.s., wrong side ● s.s.k., sl.1, k.1, p.s.s.o. ● p.2tog.b., p.2tog. through back of sts. ● 3 from 1, k.1, y.r.n., k.1 all into 1 stitch ● 6 onto 1, slip next 4 sts. onto right hand needle, pass 2nd. st. over first st. * slip this st. onto other needle, pass 2nd. st. on this needle over the st.; repeat from * 4 times more, k. the remaining st. ● s.c., start circle thus, k.1, (y.r.n., k.1) 3 times all into 1 st., turn, k.7, turn, p.7 ● cr.5b., cross 5 back thus, sl. next 2 sts. onto cable needle at back of work, k.3, k.2 from cable needle ● cr.5f., cross 5 front thus, sl. next 3 sts. onto cable needle at front of work, k.2, then k.3 from cable needle ● double rib is k.2 and p.2 alternately ● single rib is k.1 and p.1 alternately ●

MEASUREMENTS The measurements are given in centimetres followed by inches in brackets.
Underarms 120 (48) ● Side seam 40 (16) ● Length 120 (48) ● Sleeve seam 42.5 (17) ●

NOTE Instructions in brackets are worked the number of times stated after the brackets ●

BACK With size 2¾mm needles cast on 242 sts. and work in basket st. as follows:
1st. row: k.3, * p.4, k.4; repeat from * ending last repeat k.3.
2nd. row: P.3, * k.4, p.4; repeat from * ending last repeat p.3.
3rd. and **4**th. rows: As 1st. and 2nd. rows.
5th. row: As 1st row.
6th. and **7**th. rows: As 1st. and 2nd. rows.
8th. and **9**th. rows: As 1st. and 2nd. rows.
10th. row: As 1st. row.
Repeat these 10 rows 4 times more.
Decrease row: K.2, * k.2tog., k.3, sl.1, k.2tog., p.s.s.o., k.2; repeat from * to end. – 170 sts.
K. 1 row.
Now work in lace pattern as follows:
1st. pattern row: K.11, * (k.2tog., y.r.n.) 12 times, k.18, (k.2tog., y.r.n.) 12 times, k.18; repeat from * ending last repeat k.9 instead of 18.
2nd. row: All k.
3rd. row: K.9, * (y.r.n., s.s.k.) 5 times, k.1, y.r.n., sl.1, k.2tog., p.s.s.o., y.r.n., k.2, (y.r.n., s.s.k.) 6 times, k.14, (y.r.n., s.s.k.) 14 times, k.14; repeat from * ending last repeat k.7.
4th. row: P.6, * k.30, p.12, k.14, y.r.n., p.2tog.b, p.1, p.2tog., y.r.n., k.11, p.12; repeat from * ending last repeat p.8.
The last 4 rows set the position of the pattern given in the chart, work the 5th. to 96th. rows from the chart, then work the first 12 rows again. Mark each end of the last row with coloured threads to denote armhole.**
Pattern 86 rows.
To slope the shoulder: Cast off 52 sts. at the beginning of the next 2 rows. Cast off the remaining 66 sts.

FRONT Work as given for back until ** is reached.
Now work in simple pattern as follows:
1st. row: All k..
2nd. row: All p..
3rd. and **4**th. rows: All k..
Repeat these 4 rows 13 times, then work the first 3 rows again.
Now divide the sts. for the neck: Next row: K.77 and leave these sts. on a spare needle until required for right front shoulder, cast off 16, k. to end and continue on these 77 sts. for the left front shoulder.
Left front shoulder: To shape the neck: Dec. 1 st. at the neck edge on each of the next 25 rows. On 52 sts. work 1 row.
To slope the shoulder: Cast off
Right front shoulder: With right side of work facing rejoin yarn to inner edge of sts. left on spare needle and work to end of row, then work as given for left front shoulder to end.
Neckband: First join right shoulder seam. With right side of work facing, rejoin yarn at left front shoulder and using size 2¼mm needles, pick up and k. 29 sts. from left front neck edge, 16 sts. from centre front and 29 sts. from right front neck edge and 66 sts. from back neck edge.
On 140 sts. k.5 rows, then cast off loosely.

SLEEVES Both alike: First join left shoulder seam. With right side of work facing, rejoin m. and using size 2¾mm needles pick up and k.106 sts. from the armhole edge between the marking threads on back and front.
K. 1 row.
Work the 4 row simple pattern given for front yoke, 8 times.
Continuing in pattern, dec. 1 st. at each end of the next row and the 15 following 4th. rows.
On 74 sts. work 1 row.
Now work ribbing at the centre of the pattern as follows: Change to size 2¼mm needles.
1st. row: All k.
2nd. row: K.36, p.2, k.36.
3rd. row: All k..
4th. row: All p..
5th. and **6**th. rows: As 1st. and 2nd. rows.
7th. row: K.34, p.2, k.2, p.2, k.34.
8th. row: P.34, k.2, p.2., k.2, p.34.
9th. row: K.34, p.2, k.2, p.2, k.34.
10th. row: K.32, p.2, k.2, p.2, k.2, p.32.
11th. row: K.32, rib 10, k.32.
12th. row: P.32, rib 10, p.32.
Thus working 2 extra sts. in rib at each side of centre on each successive 4th. row, work a further 40 rows.
On all 74 sts. k.2 rows.
Work 20 rows in single rib, then cast off in rib.

MAKING UP Do not press. Join sleeve and side seams. ●

O = y.r.n.	□ = k.on r.s., p.on w.s.	λ = s.s.k. on r.s., p.2 tog. on w.s.	∪ = s.c.
⊀ = k 2 tog	∧ = p.on r.s., k.on w.s.	⋋ = k.2 tog. on r.s., p.2 tog. b. on w.s.	
⋋ = s.s.k.	⋏ = sl. 1, k.2 tog., p.s.s.o.	⫸ = k 2, 6 onto 1, k.2	
⩔ = 3 from 1	|·| = k.3 on r.s.	⌐⌐| = k.3 on w.s.	⋊⋉ = cr 5b.	⋊⋉ = cr.5f

GRACE

MATERIALS For the short sweater: Either 18 50 gram balls of "Patricia Roberts Cotton No. 2" or 12 50 gram hanks of "Patricia Roberts Shetland No. 2" ●

For the long sweater: Either 23 50 gram balls of "Patricia Roberts Cotton No. 2" or 15 50 gram hanks of "Patricia Roberts Shetland No. 2" ●

For either garment: A pair each of size 3mm and 3¾mm Aero knitting needles; a medium sized cable needle ●

TENSION 44 stitches – 2 repeats of the pattern – to 14 centimetres (5½ inches) in width and 44 rows – 1 repeat of the pattern – to 12 centimetres (4¾ inches) in depth, using size 3¾mm needles.

If you cannot obtain the correct tension using the size needles suggested, use larger or smaller ones accordingly.

ABBREVIATIONS K., knit ● p., purl ● st., stitch ● tog., together ● dec., decrease (by working 2 sts. tog.) ● inc., increase (by working twice into the same st.) ● single rib is k.1 and p.1 alternately ● cable 10 thus, slip next 5 sts. onto cable needle and leave at front of work, k.5, then k.5 from cable needle ● cable 7f., cable 7 front thus, slip next 4 sts. onto cable needle at front of work, k.3, then k.4 from cable needle ● cable 7b., cable 7 back thus, slip next 3 sts. onto cable needle and leave at back of work, k.4, then k.3 from cable needle ● up1, pick up the loop, which lies between the needles, slip it onto left hand needle, then k. into back of it ●

MEASUREMENTS The measurements are given in centimetres followed by inches in brackets.
Underarms 120 (47) ● Sleeve seam 42 (16½) ● Side seam short: 22.5 (9) long: 37 (14¾) ● Length short: 48 (19¼) long: 63 (25) ●

NOTE The instructions in brackets are worked the number of times stated after the brackets ●

BACK With size 3mm needles cast on 144 sts. and work 15 rows for the short sweater or 21 rows for the long one in single rib.
Increase row: Rib 4, * inc. in next st., rib 2; repeat from * ending last repeat rib 4 instead of 2. – 190 sts.
Change to size 3¾mm needles and work in pattern as follows:
1st. row: K.1, p.1, k.6, * k.2tog., k.3, p.1, k.3, up1, k.2, up1, k.3, p.1, k.3, k.2tog., k.2; repeat from * until 6 remain, k.4 more, then p.1, k.1.
2nd. row: K.13, * p.10, k.12; repeat from * ending last repeat k.1 more.
3rd. row: K.1, p.1, * k.10, p.1; repeat from * ending last repeat k.1.
4th. row: As 2nd. row.
5th. row: K.1, p.1, k.10, p.1, * cable 10, p.1, k.10, p.1; repeat from * ending last repeat k.1.
6th. to **18**th. rows: Repeat 2nd. and 3rd. rows 6 times, then work the 2nd. row again.
19th. row: As 5th. row.
20th. and **21**st. rows: As 2nd. and 3rd. rows.
22nd. row: As 2nd. row.
23rd. row: K.1, p.1, k.6, * up1, k.3, p.1, k.1, p.1, k.1, p.2tog., k.1, p.1, k.2tog., p.1, k.1, p.2, k.3, up1, k.2; repeat from * ending last repeat k.4 more, p.1, k.1.
24th. row: K.1, p.1, k.10, * (k.1, p.1) 5 times, k.2, p.10; repeat from * ending last repeat k.2.
25th. row: K.1, p.1, k.10, p.1, * (k.1, p.1) 4 times, k.1, p.2, k.10, p.1; repeat from * ending last repeat k.1.
26th. row: As 24th. row.
27th. row: K.1, p.1, k.3, cable 7 f., k.3, p.1, * (k.1, p.1) 4 times, k.1, p.2, cable 7f., k.3, p.1; repeat from * ending last repeat k.1.
28th., **29**th. and **30**th. rows: As 24th. to 26th. rows.
31st. row: K.1, p.1, k.3, cable 7b., p.1, * (k.1,

p.1) 4 times, k.1, p.2, k.3, cable 7 b., p.1; repeat from * ending last repeat k.1.
32nd to **39**th. rows: As 24th. to 31st. rows.
40th to **44**th. rows: As 24th. to 28th. rows.
The last 44 rows form the pattern; repeat them once more for the short sweater or twice more for the long one, marking each end of the 20th. row of the last pattern repeat, with coloured threads to denote armholes.
Work the first 22 pattern rows again, then continue as follows:
*****Next row: K.1, p.1, k.6, * up1, k.3, p.2, k.10, p.2, k.3, up1, k.2; repeat from * until 6 remain, k.4, p.1, k.1. – 206 sts.
Next row: K.2, * p.10, k.2; repeat from * to end.
Work in all over cable pattern as follows:
1st. row: K.1, p.1, * k.10, p.2; repeat from * ending last repeat p.1, k.1, instead of p.2.
2nd. row: K.2, * p.10, k.2; repeat from * to end.
3rd. row: K.1, p.1, * cable 7f., k.3, p.2, cable 10, p.2; repeat from * until 12 remain, cable 7f., k.3, p.1, k.1..
4th. and each wrong side row: As 2nd. row.
5th. row: As 1st. row.
7th. row: K.1, p.1, k.3, cable 7b., * p.2, k.10, p.2, k.3, cable 7b.; repeat from * until 2 remain, p.1, k.1.
9th. row: As 1st. row.
11th. row: K.1, p.1, cable 7f., k.3, * p.2, k.10, p.2, cable 7f., k.3; repeat frm * until 2 remain, p.1. k.1.
13th. row: As 1st. row.
15th. row: As 7th. row.
17th. row: As 1st. row.
19th. row: As 3rd. row.
21st. row: As 1st. row.
23rd. row: As 7th. row.
24th. row: As 2nd. row.****
The last 24 rows form the pattern. Work the first 22 rows again.
To slope the shoulders: Continuing in pattern as set, cast off 73 sts. at the beginning of the next 2 rows.
Change to size 3mm needles and on 60 sts. work 16 rows in single rib, then cast off loosely using a size larger needle.
FRONT Work as given for back until **** is reached and the 24 row all over cable pattern has been worked, then work the first 5 of these rows again.
Divide the sts. for the neck: Next row: Pattern 93 and leave these sts. on a spare needle until required for right shoulder, cast off 20 sts., pattern to end and continue on these 93 sts. for the left front shoulder.
Left front shoulder: To shape the neck: Work 1 row, back to neck edge.
****C**ast off 4 sts. at the beginning of the next row and the 4 following alternate rows.
On 73 sts. pattern 6 rows.
To slope the shoulder: Cast off.
Right front shoulder: With right side of work facing rejoin yarn to inner edge of sts. left on spare needle and work as given for left front shoulder from ** to end.
Front Neckband: With right side of work facing rejoin yarn to left front shoulder and using size 3mm needles, pick up and k. 18 sts. from left front neck edge, 20 sts. from centre front neck edge and 18 sts. from right front neck edge.
On 56 sts. work 15 rows in single rib, then cast off in rib loosely, using a size larger needle.
SLEEVES Both alike: With size 3mm needles cast on 68 sts. and work 15 rows in single rib.
Increase row: * Rib 1, inc. in next st.; repeat from * to end. – 102 sts.
Change to size 3¾mm needles and work the first 22 pattern rows given at beginning of back.

Continuing in pattern as set and working the extra sts. into the pattern as they occur, inc. 1 st. at each end of the next row and the 21 following 4th. rows. – 146 sts.
Pattern 3 rows more.
Now work as given for back from *** to **** noting that after the increase row there will be 158 sts. Cast off in pattern.
MAKING UP Do not press. Join shoulder seams. Set in sleeves between the marking threads on back and front. Join sleeve and side seams. Fold neckband in half to wrong side and neatly sew in place ●

"Raoul", left, the modern Fair-Isle – note the raised patterning. To knit in cotton or lambswool for men, women and children.

Romantic "Zee-zee, right, a simple to knit easy to wear version of Tinsel. The pattern is on page 118.

MATERIALS 4 (5) (6) (8) (8) 25 gram balls of "Patricia Roberts" "Fine Cotton" or "Lurex No. 2" in main colour 6 (7) (9) (13) (13) balls in contrast a., 2 (3) (4) (5) (5) in contrast c. and 1 (1) (2) (2) (2) in each of the 3 other contrasts●

This design may also be knitted in either "Patricia Roberts Lambswool No. 1" in 25 gram balls or "Shetland" in 28 gram hanks. It will require 4 (4) (5) (7) (7) balls or hanks in main colour, 5 (6) (8) (10) (10) in contrast a. 2 (2) (3) (4) (4) in contrast c. and 1 (1) (2) (2) (2) in each of the 3 other contrasts●

A pair each of size 2¼mm and 3mm Aero knitting needles● a fine cable needle●

TENSION 32 stitches — 2 repeats of the pattern to 9 centimetres (3¾ inches) in width and 88 rows — 1 repeat of the pattern to 23 centimetres (9¼ inches) in depth, using size 3mm needles.

If you cannot obtain the correct tension using the size needles suggested, use larger or smaller ones accordingly●

It is most important to work at the correct tension●

ABBREVIATIONS K., knit● p., purl● st., stitch● tog., together● dec., decrease (by working 2 sts. tog.)● inc., increase (by working twice into same st.)● single rib is k.1 and p.1 alternately● sl., slip● p.s.s.o., pass sl. st. over● s.s.k., sl.1, k.1, p.s.s.o.● m., main colour● a., first contrast● b., second contrast● c., third contrast● d., fourth contrast● e., fifth contrast● h.b., half bobble thus, with a. k. into back and front of next st., turn, k.2, turn, p.2● 1 into 3, k. into back, then into front of next st., then pick up the strand between the 2 sts. just made and k. into it● cr.3f., with m. k. into back of 3rd st. on left hand needle, with a. p. 1st and 2nd sts.● cr.3b., sl. next st. onto cable needle at back of work, with a. p.2, with m. k.1 from cable needle● m.b., with a. 1 into 3, turn, k.3, turn, p.3, turn, k.3, turn, with m. p.3tog.● c.4f., slip next 2 st. onto cable needle at front of work, with appropriate colour k.2, then with a. p.2 from cable needle● c.4b., slip next 2 sts. onto cable needle at back of work, with a. p.2, then with appropriate colour k.2 from cable needle● 4 onto 1, slip first 3 sts. from left hand needle onto right hand needle, pass the 2nd of these sts. over the first st., slip this first st. back to left hand needle, pass next st. over this st., transfer st. back to right hand needle, *pass 2nd st. on needle over this st., transfer back to left hand needle, pass next st. over it, with m. or c. as appropriate k. this st.● 2 onto 1, pass first 2 sts. from left hand needle onto right hand needle, work as for 4 onto 1 from * to end● up 1, pick up the loop which lies between the needles, slip it onto left hand needle, then k. into back of it●

NOTE The instructions are given for the 3 year size. Where they vary, work the figures in the first brackets for the 5 year size; those in the second brackets for the 8 year size; those in the third brackets for the woman's size and those in the fourth brackets for the man's size●

Special Notes: When counting, where extra sts. have been made in a. count the sets of 2 sts. as 1st● For easier working, before commencing work read through the pattern and underline the number of sts. or rows to be worked for the relevant size.

MEASUREMENTS The measurements are given in centimetres followed by inches in square brackets.
Sizes: 3 yrs (5 yrs) (8 yrs) (woman's) (man's)● Underarms: 75 [30] (84 [33¾]) (94 [37½]) (112.5 [45]) (112.5 [45])● Side seams: 28.5 [11½] (31.5 [13]) (37.5 [15])

(42.5 [17]) (42.5 [17])● Length: 39 [15¾] (46 [18½]) (53 [21¼]) (65 [26]) (65 [26])● Sleeve seam 18.5 [7½] (26 [10½]) (32.5 [13]) (41 [16½]) (46 [18½])●

BACK With size 2¼mm needles and m. cast on 86 (97) (108) (129) (129) sts. and work 17 (21) (25) (29) (29) rows in single rib.
Increase row: Rib 1, *up 1, rib 2; repeat from * ending last repeat rib 1 (2) (3) (2) (2). – 129 (145) (161) (193) (193) sts.

Change to size 3mm needles and work in pattern as follows. Take care not to pull colours not in use tightly across the back of the work.
1st to **4**th rows: With a. all k.
5th row: With b. all k.
6th row: With b. all p.
7th row: With b. k.3, *with a. h.b., with b. k.3; repeat from * ending last repeat k.1.
8th row: With b. p.1, *slip next 2 sts. onto cable needle at back of work, with b. p.2, with a. k.2 from cable needle, with b. p.1; repeat from * to end.
9th row: With b. k.1, *s.s.k., k.3; repeat from * to end.
10th row: With b. all p.
11th to **14**th rows: With a. all k.
15th row: With m. all k.
16th row: With m. all p.
17th row: With m. k.1, *sl.2, k.2; repeat from * to end.
18th row: With m. p.2, *sl.2, p.2; repeat from * ending p.1 instead of 2.
19th and **20**th rows: With a. k.2 rows.
21st row: With c. sl.1, *k.2, sl.2; repeat from * to end.
22nd row: With c. sl.2, *p.2, sl.2; repeat from * ending sl.1 instead of 2.
23rd and **24**th row: With c. k.1 row and p.1 row.
25th row: With a. inc., *still with a. up 1, with c. s.s.k., k.2, with a. h.b., with c. k.5, with a. h.b., with c. k.2, k.2tog., with a. up 1, 1 into 3; repeat from * ending last repeat inc. instead of 1 into 3.
26th row: With a. k.3, *with c. p.3, with a. k.2, with c. p.5, with a. k.2, with c. p.3, with a. k.5; repeat from * ending last repeat with a. k.3.
27th row: With c. k.1, *(with c. and a. c.4f., with c. k.1) twice, (with c. and a. c.4b., with c. k.1) twice; repeat from * to end.
28th row: With c. p.3, *with a. k.2, with c. p.3, with a. k.5, with c. p.3, with a. k.2, with c. p.5; repeat from * ending last repeat with c. p.3.
29th row: With a. inc., *still with a. up 1, with c. s.s.k., with c. and a. c.4f., with c. up 1, k.1, 4 onto 1 – see abbreviations, k.1, up 1, with c. and a. c.4b., with c. k.2tog., with a. up 1, 1 into 3; repeat from * ending last repeat inc. instead of 1 into 3.
30th row: With a. k.3, *with c. p.3, with a. k.2, with c. p.5, with a. k.2, with c. p.3, with a. k.5; repeat from * ending last repeat k.3.
31st row: With c. k.1, *(with c. and a. c.4f., with c. k.1) twice, (with c. and a. c.4b., with c. k.1) twice; repeat from * to end.
32nd row: With c. p.3, *with a. k.2, with c. p.3, with a. k.5, with c. p.3, with a. k.2, with c. p.5; repeat from * ending with c. p.3.
33rd row: With c. k.3, *s.s.k., k.2, up 1, k.1, 4 onto 1, k.1, up 1, k.2, s.s.k., k.5; repeat from * ending last repeat k.3.
34th to **36**th rows: Using c. instead of m. work as given for 16th to 18th rows.
37th to **42**nd rows: As 19th to 24th rows.
43rd to **46**th rows: With a. all k.
47th and **48**th rows: Using d. instead of b. as 5th and 6th rows.
49th row: With d. k.1, *with a. h.b., with d. k.3; repeat from * to end.
50th row: With d. p.1, *sl. next 2 sts. onto

cable needle at front of work – wrongside, with a. k.2, with d. p.2 from cable needle, with d. p.1; repeat from * to end.
51st row: With d. k.3, *s.s.k., k.3; repeat from * ending k.1 instead of k.3.
52nd row: With d. all p.
53rd and **54**th rows: With a. all k.
55th and **56**th rows: With m. k.1, *p.1, k.1; repeat from * to end.
The last 2 rows set the position of the moss st. now referred to as m.st.
57th row: With a. inc., *still with a. up 1, with m. s.s.k., p.1, k.1, with a. h.b., with m. m.st.5, with a. h.b., with m. k.1, p.1, k.2tog., with a. up 1, 1 into 3; repeat from * ending inc. instead of 1 into 3.
58th row: With a. k.3, *with m. k.1, p.1, k.1, with a. k.2, with m. m.st.5, with a. k.2, with m. m.st.3, with a. k.5; repeat from * ending last repeat k.3.
59th row: With m. k.1, *cr.3f., with m. p.1, k.1, with m. and a. c.4f., with m. k.1, with m. and a. c.4b., with m.k.1, p.1, cr.3b., with m. k.1; repeat from * to end.
60th row: With m. k.1, *p.1, with a. k.2, with m. (p.1, k.1) twice, with a. k.5, with m. (k.1, p.1) twice, with a. k.2, with m. p.1, k.1; repeat from * to end.
61st row: With m. k.1, *p.1, cr.3f., with m. k.1, p.1, up 1, p.1, 4 onto 1, p.1, up 1, p.1, k.1, cr.3b., with m. p.1, k.1; repeat from * to end.
62nd row: With m. k.1, *p.1, k.1, with a. k.2, with m. (k.1, p.1) 4 times, k.1, with a. k.2, with m. k.1, p.1, k.1; repeat from * to end.
63rd row: With a. m.b., *with m. p.1, k.1, s.s.k., k.1, p.1, k.2tog., with a. up 1, 1 into 3, up 1, with m. k.2tog., p.1, k.1, s.s.k., k.1, p.1, with a. m.b.; repeat from * to end.
64th row: With m. m.st.7, *with a. k.5, with m. m.st.13; repeat from * ending last repeat m.st.7.
65th row: With m. m.st.5, *with e. and a. c.4b., with e. k.1, with e. and a. c.4f., with m. m.st.9; repeat from * ending last repeat m.st.5.
66th row: With m. m.st.5, *with a. k.2, with e. p.1, k.1, p.1, k.1, p.1, with a. k.2, with m. m.st.9; repeat from * ending last repeat m.st.5.
67th row: With m. m.st.3, *with e. and a. c.4b., with e. k.1, p.1, with a. h.b., with e. p.1, k.1, with e. and a. c.4f., with m. m.st.5; repeat from * ending last repeat m.st.3.
68th row: With m. m.st.3, *with a. k.2, with e. (p.1, k.1) twice, a. k.2, with e. (k.1, p.1) twice, with a. k.2, with m. m.st.5; repeat from * ending m.st.3.
69th row: With m. k.1, *with e. and a. c.4b., with e. k.1, p.1, with a. h.b., with e. p.1, s.s.k., p.1, with a. h.b., with e. p.1, k.1, with e. and a. c.4f., with m. k.1; repeat from * to end.
70th row: With a. k.3, *with e. (p.1, k.1) twice, (with a. k.2, with e. k.1, p.1, k.1) twice, with e. p.1, with a. k.5; repeat from * ending k.3.
71st row: With e. 2 over 1, *still with e. p.1, up 1, p.1, with a. h.b., with e. p.1, s.s.k., p.1, k.1, p.1, s.s.k., p.1, with a. h.b., with e. p.1, up 1, p.1, 4 over 1; repeat from * ending last repeat 2 over 1.
72nd row: With e. (p.1, k.1) twice, *with a. k.2, with e. rib 7 as set, with a. k.2, with e. rib 7; repeat from * ending rib 4.
73rd row: With e. k.1, p.1, *with a. h.b., with e. p.1, s.s.k., p.1, k.2tog., with a. up 1, 1 into 3, up 1, with e. (s.s.k., p.1) twice, with a. h.b., with e. rib 3; repeat from * ending rib 2.
74th row: With e. rib 2, *with a. k.2, with e. rib 4, with a. k.5, with e. rib 4, with a. k.2, with e. rib 3; repeat from * ending rib 2.

Continued on page 119●

"Wallis", a simple to
knit chenille blouson.
The ribbed edgings can
be worked in cotton or
in Shetland Tweed, for
spring or autumn.

"Wallis", a simple to
knit chenille blouson.
The ribbed edgings can
be worked in cotton or
in Shetland Tweed, for
spring or autumn.

needles, slip it onto left hand needle, then k. into back of it● sl., slip● p.s.s.o., pass sl. st. over● m., main yarn● c., contrast yarn●

MEASUREMENTS The measurements are given in centimetres followed by inches in square brackets.
Underarms 113 [45.5] (113 [45.5])● Side seam 40 [15¾] (45 [17½])● Length 65 [25½] (73 [28¾])● Sleeve seam 40 [16] (45 [18])●

NOTE The instructions are given for the woman's size. Where they vary, work the instructions in brackets for the man's size●

SPECIAL NOTE When knitting with Chenille. It is essential to check ones tension before commencing work and if necessary to change needles accordingly●

BACK With size 2¾mm needles and c. cast on 132 sts. and work 23 rows in twisted rib. Break of c., join in m. and p.1 row.
Change to size 3¼mm needles and with m. work in pattern as follows: **1**st. row: k.1, p. until 1 remains, k.1.
2nd. row: All k..
3rd. row: K.1, p.1, *k.8, p.2; repeat from * ending last repeat p.1, k.1 instead of p.2.
4th. row: K.2, * p.8, k.2; repeat from * to end.
5th and **6**th. rows: As 3rd. and 4th rows.
7th. row: K.1, p.1, cable 8, p.2, * k.8, p.2, cable 8, p.2; repeat from * ending last repeat p.1, k.1.
8th. row: As 4th. row.
9th. to **20**th. rows: Repeat 3rd. and 4th. rows 6 times.
21st. row: As 7th. row.
22nd. row: As 4th row.
23rd. to **26**th rows: Repeat 3rd. and 4th. rows twice.
27th. row: K.1, p. until 1 remains, k.1.
28th. row: All k..
29th. to **32**nd. rows: Repeat 3rd. and 4th. rows twice.
33rd. row: K.1, p.1, k.8, p.2, * cable 8, p.2, k.8, p.2; repeat from * ending last repeat p.1, k.1.
34th. row: As 4th. row.
35th. to **46**th. rows: Repeat 3rd. and 4th. rows 6 times.
47th row: As 33rd. row.
48th. row: As 4th. row.
49th. to **52**nd. rows: Repeat 3rd. and 4th. rows twice.
The last 52 rows form the pattern; repeat them once more, then work the first 2 (18) rows again.
To shape the armhole: Continuing in pattern as set, cast off 4 sts. at the beginning of the next 2 rows, then dec. 1 st. at each end of the next row and the 5 following alternate rows.
On 112 sts. pattern 61 (71) rows.
To slope the shoulders: Cast off 9 sts. at the beginning of the next 8 rows.
Cast off the remaining 40 sts.

FRONT First work the pocket backs: 2 alike: With size 3¼mm needles and m. cast on 30 sts. and work 41 rows in twisted rib, then leave these sts. on a stitch-holder until required.
With size 2¾mm needles and c. cast on 132 sts. and work as given for back until 42 (68) rows have been worked in pattern.
1st. Pocket row: Pattern 10, cast off 30 pattern next 51 sts., cast off 30, pattern to end.
2nd. Pocket row: Pattern 10, pattern across the 30 sts. of one pocket back, pattern 52, pattern across the 30 sts. of other pocket back, pattern 10.
Pattern 35 (9) rows.
Now divide the sts. for the front opening: Next row: Pattern 62 and leave these sts. on a spare needle until required for right half front, pattern 8 and leave these sts. on a stitch-holder, work to end and continue on these 62 sts. for the left half front.

Left half front: Continuing in pattern as set and, knitting the first and last st. of each row, work 26 (42) rows.
***T**o shape the armhole: Cast off 4 sts. at the beginning of the next row, then dec. 1 st. at the armhole edge on the 6 following alternate rows.
On 52 sts. work 38 (48) rows, ending at inner edge.
To shape the neck: Cast off 2 sts. at the beginning of the next row, then dec. 1 st. at the neck edge on each of the next 14 rows.
On 36 sts. pattern 8 rows.
To slope the shoulder: Cast off 9 sts. at the beginning of the next row and the 2 following alternate rows. On 9 sts. work 1 row, then cast off.
Right half front: With right side of work facing rejoin yarn to inner edge of the sts. left on spare needle and work to end of row, then work as given for left half front to end.
Buttonhole band: With right side of work facing rejoin m. to the 8 sts. left on stitch-holder and using size 3¼mm needles k. 1 row increasing 1 st. at each end.
On 10 sts. k.5 (9) rows.
1st. Buttonhole row: K.4, cast off 2, k. to end.
2nd. Buttonhole row: K.4, turn, cast on 2, turn, k. to end.
K. 20 rows.
Repeat the last 22 rows 2 (3) times more, then work the 2 buttonhole rows again.
K. 4 rows, then cast off.
Button band: With size 3¼mm needles and m. cast on 10 sts. and k. 78 (104) rows, then cast off.
Collar: With size 2¾mm needles and c. cast on 117 sts. and work 4 rows in twisted rib.
Dec. row: Rib 4, sl.1, k.2tog., p.s.s.o., rib until 7 remain sl.1, k.2tog., p.s.s.o., rib 4.
Rib 3 rows.
Repeat the last 4 rows 4 times more. − 97 sts.
Cast off loosely in rib.
Pocket flaps: 2 alike: With size 3¼mm needles and m. cast on 30 sts. and k. 8 rows.
Next row: Sl.1, k.2tog., p.s.s.o., k. until 3 remain, sl.1, k.2tog., p.s.s.o..
Repeat the last row 6 times more, then take the 2 remaining sts. tog. and fasten off.
SLEEVES Both alike: With size 2¾mm needles and c. cast on 52 sts. and work 23 rows in twisted rib. Break off c. join in m. and p.1 row.
Change to size 3¼mm needles and with m. work 26 rows in pattern as given for back.
Continuing in pattern and working the extra sts. into the pattern as they occur, inc. 1 st. at each end of the next row and the 19 following 4th rows.
On 92 sts. pattern 3 (19) rows.
To shape the sleevetop: For the woman's size: Cast off 4 sts. at the beginning of the next 2 rows.
For the man's size: Mark each end of the last row with coloured threads, then pattern 4 rows.
For either size: Dec. 1 st. at each end of the next 24 (28) rows. − 36 sts.
Cast off 3 sts. at the beginning of the next 4 rows and 4 sts. on the 4 following rows.
Cast off the remaining 8 sts.

MAKING UP Do not press. Join shoulder seams. Set in sleeves, for the woman's matching the cast off groups at underarms and for the man's matching the row ends above the marking threads on the sleeves to the cast off groups on back and front. Join sleeve and side seams. Sew cast off edge of collar in place, all round neck edge. Sew buttonhole band in place, then sew button band in position, so that the cast on edge is sewn behind buttonhole band. Sew pocket backs and pocket flaps in place. Make buttonholes in flaps. Sew on buttons ●

MATERIALS 14 (16) 50 gram balls of "Patricia Roberts Chenille" in main colour and 2 50 gram balls or hanks of either "Patricia Roberts Cotton No. 2 or Shetland No. 2" in a toning shade● A pair each of size 2¾mm and 3¼mm Aero knitting needles and a medium sized cable needle; 6 (7) buttons●
TENSION 20 stitches − 1 repeat of the pattern to 9 centimetres (3½ inches) in width and 52 rows − 1 repeat of the pattern − to 16 centimetres (6¼ inches) in depth, using size 3¼mm needles●
If you cannot obtain the correct tension using the size needles suggested, use larger or smaller ones accordingly●
ABBREVIATIONS K., knit● p., purl● st., stitch● tog., together● dec., decrease (by working 2 sts. tog.)● inc., increase (by working twice into same st.)● k. or p.1b., k. or p.1 into back of st.● twisted rib is k.1b. and p.1b. alternately● cable 8 thus, slip next 4 sts. onto cable needle and leave at front of work, k.4, then k.4 from cable needle● up1, pick up the loop, which lies between the

Left: "Juliette" and
"Greco". "Juliette" is
knitted in pure wool
and "Greco" in
Shetland Tweed, both
perfect for a country
weekend.
Right: "Wallis" for a
man.

MATERIALS 9 (10)100 gram balls of "Patricia Roberts Extra Thick Wool" ● a pair each of size 3¾mm and 4½mm Aero knitting needles, a large cable needle ●
TENSION 12 stitches to 5.7 centimetres (2¼ inches) and 24 rows to 9 centimetres (3½ inches) over the basket stitch using size 4½mm needles ●
If you cannot obtain the correct tension using the size needles suggested, use larger or smaller ones accordingly ●
ABBREVIATIONS K., knit ● p., purl ● st., stitch ● tog., together ● dec., decrease (by working 2 sts. tog.) ● inc., increase (by working twice into same st.) ● double rib is k.2 and p.2 alternately ● up 1 is pick up the loop that lies between the needles, slip it onto left hand needle and k. into back of it ● cable 8 thus, slip next 4 sts. onto cable needle at front of work, k.4 then k.4 from cable needle ●
MEASUREMENTS The measurements are given in centimetres followed by inches in brackets.
Underarms: 114 (45) ● Side seam 49 (19½) ● Length: 72 (28½) ● Sleeve seam: woman's 42 (16½) ● man's 47 (18¼) ●
NOTE Instructions in brackets are worked the number of times stated after the last bracket ●
BACK With size 3¾mm needles cast on 122 sts. and work 22 rows in double rib, beginning right side rows with k.2 and wrong side rows with p.2.
Change to size 4½mm needles and work in pattern as follows:
1st row: K.1, p.3, * k.6, p.6; repeat from * ending last repeat p.3, k.1.
2nd row: K.4, * p.6, k.6; repeat from * ending last repeat k.4.
3rd to **6**th rows: repeat 1st and 2nd rows twice.
7th row: K.4, * p.6, k.6; repeat from * ending last repeat k.4.
8th row: K.1, p.3, * k.6, p.6; repeat from * ending last repeat p.3, k.1.
9th to **12**th rows: Repeat 7th and 8th rows twice.
The last 12 rows form the basket stitch. Repeat them 3 times more then work the first 6 rows again.
Now work in basket stitch as set with cables as follows:
1st row: K.4, p.6, (k.6, p.6) 4 times, k.2, up1, k.2, up1, k.2, (p.6, k.6) 4 times, p.6, k.4. – 124 sts.
2nd row: K.1, p.3, k.6, (p.6, k.6) 4 times p.8, (k.6, p.6) 4 times, k.6, p.3, k.1.
3rd row: K.4, p.6, (k.6, p.6) 4 times, k.8, (p.6, k.6) 4 times, p.6, k.4.
4th and **5**th rows: As 2nd and 3rd rows.
6th row: As 2nd row.
7th row: K.1, p.3, (k.6, p.6) 4 times, k.5, p.1, cable 8, p.1, k.5, (p.6, k.6) 4 times, p.3, k.1.
8th row: K.4, p.6, (k.6, p.6) 4 times, p.5, k.1, p.8, k.1, p.5, (k.6, p.6) 4 times, k.4.
9th. row: K.1, p.3, (k.6, p.6) 4 times, k.5, p.1, k.8, p.1, k.5, (p.6, k.6) 4 times, p.3, k.1.
10th and **11**th rows: As 8th and 9th rows.
12th row: As 8th row.
13th row: As 3rd row.
14th to **18**th rows: As 2nd to 6th rows.
19th row: K.1, p.3, (k.6, p.6) 3 times, k.2, up1, k.2, up1, k.2, p.6, k.5, p.1, cable 8, p.1, k.5, p.6, k.2, up1, k.2, up1, k.2, (p.6, k.6) 3 times, p.3, k.1. – 128 sts.
20th row: K.4, (p.6, k.6) 3 times, p.8, k.6, p.5, k.1, p.8, k.1, p.5, k.6, p.8, (k.6, p.6) 3 times, k.4.
21st row: K.1, p.3, (k.6, p.6) 3 times, k.8, p.6, k.5, p.1, k.8, p.1, k.5, p.6, k.8, (p.6, k.6) 3 times, p.3, k.1.
22nd and **23**rd rows: As 20th and 21st rows.

24th rows: As 20th row.
25th row: K.4, p.6, (k.6, p.6) twice, k.5, p.1, cable 8, p.1, k.5, p.6, k.8, p.6, k.5, p.1, cable 8, p.1, k.5, (p.6, k.6) twice, p.6, k.4.
26th row: K.1, p.3, k.6, (p.6, k.6) twice, p.5, k.1, p.8, k.1, p.5, k.6, p.8, k.6, p.6, k.1, p.8, k.1, p.5, (k.6, p.6) twice, k.6, p.3, k.1.
27th row: K.4, p.6, (k.6, p.6) twice, k.5, p.1, k.8, p.1, k.5, p.6, k.8, p.6, k.5, p.1, k.8, p.1, k.5, (p.6, k.6) twice, p.6, k.4.
28th and **29**th rows: As 26th and 27th rows.
30th row: As 26th.
31st row: K.1, p.3, (k.6, p.6) 3 times, k.8, p.6, k.5, p.1, cable 8, p.1, k.5, p.6, k.8, (p.6, k.6) 3 times, p.3, k.1.
32nd to **36**th rows: As 20th to 24th rows.
37th row: K.4, p.6, k.6, p.6, k.2, up1, k.2, up1, k.2, p.6, k.5, p.1, cable 8, p.1, k.5, p.6, k.8, p.6, k.5, p.1, cable 8, p.1, k.5, p.6, k.2, up1, k.2, up1, k.2, p.6, k.6, p.6, k.4. – 132 sts.
38th rows: K.1, p.3, k.6, p.6, (k.6, p.8, k.6, p.5, k.1, p.8, k.1, p.5) twice, k.6, p.8, k.6, p.6, k.6, p.3, k.1.
39th row: K.4, p.6, k.6, (p.6, k.8, p.6, k.5, p.1, k.8, p.1, k.5) twice, p.6, k.8, p.6, k.6, p.6, k.4.
40th and **41**st rows: As 38th and 39th rows.
42nd. row: As 38th. row
43rd. row: K.1, p.3, k.6, p.6, (k.5, p.1, cable 8, p.1, k.5, p.6, k.8, p.6) twice, k.5, p.1, cable 8, p.1, k.5, p.6, k.6, p.3, k.1.
44th row: K.4, p.6, k.6, p.5, k.1, p.8, k.1, p.5, (k.6, p.8, k.6, p.5, k.1, p.8, k.1, p.5) twice, k.6, p.6, k.4.
45th row: K.1, p.3, k.6, p.6, (k.5, p.1, k.8, p.1, k.5, p.6, k.8, p.6) twice, k.5, p.1, k.8, p.1, k.5, p.6, k.6, p.3, k.1.
46th and **47**th rows: As 44th and 45th rows.
48th row: As 44th row.
49th row: K.4, p.6, k.6, (p.6, k.8, p.6, k.5, p.1, cable 8, p.1, k.5) twice, p.6, k.8, p.6, k.6, p.6, k.4.
50the to **54**th rows: As 38th to 42nd rows.
55th row: K.1, p.3, k.2, up1, k.2, up1, k.2, p.6, (k.5, p.1, cable 8, p.1, k.5, p.6, k.8, p.6) twice, k.5, p.1, cable 8, p.1, k.5, p.6, k.2, up1, k.2, up1, k.2, p.3, k.1. – 136 sts.
56th row: K.4, (p.8, k.6, p.5, k.1, p.8, k.1, p.5, k.6) 3 times, p.8, k.4.
Continue in cable and basket stitch as follows:
1st row: K.1, p.3, (k.8, p.6, k.5, p.1, k.8, p.1, k.5, p.6) 3 times, k.8, p.3, k.1.
2nd row: K.4, (p.8, k.6, p.5, k.1, p.8, k.1, p.5, k.6) 3 times, p.8, k.4.
3rd and **4**th rows: As 1st and 2nd rows.
Mark each end of the last row with coloured threads to denote armholes.
5th row: K.3, p.1, (cable 8, p.1, k.5, p.6, k.8, p.6, k.5, p.1) 3 times, cable 8, p.1, k.3.
6th row: K.1, p.2, k.1, (p.8, k.1, p.5, k.6, p.8, k.6, p.5, k.1) 3 times, p.8, k.1, p.2, k.1.
7th row: K.3, p.1, (k.8, p.1, k.5, p.6, k.8, p.6, k.5, p.1) 3 times, K.8, p.1, k.3.
8th and **9**th rows: As 6th and 7th rows.
10th row: As 6th row.
11th row: K.1, p.3, (k.8, p.6, k.5, p.1, cable 8, p.1, k.5, p.6) 3 times, k.8, p.3, k.1.
12th row: As 2nd row. **
Repeat the last 12 rows 4 times more.
To slope the shoulders: Cast off 15 sts. at the beginning of the next 6 rows.
Leave the remaining 46 sts. on a stitch-holder until required for collar.

FRONT Work as given for back until ** is reached.
Repeat the last 12 rows twice more, then work the first 3 rows again.
Now divide the sts. for the neck: Next row: Pattern 57 and leave these sts. on a spare needle until required for right front shoulder, pattern 22 and leave these sts. on a stitch-holder until required for collar, pattern to end

and continue on these 57 sts. for the left front shoulder.
Left front shoulder: to shape the neck: Continuing in pattern as set, dec. 1 st. at the neck edge on each of the next 12 rows.
On 45 sts. pattern 8 rows.
To slope the shoulder: Cast off 15 sts. at the beginning of the next row and the following alternate row. On 15 sts. work 1 row then cast off.
Right front shoulder: With right side of work facing, rejoin yarn to inner edge of sts. left on spare needle and work to end of row, then work as given for left front shoulder to end.
Collar: First join right shoulder seam. With right side of work facing, rejoin yarn at left front neck edge and using size 3¾mm needles pick up and k. 22 sts. from left front neck edge, k. across the 22 sts. at centre front neck, pick up and k. 22 sts. from right front neck edge, then k. across the 46 sts. at back neck edge. – 112 sts.
Work 59 rows in double rib, then cast off in rib loosely, using a size larger needle.
SLEEVES Both alike: With size 3¾mm needles cast on 44 sts. and work 21 rows in double rib.
Increase row: Rib 3. * up1, rib 2; repeat from * ending last repeat rib 3. – 64 sts.
Change to size 4½mm needles and work in pattern as follows:
1st row: P.4, (k.6, p.6) twice, k.8, (p.6, k.6) twice, p.4.
2nd row: K.4, (p.6, k.6) twice, p.8, (k.6, p.6) twice, k.4.
3rd and **4**th rows: As 1st and 2nd rows.
5th and **6**th rows: As 1st and 2nd rows.
7th row: K.4, p.6, k.6, p.6, k.5, p.1, cable 8, p.1, k.5, p.6, k.6, p.6, k.4.
8th row: P.4, k.6, p.6, k.6, p.5, k.1, p.8, k.1, p.5, k.6, p.6, k.6, p.4.
9th row: K.4, p.6, k.6, p.6, k.5, p.1, k.8, p.1, k.5, p.6, k.6, p.6, k.4.
10th and **11**th rows: As 8th and 9th rows.
12th row: As 8th row.
The last 12 rows form the pattern, continuing in pattern and working the extra sts. into the basket st. pattern as they occur, inc. 1 st. at each end of the next row and the 19 following 4th rows.
On 104 sts. pattern 7 rows, for the woman's size or 19 rows for the man's.
Cast off in pattern loosely.
MAKING UP Do not press. Join left shoulder seam continuing and reversing seam across collar. Neatly sew cast off edge of sleeves to the row ends between the marking threads on back and front. Join sleeve and side seams. ●

GRECO

MATERIALS 11 (12) 100 gram hanks of "Patricia Roberts Extra Thick Shetland Tweed" ● a pair each of size 4mm and 5mm Aero knitting needles; a thick cable needle ●
TENSION 18 stitches to 10 centimetres (4 inches) and 13 rows to 5 centimetres (2 inches) over the basket stitch using size 5mm needles ●
If you cannot obtain the correct tension using the needles suggested, use larger or smaller needles accordingly ●
ABBREVIATIONS As given for "Juliette" ●
MEASUREMENTS The measurements are given in centimetres followed by inches in brackets ●
Underarms 132.5 (53) ● Side seam 51 (20½) ● Length 75 (30) ● Sleeve seam woman's 44 (17.5) ● man's 49 (19.5) ●
TO WORK Work exactly as given for "Juliette".

"Greco", for the
existentialist look. For
more classic attire knit
it in brown or beige
tweed.

"Charlie" chunky "Aran" style jackets with a difference. King Charles spaniels and Argyll motifs are cleverly interspersed in the pattern. The instructions for the hat are given on page 41.

MATERIALS Either 14 100 gram balls of "Patricia Roberts Extra Thick Wool" or 15 100 gram hanks of "Patrica Roberts Extra Thick Shetland Tweed" in main colour, plus 2 20 gram balls of "Patrica Roberts Angora" in each of 3 contrast colours and a small ball in 4th. contrast● a pair each of size 3¾mm and 4½mm Aero knitting needles; a large cable needle; a 50 centimetre (20 inch) open ended zip fastener●

TENSION 36 stitches – 1 repeat of the pattern – to 13 centimetres (5¼ inches) in width and 56 rows – 1 repeat of the pattern – to 18 centimetres (7 inches) in depth●

If you cannot obtain the correct tension using the size needles suggested, use larger or smaller ones accordingly●

ABBREVIATIONS K., knit● p., purl● st., stitch● tog., together● dec., decrease (by working 2 sts. tog.)● inc., increase (by working twice into same st.)● double rib is k.2 and p.2 alternately● single rib is k.1 and p.1 alternately● up1, pick up the loop, which lies between the needles, slip it onto left hand needle and k. into back of it● c.6f., cable 6 front, thus, slip next 3 sts. onto cable needle and leave at front of work, k.3, then k.3 from cable needle● c.6b., cable 6 back, thus, slip next 3 sts. onto cable needle at back of work, k.3, then k.3 from cable needle● s.s., stocking stitch is k. on the right side and p. on the wrong side● m., main colour● a., first contrast colour● b., second contrast● c., third contrast● d., fourth contrast●

MEASUREMENTS The measurements are given in centimetres followed by inches in brackets.
Underarms 136 (55)● Side seam 47 (18½)● Length 74 (29)● Sleeve seam 43.5 (17)●

NOTE The contrast colours in "Angora" are used double through out●

BACK With size 3¾mm needles and m. cast on 162 sts. and work 35 rows in double rib.
Increase row: Rib 6, * up1, rib 6; repeat from * to end. – 188 sts.
Change to size 4½mm needles and work in pattern as follows: **1**st. row: All k..
2nd. row: K.1, p.6, *k.12, p.6; repeat from * ending last repeat k.1.
3rd. row: K.1, c.6f., * k.30, c.6f.: repeat from * ending last repeat k.1.
4th., **6**th. and **8**th. rows: As 2nd. row.
5th. row: all k..
7th. row: K.19, *c.6f., k.30: repeat from * ending last repeat k.19 instead of 30.
9th. row: K.16, * c.6b., c.6f., k.24; repeat from * ending last repeat k.16.
10th. row: K.1, p.6, * k.9, p.3, k.6, p.3, k.9, p.6; repeat * ending last repeat k.1 more.
11th. row: As 3rd. row.
12th. row: As 10th. row.
13th. row: K.4, * c.6f, k.3, c.6b., k.6, c.6f., k.3, c.6b.; repeat from * ending last repeat k.4.
14th. row: K.7, * p.3, k.3, p.3, k.12, p.3, k.3, p.3, k.6; repeat from * ending last repeat k.7 instead of 6.
15th. row: K.7, * c.6f., k.18, c.6b., k.6; repeat from * ending last repeat, k.1 more.
16th. row: K.10, * p.6, k.12; repeat from * ending last repeat k.10 instead of 12.
17th. row: K.10, * c.6f, k.12, c.6b., k.12; repeat from * ending last repeat k.10 instead of 12.
18th. row: As 16th row.
19th. row: K.13, * c.6f., k.6, c.6b, k.18; repeat from * ending last repeat k.13.
20th. row: K.10, * p.3, k.3, p.3, k.6, p.3, p.3, k.12; repeat from * ending last repeat k.10.
21st. row: K.7, * c.6b., k.3, c.6f., c.6b., k.3, c.6f., k.6; repeat from * ending last repeat k.7.
22nd. row: K.7, * p.3, k.9, p.6, k.9, p.3, k.6; repeat from * ending last repeat k.7.

23rd. row: K.19, * c.6f., k.30; repeat from * ending last repeat k.19.
24th. row: K.7, * p.3, k.9, p.6, k.9, p.3, k.6; repeat from * ending last repeat k.7.
25th. row: K.4, * c.6b., k.24, c.6f.; repeat from * until 4 remain, k.4.
26th. to **32**nd. rows: As 2nd. to 8th. rows.
33rd. to **36**th. row: As 1st. to 4th. rows.
37th. row: K.4, * c.6f., k.24, c.6b.; repeat from * until 4 remain, k.4.
38th. to **40**th. rows: As 22nd. to 24th. rows.
41st. row: K.7, * c.6f., k.3, c.6b., c.6f., k.3, c.6b., k.6; repeat from * ending last repeat k.7, instead of k.6.
Now work the Argyll and Dog motifs from the charts, but positioned as follows. Use seperate balls of m. at each side of motifs, so that the colours not in use are not taken across the back of the work. Note that the angora colours are used double.
42nd. row: Working in pattern as for 20th. row, with m. pattern 57, with a. p.2 for Argyll motif, with m. pattern 68, with b. p.6 for dog motif, with m. pattern 55.
Now working the motifs from the charts as set, continue as follows:
43rd. row: K.13, * c.6b., k.6, c.6f., k.18; repeat from * ending last repeat k.13.
44th. row: As 16th. row.
45th. row: K.10, * c.6b., k.12, c.6f., k.12; repeat from * ending last repeat k.10.
46th. row: As 16th. row.
47th. row: K.7, * c.6b., k.18, c.6f., k.6; repeat from * ending last repeat k.7.
48th. row: As 14th. row.
49th. row: K.4, * c.6b., k.3, c.6f., k.6, c.6b., k.3, c.6f.; repeat from * ending last repeat k.4.
50th. row: As 10th. row.
51st. row: K.1, * c.6f., k.30; repeat from * until 7 remain, c.6f., k.1.
52nd. row: K.1, p.6, * k.9, p.3, k.6, p.3, k.9, p.6; repeat from * ending last repeat k.1.
53rd. row: K.16, * c.6f., c.6b., k.24; repeat from * ending last repeat k.16.
54th. row: K.1, p.6, * k.12, p.6; repeat from * ending last repeat k.1.
55th. row: K.19, * c.6f., k.30; repeat from * ending last repeat k.19 instead of 30.
56th. row: As 2nd. row.
The last 56 rows form the cable pattern. Work the first 20 rows to complete motifs. Then work the 21st. to 56th. with m. in cable pattern, marking each end of the last row with coloured threads to denote armholes.
Work the first 13 pattern rows again.
Now work Dog and Argyll motifs again as follows: **N**ext row: with m. pattern 37 as for 14th. pattern row, with b. p.6 for dog motif, with m. pattern 104, with a. p.2 for Argyll, with m. pattern 39.
The last row sets the position of the motifs. Work the 15th. to 48th. rows in cable pattern with motifs as set.
With m. only pattern 30 rows.
To slope the shoulders: Continuing in pattern as set, cast off 23 sts. at the beginning of the next 6 rows. Cast off the remaining 50 sts.

LEFT FRONT First work the pocket back: With size 3¾mm needles and m. cast on 36 sts. and work 36 rows in s.s., then leave these sts. on a stitch holder until required.
With size 4½mm needles and m. cast on 86 sts. and work 35 rows in double rib.
Increase row: Rib 4, * up1, rib 7; repeat from * ending last repeat rib 5. – 98 sts.
Change to size 4½mm needles and work in pattern as follows:
1st. row: All k..
2nd. row: K.1, p.6, * k.12, p.6; repeat from * ending last repeat k.1.
3rd. row: K.1, * c.6f., k.30; repeat from * ending last repeat k.19.
4th. **6**th. and **8**th. rows: As 2nd. row.

5th. row: All k..
7th. row: K.19, * c.6f., k.30; repeat from * ending last repeat k.1, instead of 30.
9th. row: K. 16, c.6b., * c.6f., k.24, c.6b.; repeat from * until 4 remain k.4.
10th. row: K.7, p.3, k.9, p.6, * k.9, p.3, k.6, p.3, k.9, p.6; repeat from * until 1 remains, k.1.
11th. row: As 3rd. row.
12th. row: As 10th. row.
The last 12 rows set the position of the pattern, given for the back. Work the 13th. to 39th. rows as set.
Pocket row: Pattern 40, slip next 36 sts. onto a stitch-holder at front of work until required and in their place, pattern across the 36 sts. of pocket back, pattern 22.
Pattern 1 row.
Now work the dog motif. Next row: with m. pattern 37 as set, with b., p.6 for dog motif, with m. pattern 55.
Continuing in pattern with dog motif as set, pattern 34 rows to compete motif.
Pattern 36 rows, marking the end of the last row with a coloured thread to denote armhole.
To slope the front edge: Maintaining the continuity of the pattern, dec. 1 st. at the end – front edge on the next row and the 6 following alternate rows. – 91 sts.
Next row: With m. pattern 50, with a. p.2 for the Argyll motif, with m. pattern 39.
The last row sets the position of the Argyll motif. Continuing in pattern with motif as set, dec. 1 st. at the end of the next row and the 21 following alternate rows.
On 69 sts. pattern 21 rows.
To slope the shoulder: Cast off 23 sts. at the beginning of the next row and the following alternate row. On 23 sts. work 1 row, then cast off.
Pocket top: With right side of work facing rejoin m. to the 36 sts. on stitch-holder and using size 3¾mm needles work 6 rows in double rib, then cast off in rib.

RIGHT FRONT Work as given for left front until the first 2 pattern rows have been worked.
3rd. row: K.19, * c.6f., k.30; repeat from * ending last repeat k.1.
4th., **6**th. and **8**th. rows: As 2nd. row.
5th. row: All k.
7th. row: K.1, * c.6f., k.30; repeat from * ending last repeat k.19.
9th. row: K.4, * c.6f., k.24, c.6b.; repeat from * until 22 remain, c.6f., k.16.
10th. row: K.1, p.6, k.9, p.3, * k.6, p.3, k.9, p.6, k.9, p.3; repeat from * until 7 remain, k.7.
11th. row: As 3rd. row.
12th. row: As 10th. row.
The last 12 rows set the position of the pattern, given for back. Work the 13. to 39th. rows as set.
Pocket row: Pattern 22, slip next 36 sts. onto a stitch holder until required and in their place pattern across the 36 sts. of pocket back, pattern 40.
Work 1 row.
Now work the Argyll motif. Next row: With m. pattern 57, with a. p.2 for Argyll motif, with m. pattern 39.
Continuing in pattern, with motif as set, work 34 rows to complete motif.
Pattern 36 rows, marking the beginning of the last row with a coloured thread to denote armhole.
To slope the front edge: Maintaining the continuity of the pattern, dec. 1 st. at the beginning – front edge on the next row and the 6 following alternate rows.
Next row: With m. pattern 37, with b. p.6 for dog motif, with m. pattern 48.
The last row sets the position of the motif. Continuing in pattern with motif as set, dec. 1

st. at the beginning of the next row and the 21 following alternate rows.

On 69 sts. pattern 22 rows.

To slope the shoulder: Work as given for left front shoulder to end, including pocket top.

COLLAR With size 3¾mm needles and m. cast on 144 sts. and work 2 rows in single rib. **W**ork turning rows as follows: **1**st. and **2**nd. turning rows: Rib 142, turn, rib 140, turn. **3**rd. and **4**th. turning rows: Rib 138, turn, rib 136, turn.

Thus working 2 sts. less before turning on each successive repeat; repeat the last 2 turning rows 20 times. Rib to end of row. **O**n all 144 sts. rib 3 rows.

1st. and **2**nd. turning rows: Rib 96, turn, rib 56, turn. **3**rd. and **4**th. turning rows: Rib 58, turn, rib 60, turn.

Thus working 2 sts. more before turning on each successive repeat; work the last 2 turning rows 21 times.

On all 144 sts. rib 2 rows, then cast off in rib.

SLEEVES Both alike: With size 3¾mm needles and m. cast on 42 sts. and work 23 rows in double rib.

Increase row: Rib 2, * up1, rib 1; repeat from * ending last repeat rib 3. – 80 sts.

Change to size 4½mm needles and work 24 rows in pattern as given for back.

Continuing in main pattern given for back, and working the extra sts. into the pattern as they occur, inc. 1 st. at each end of the next row and the 21 following 4th. rows. If desired, dog and Argyll motifs may be worked on the sleeves, commencing as follows at the 42nd. pattern row, when there will be 90 sts. 42nd. row: With m. pattern 26, with a. p.2 for Argyll motif, with m. pattern 32, with b. p.6 for dog motif, with m. pattern 24.

On 124 sts. pattern 3 rows, then cast off loosely.

MAKING UP Do not press. Join shoulder seams. Set in sleeves. Join sleeve and side seams. Neatly sew pocket backs and row ends of pocket tops in place. Fold collar in half and sew cast on and cast off edges all round neck edge, beginning and ending at first front edge decreases. Neatly sew zip fastener in place. ●

SCARF

MATERIALS 4 100 gram hanks or balls of either "Patricia Roberts Extra Thick Shetland Tweed" or "Patricia Roberts Extra Thick Wool" and oddments of "Patricia Roberts Angora" in each of 4 contrast colours. If you wish to knit the scarf without the motifs, omit the angora and add 1 extra ball or hank of main yarn ● This design is available as a knit kit, including small balls of angora ● A pair of size 4½mm Aero knitting needles; a thick cable needle ●

TENSION AND MEASUREMENTS Worked at a tension of 9 stitches – 1 repeat of the cable pattern – to 3 centimetres (1¼ inches) in width and 12 rows to 5 centimetres (2 inches) in depth, using size 4½mm needles, the scarf will measure 21 centimetres (8¾ inches) in width and 196 centimetres (78½ inches) in length ●

If you cannot obtain the correct tension using the size needles suggested, use larger or smaller ones accordingly ●

ABBREVIATIONS K., knit ● p., purl ● st., stitch ● c.6f, cable 6 front thus, slip next 3 stitches onto the cable needle and leave at front of work, k.3, then k.3 from cable needle ● c.6b., cable 6 back thus, slip next 3 stitches onto a cable needle and leave at back of work, k.3, then k.3 from cable needle ● stocking stitch is k. on the right side and p. on the wrong side ● m., main colour ● a., first contrast colour ● b., second contrast colour ● c., third contrast colour ● d., fourth contrast ● r.s. right side ● w.s. wrong side ●

TO WORK With size 4½mm needles and m. cast on 64 sts. and work in cable pattern as follows:

1st. row: K.1, * p.1, k.6, p.1, k.1; repeat from * to end.

2nd. row: K.2, * p.6, k.1, p.1, k.1; repeat rom * ending last repeat k.2 instead of k.1, p.1, k.1.

3rd. and **4**th. rows: As 1st. and 2nd. rows.

5th. row: K.1, * p.1, c.6f., p.1, k.1; repeat from * to end.

6th. row: As 2nd. row.

7th. and **8**th. rows: As 1st. and 2nd. rows.

Repeat these 8 rows 3 times, then work the first 6 rows again. Now work either the Argyll or the dog motif, continuing in cable pattern at each side of the stitches given in the chart. Use separate balls of m. at each side of the motif and separate small balls of contrasts for each section of the pattern. Unless indicated the picture pattern is worked in stocking stitch. The angora contrasts are used double through out.

Next row: With m. k.1, p.1, k.6, p.1, k.1, p.1, k.6, p.1, k.1, p.1, k.6, c.6b., c.6f., k.6, p.1, k.1, p.1, k.6, p.1, k.1, p.1, k.6, p.1, k.1.

Next row: With m. k.2, p.6, k.1, p.1, p.6, k.1. p.1, k.1, p.6, then from the chart, p.3, with colours from appropriate chart p.6, with m. p.3, with m. pattern to end as set.

Work a further 36 rows from the chart, while continuing in cable pattern as set at each side. This completes the motif.

Work the 5th. to 8th. cable rows.

Repeat the 8 cable rows 49 times.

Cast off in pattern

Tassels: To make one tassel: Cut 12 lengths of m. each 30 centimetres (12 inches) long. Fold these in half. Insert a crochet hook into one end of cast on edge and draw the looped ends through, pass cut ends through looped ends and pull firmly. Make a further 6 tassels evenly spaced, along this edge. Now make 7 tassels in the same way along the cast off edge. ●

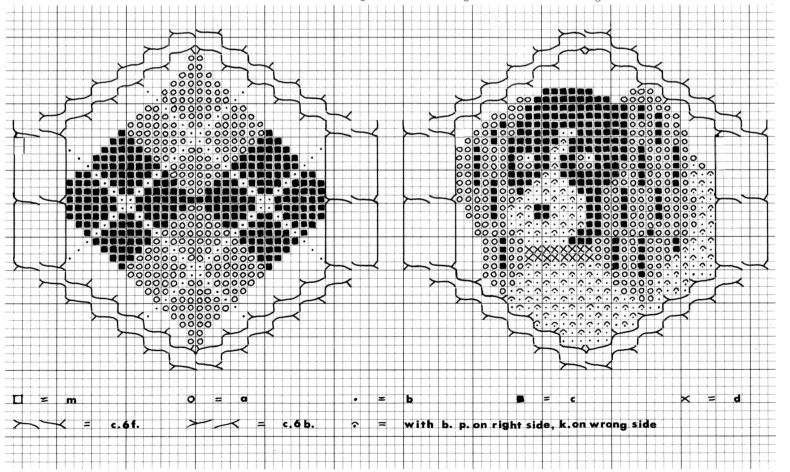

□ = m	O = a	• = b	■ = c	X = d

⟩⟨ = c.6f.   ⟩⟨ = c.6b.   ⌒ = with b. p. on right side, k. on wrong side

MATERIALS For the multi-colour version: 11 100 gram hanks of "Patricia Roberts Extra Thick Shetland Tweed" in main colour and in either the same yarn or in "Patricia Robert Extra Thick Wool" 2 hanks or balls in each of the contrasts coloured red and blue in the chart and 1 hank or ball in each of the 2 other colours.

For the one colour version: 12 100 gram balls of "Patricia Roberts Extra Thick Wool". ● Either version ● a pair each of size 3¾mm and 4mm Aero knitting needles ● a medium size cable needle ●

TENSION The tension is based on a stocking stitch tension of 10 stitches and 14 rows to 4 centimetres (2 inches) using size 4mm needles.

Knit a test square before commencing work and if you cannot obtain the correct tension using the size needles suggested, use larger or smaller ones accordingly.

Worked at this tension 1 repeat of the pattern – 42 sts. will measure 15 centimetres (6 inches) in width and 84 rows will measure 30 centimetres (12 inches) in depth ●

ABBREVIATIONS As given for Martinique ●
MEASUREMENTS The measurements are given in centimetres followed by inches in brackets ●
Underarms (including front bands) 124 (49¾) ● Side seam 37 (14¾) ● Length 64 (25¾) ● Sleeve seam 41 (16½) ●

MULTICOLOUR As given for Martinique.
BACK With size 3¾mm needles cast on 114 sts. and work 17 rows in single rib.

Increase row: Rib 2, * up 1, rib 2; repeat from * to end.

Change to size 4mm needles and on 170 sts. work as follows:

Work the first 152 pattern rows given for Martinique sweater, marking each end of the 86th pattern row with coloured threads to denote armhole.

To slope the shoulder: Continuing in pattern as set, cast off 11 sts. at the beginning of the next 10 rows. Cast off the remaining 60 sts.

LEFT FRONT With size 3¾mm needles and m. cast on 58 sts. and work 17 rows in single rib.

Increase row: Rib 2, * up 1, rib 2; repeat from * to end. – 86 sts.

Change to size 4mm needles and work 32 rows in pattern as given for back.

Divide the sts. for the pocket as follows:

Next row: Pattern 27, and leave these sts. on a spare needle, pattern 32 and leave these sts. for pocket back, onto the spare needle pattern to end and leave these 54 sts. in all until required.

Pocket back: With wrong side of work facing rejoin m. to the 32 sts. of pocket back and beginning with a p. row s.s. 2 rows.

With the colour indicated by red in the chart, p. 2 rows. With m.p.1 row, then k.1 row.

Repeat the last 4 rows 11 times.

With wrong side of work facing rejoin m. to the sts. on spare needle and work as follows:
Next row: Pattern 27, then pattern as set for 34th pattern row across the 32 sts. of pocket back, pattern to end.

Work the 35th to 133rd pattern rows, marking the armhole edge on the **86**th pattern row with a coloured thread to denote armhole.

Work 1 extra row here when working right front.

To shape the neck: Cast off 17 sts. at the beginning of the next row, then dec. 1 st. at the neck edge on each of the next 14 rows.

On 55 sts. pattern 4 rows.

To slope the shoulder: Cast off 11 sts., at the beginning of the next row and the 3 following alternate rows. On 11 sts. work 1 row, then cast off.

RIGHT FRONT Work as given for left front, working 1 extra row before shaping the neck.
SLEEVES Both alike ● With size 3¾mm needles and m. cast on 58 sts. and work 25 rows in single rib.

Increase row: Rib 2, * up 1, rib 2; repeat from * to end. – 86 sts.

Change to size 4mm needles and work the first 6 rows in pattern as for back.

Working the extra sts. into the pattern as they occur, inc. 1 st. at each end of the next row and the 20 following 4th rows. On 128 sts. pattern 3 rows, then cast off.

EXTRAS Buttonband: With size 3¾mm needles and m. cast on 14 sts. and work 14 rows in single rib, leave m. hanging. Join in the colour indicated by blue in the chart and k.4 rows. With m. rib 26 rows.

Repeat the last 30 rows 3 times then work the first 20 rows again. Cast off in rib.
Buttonhole band: With size 3¾mm needles and m. cast on 14 sts. and work 14 rows in single rib, leave m. hanging. Join in the colour indicated by blue in the chart and k.1 row.

1st. Buttonhole row: K.5, cast off 4, k. to end.
2nd. Buttonhole row: K.5, turn, cast on 4 over those cast off, turn, k. to end.
K. 1 row more.
With m. work 26 rows in single rib.
Repeat the last 30 rows 3 times, then work the first 20 rows again. Cast off in rib.

COLLAR With size 3¾mm needles and m. cast on 120 sts. and work 4 rows in single rib.
Decrease row: Rib 2, sl 1, k.2tog., p.s.s.o., rib until 5 remain, sl.1, k.2tog., p.s.s.o., rib 2.
Rib 5 rows.

Repeat the last 6 rows once more. – 112 sts.

Decrease row: K.3, * k.2tog., k.2; repeat from * ending last repeat k.3. – 85 sts.

Next row: K.2, up 1, k. until 2 remain, up 1, k.2.

Repeat the last row 4 times more.

1st. Buttonhole row: K. until 9 remain, cast off 4, k. to end.

2nd. Buttonhole row: K.5, turn, cast on 4, turn, k. to end.

K. 4 rows, then cast off.

MAKING UP Join shoulder seams. Sew cast off edges of sleeves to the row ends between the marking threads. Join sleeve and side seams. Neatly sew button and buttonhole bands in place. Join row ends of pocket backs. Sew cast off edge of collar in place all round neck edge, including frontbands. Sew on button. ●

CHARLIE HAT

MATERIALS 2 100 gram hanks or balls of either "Patricia Roberts Extra Thick Shetland Tweed" or "Patricia Roberts Extra Thick Wool" ● a pair each of size 4mm and 3¾mm Aero knitting needles ●

TENSION 14 stitches and 13 rows to 5 centimetres (2 inches) over the single rib using size 3¾mm needles ●
If you cannot obtain the correct tension using the size needles suggested use larger or smaller ones accordingly.

ABBREVIATIONS K., knit ● p., purl ● st., stitch ● tog., together ● sl., slip ● p.s.s.o., pass sl. st over ● single rib is k.1 and p.1 alternately ● double rib is k.2 and p.2 alternately ●

TO WORK With size 4mm needles cast on 136 sts. and work 60 rows in double rib.
Change to size 3¾mm needles and work 30 rows in single rib.

1st. Decrease row: Rib 7, * sl.1, k2tog., p.s.s.o., rib 14; repeat from * ending last repeat rib 7. – 120 sts.

Rib 3 rows.

2nd. Decrease row: Rib 6, * sl.1, k2tog., p.s.s.o., rib 12; repeat from * ending last repeat rib 6. – 104 sts.

Thus working 1st. less before, 2 sts. less between and 1st. less after the decreases on each successive repeat of the decrease row, repeat the last 4 rows twice more, then work decrease rows on the 3 following alternate rows. – 24 sts.

Next row: * P.2tog.; repeat from * to end. – 12 sts.

Break off yarn leaving a long end. Thread through the remaining 13 sts. draw up, and with this end join row end edges. Roll over double rib edging. ●

168

160

144

128

112

96

80

64

48

32

16

1

□	=	k. on r.s. p. on w.s.	⋌	=	k. 2 tog.	O	=	y.r.n.	⋎	=	3 from 1	⟋⟍	=	c.10 f.
∧	=	p. on r.s. k. on w.s.	⋋	=	s.s.k.	⋁	=	upl	⤬	=	2 from 2		=	c.8 f.
	=	c. bf.	⋏	=	p. 2 tog.	⋁	=	inc.					=	c.8 b.

45

MATERIALS For the sweater: Either 10 100 gram balls of "Patricia Roberts Extra Thick Wool" or 11 100 gram hanks of "Patricia Roberts Extra Thick Shetland Tweed" in main colour, plus in either of these yarns 2 balls or hanks in first contrast – sand – and 1 ball or hank in each of the other 5 contrast colours● A pair each of 3¾mm and 4½mm Aero knitting needles, a large cable needle● For the jacket: Add 1 ball or hank in main colour and 5 buttons.

TENSION Based on a stocking stitch tension of 10 stitches and 14 rows to 5 centimetres (2 inches) using size 4½mm needles, 1 repeat of the pattern – 42 sts. will measure 15 centimetres (6 inches) in width and 84 rows will measure 30 centimetres (12 inches) in depth●

If you cannot obtain the correct stocking stitch tension using the size needles suggested, use larger or smaller needles accordingly●

ABBREVIATIONS K., knit● p., purl● st., stitch● tog., together● dec., decrease (by working 2 sts. together)● inc., increase (by working twice into same st.)● 3 from 1, k. into front, back, then front again of same st.● sl. slip● p.s.s.o., pass sl. st. over● s.s.k., sl.1, k.1, p.s.s.o.● c.8b., cable 8 back, slip next 4 sts. onto cable needle and leave at back of work, k.4, then k.4 from cable needle● c.8f., cable 8 front, as c.8b., but leaving sts. on cable needle at front of work● up1., pick up the loop, which lies between the needles, slip it onto left hand needle, then k. into back of it● y.r.n., yarn round needle● c.6f., cable 6 front thus, slip next 3 sts. onto a cable needle at front of work, k.3, then k.3 from cable needle● c.10f., cable 10 front thus, slip next 5 sts. onto cable needle at front of work, k.5, then k.5 from cable needle● 2 from 2, k.2tog., into front of 2 sts., then p.2tog. into the back of them●

MEASUREMENTS The measurements are given in centimetres followed by inches in brackets.
Underarms sweater: 120 (48) Jacket: 125 (50)● Side seam 52 (20¾)● Length 77 (30¾)● Sleeve seam 42.5 (17)●

SWEATER

BACK With size 3¾mm needles and m. cast on 114 sts. and work 19 rows in single rib.
Increase row: P.2, * up1, p.2; repeat from * to end. – 170 sts.
Change to size 4½mm needles and work in pattern as follows. Use separate balls of contrast colour for each motif and separate balls of m. at each side of the larger motifs. Take care not to pull colours not in use tightly across the back of the work.
1st. row: With m. k.1, with colours given in chart, work the 84 st. chart pattern twice, with m. k.1.
Beginning and ending each row with k.1, work the 2nd. to 34th. rows from the chart.
Now increasing 1 st. at the beginning and decreasing 1 st. at the end of each right side row, to keep the pattern correct, work the 35th. to 50th. pattern rows.
Work the 51st. to 118th. pattern rows straight.
Now, increasing 1 st. at the beginning and decreasing 1 st. at the end of each right side row, work the 119th. to 134th. rows; marking each end of the 128th. pattern row with coloured threads to denote armholes.
Work the 135th. to 168th. rows straight, then work the first 20 pattern rows again.
To slope the shoulders: Cast off 11 sts. at the beginning of the next 10 rows, then cast off the remaining 60 sts.

FRONT Work as given for back until 141 rows have been worked in pattern and the armholes have been marked.
Now divide the sts. for the neck: Next row: Pattern 75 and leave these sts. on a spare needle until required for right front shoulder, cast off 20, pattern to end and continue on these 75 sts. for the left front shoulder.
Left front shoulder: To slope the neck: Dec. 1 st. at the end of the next row and the 19 following alternate rows.
On 55 sts. work 7 rows.
To slope the shoulder: Cast off 11 sts. at the beginning of the next row and the 3 following alternate rows. On 11 sts. work 1 row, then cast off.
Right front shoulder: With right side of work facing rejoin yarn to inner edge of sts. left on spare needle and work to end of row, then work as given for left front shoulder to end.
Collar: With size 3¾mm needles and m. cast on 24 sts. and work 2 rows in single rib.
Continuing in rib, inc. 1 st. at the end of the next row and the 19 following alternate rows. On 44 sts. rib 93 rows.
Dec. 1 st. at the end (shaped edge) on the next row and the 19 following alternate rows. On 24 sts. rib 2 rows, then cast off in rib.
SLEEVES Both alike: With size 3¾mm needles and m. cast on 58 sts. and work 19 rows in single rib, then work the increase row given for back. – 86 sts.
Change to size 4½mm needles and work 66 rows in pattern as for back, increasing 1 st. at the beginning and decreasing 1 st. at the end of the 35th. to 49th. rows inclusive. to keep the pattern correct.
Maintaining the continuity of the pattern and working the extra sts. in garter st. as they occur, inc. 1 st. at each end of the next row and the 16 following alternate rows.
On 120 sts. pattern 3 rows, then cast off.
MAKING UP Do not press. Join shoulder seams. Set in sleeves, between the marking threads on back and front. Join sleeve and side seams. Sew collar in place, so that shaped row end edges are sewn to the shaped edges of neck and the cast on and cast off sts. are sewn to the sts. cast off at centre front.

JACKET

BACK As given for sweater.
LEFT FRONT With size 3¾mm needles and m. cast on 58 sts. and work 19 rows in single rib, then work the increase row given for back. – 86 sts.
Change to size 4½mm needles and work 124 rows in pattern from chart as for back. Work 1 extra row here, when working right front.
To slope the front edge: Dec. 1 st. at the end of the next row and at the same edge on the 30 following alternate rows, but marking the armhole edge with a coloured thread on the 128th pattern row. – 55 sts.
Work 3 rows ending at armhole edge.
To slope the shoulder: Cast off 11 sts. at the beginning of the next row and the 3 following alternate rows. On 11 sts. work 1 row, then cast off.
RIGHT FRONT Work as given for left front, noting the variation in the rows before sloping front edge.
Frontband: With size 3¾mm needles and m. cast on 10 sts. and work 6 rows in single rib.
1st. Buttonhole row: Rib 3, cast off 4, rib to end.
2nd. Buttonhole row: Rib 3, turn, cast on 4, turn, rib to end.
Rib 32 rows.
Repeat the last 34 rows 3 times, then work the 2 buttonhole rows again.

Rib 352 rows, then cast off in rib.
Pocket backs 2 alike: With size 4½mm needles and m. cast on 35 sts. and work 36 rows in single rib, then cast off.
SLEEVES As given for sweater.
MAKING UP Do not press. Join shoulder seams. Set in sleeves, between the marking threads on back and front. Join sleeve and side seams, inserting pockets 8 centimetres (3 inches) above ribbing and sewing them in place neatly on wrong side of fronts. Neatly sew frontband in place, so that the last buttonhole is in line with the first front edge decrease. Sew on buttons. ●

MARILYN

MATERIALS 7 50 gram balls of "Woollybear Shetland Fleck" and 17 25 gram balls of "Woollybear 100% Mohair"● a pair of size 5½ mm needles● 7 buttons● 2 shoulder pads●

TENSION 8 stitches and 10 rows to 5 centimetres (2 inches) over the pattern using size 5½ mm needles●
If you cannot obtain the correct tension using the size needles suggested, use larger or smaller ones accordingly●

ABBREVIATIONS K., knit● p., purl● st., stitch● tog., together● dec., decrease (by working 2 sts. tog.)● inc., increase (by working twice into same st.)● single rib is k.1 and p.1 alternately●

NOTE The instructions are given for the small size. Where they vary work the instructions in the first brackets for the medium size and the figures in the second brackets for the large size●

MEASUREMENTS The measurements are given in centimetres followed by inches in brackets●
Underarms – fastened 105 [42] (110 [44]) (115 [46])● Side seam 40 (16)● Length 65 (26)● Sleeve seam 37.5 (15)●

BACK With size 5½ mm needles and one strand each of "Shetland Fleck" and "Mohair", together, cast on 84 (88) (92) sts. and work 4 rows in single rib. Now work in pattern as follows:
1st row: *P.1, k.1; repeat from * to end.
2nd row: As 1st row.
3rd row: *K.1, p.1; repeat from * to end.
4th row: As 3rd row.
The last 4 rows form the pattern; repeat them 18 times more. Work should now measure 40 centimetres (16 inches) from beginning.
To shape the armholes: Maintaining the continuity of the pattern as set, cast off 4 sts. at the beginning of the next 2 rows, then dec. 1 st. at each end of the next 5 (6) (7) rows.
On 66 (68) (70) sts. pattern 39 (38) (37) rows.
To slope the shoulders: Cast off 9 (10) (11) sts. at the beginning of the next 2 rows, then 10 sts. at the beginning of the next 2 rows. Cast off the remaining 28 sts.

LEFT FRONT First knit the pocket backs.
Large pocket back: With size 5½ mm needles and the two yarns together, cast on 24 sts. and work 24 rows in pattern as given for back, then leave these sts. on a stitch-holder until required.
Small pocket back: With size 5½ mm needles and both yarns together cast on 16 sts. and work 20 rows in pattern, then leave these sts. on a stitch-holder until required.
With size 5½ mm needles and both yarns together, cast on 54 (56) (58) sts. and work 4 rows in single rib.
Work the 4 pattern rows given for back 6 times.
Pocket row: Slip first 24 sts. onto stitch-holder until required and in their place, pattern across the 24 sts. of large pocket back, pattern to end.
Pattern 27 rows.
1st Buttonhole row: Pattern until 6 sts. remain, cast off 2, pattern to end.
2nd Buttonhole row: Pattern 4, turn, cast on 2 over those cast off, turn, pattern to end.
Pattern 22 rows.
To shape the armhole: Cast off 4 sts. at the beginning of the next row, then dec. 1 st. at the armhole edge on each of the next 5 (6) (7) rows. On 45 (46) (47) work 2 (1) (nil) rows.
Pocket row: Pattern 2, slip next 16 sts. onto a stitch-holder until required and in their place work across the 16 sts. of small pocket back, pattern to end.

On 45 (46) (47) sts. pattern 8 rows.
**To shape the lapel: Dec. 1 st. at the beginning of the next row and at the same edge on each of the next 3 rows.
Cast off in pattern 10 sts., marking the 6th of these sts. with a coloured thread, at the beginning of the next row. Cast off 4 sts. at the beginning of the 2 following alternate rows. Dec 1 st. at the end of the next row and at the same edge on each of the next 3 rows. On 19 (20) (21) sts. pattern 16 rows.
To slope the shoulder: Cast off 9 (10) (11) sts. at the beginning of the next row. On 10 sts., work 1 row, then cast off.
Pocket tops, alike: With right side of work facing rejoin both yarns together to the sts. left on stitch-holder. With size 5½ mm needles work 4 rows in single rib, then cast off in rib.

RIGHT FRONT Work as given for left front, but omitting small pocket back, until 24 rows have been worked in pattern.
Pocket row: Pattern (30) (32) (34), slip next 24 sts. onto a stitch-holder until required, in their place, pattern across the 24 sts of pocket back.
Pattern 1 row.
1st Buttonhole row: Pattern 4, cast off 2, pattern to end.
2nd Buttonhole row: Pattern until 4 remain, turn, cast on 2, turn, pattern to end.
Pattern 24 rows, then work the 2 buttonhole rows again. Pattern 23 rows.
To shape the armhole: Cast off 4 sts. at the beginning of the next row, then dec. 1 st. at the armhole edge on each of the next 5 (6) (7) rows.
On 45 (46) (47) sts. pattern 11 (10) (9) rows.
To shape the lapel: Work as given for left front from ** to end, including the pocket top.

EXTRAS The collar● With size 5½ mm needles and both yarns together, cast on 76 sts. and work 10 rows in single rib. Mark each end of the last row with coloured threads. Dec. 1 st. at each end of the next 4 rows, then cast off 4 sts. at the beginning of the 4 following rows. Cast off the remaining 52 sts. in rib.
Epaulettes 2 alike● With size 5½ mm needles and both yarns together, cast on 8 sts. and work 20 rows in single rib. Dec. 1 st. at each end of the next 3 rows. Take the 2 remaining sts. tog. and fasten off.
Shoulder pad covers 2 alike● With size 5½ mm needles and both yarns, cast on 26 sts. and pattern 8 rows as given for back. Dec. 1 st. at each end of the next row and the 3 following alternate rows. Work 1 row, then dec. 1 st. at each end of the next 8 rows. Take the 2 remaining sts. tog. and fasten off.
SLEEVES Both alike● With size 5½ mm needles and both yarns together, cast on 46 (48) (50) sts. and work 20 rows in single rib.
Work 8 rows in pattern as for back.
Working the extra sts. into the pattern as they occur, inc. 1 st. at each end of the next row and the 7 following 6th rows.
On 62 (64) (66) sts. pattern 5 rows.
To shape the sleevetop: Cast off 4 sts. at the beginning of the next 2 rows. Dec. 1 st. at each end of the next row and the 7 following alternate rows. Work 1 row straight, then dec. at each end of the next 12 rows. – 14 (16) (18) sts.
Cast off 3 sts. at the beginning of the next 4 rows. Cast off the remaining 2 (4) (6) sts.
MAKING UP Pin out to size and press very lightly on the wrong side with a warm iron over a damp cloth. Join shoulder seams. Set in sleeves. Join sleeve and side seams. Sew row ends of pocket tops in place. Neatly sew cast off and row end edges of collar, between the marking threads, to neck edge between its marking threads. Sew on

buttons. Sew cast on edge of shoulder pad covers to wrong side of sleevetop seam. Insert shoulder pads and catch row end edges of covers in place. Sew cast on edges of epaulettes in position, then secure with buttons. ●

POPPY Continued from page 101

k.15, with b. p.5, with m. k.11.
The last 12 rows set the position of the pattern. Work the **13**th to **16**th rows as set.
Continuing in pattern and working the extra sts. into the pattern as they occur, inc. 1 st. at each end of the next row and the 12 following 8th rows. On 89 sts., pattern 7 rows. Mark each end of the last row with coloured threads.
With m. work 14 rows in garter st. only, then cast off loosely.
MAKING UP Pin out to size and press very lightly on the wrong side with a cool iron over a dry cloth. Join shoulder seams. Join side seams. Join sleeve seams up to marking threads. Matching these marking threads to those at underarms, sew the row ends at top of sleeves above marking threads to the cast off groups at underarms. Sew cast off edge of sleeves to row ends of armhole edges. Join cast off edges of collars, then sew shaped row end edges of buttonhole band and buttonband in place, up right front, round neck edge and down left front. Sew pocket backs and row ends of pocket tops in place. Sew on buttons. ●

SHEBA Continued from page 51

sts. up to first front edge dec. and 50 sts. up to shoulder. – 140 sts.
1st Buttonhole row: K.50, *cast off 3; k. next 17 sts.; repeat from * ending last repeat k. next 2 sts.
2nd Buttonhole row: K.3, *turn, cast on 3, turn, k.18; repeat from * ending last repeat k.50.
K.1 row, then cast off using a size larger needle.
SLEEVES Both alike.● With size 3 mm needles and m. cast on 56 sts. and work 15 rows in single rib.
Increase row: Rib 1, *up 1, rib 2; repeat from * ending last repeat rib 1. – 84 sts.
Join in c., change to size 5 mm needles and work 220 rows in pattern as given for back. Break off m.
Change to size 3¾ mm needles and with c. k.6 rows, then cast off.
Underarm pieces Both alike● With size 3¾ mm needles and m. cast on 3 sts. and k.2 rows, then, working in garter stitch, inc. 1 st. at each end of the next row and the 5 following alternate rows. On 15 sts. work 3 rows, marking each end of the 2nd row with coloured threads. Dec. 1 st. at each end of the next row and the 5 following 6th rows. Take the 3 remaining sts. tog. and fasten off.
MAKING UP Pin out to size – and press lightly on the wrong side with a warm iron over a damp cloth. Join shoulder seams. Sew cast off edge of sleeves to row ends between the marking threads on back and front. Matching the marking threads on underarm pieces to those on back and front pin the underarm pieces in place so that the 16 row ends up to the markings are pinned to row ends of back and front and those above the marking threads are pinned to those on sleeves. Join sleeve and side seams, insetting underarm pieces. Neatly sew pocket backs and row ends of pocket tops in place. Sew on buttons. ●

Daytime pyjamas, by
"Kamikaze", topped by
"Marilyn" jacket, knitted
in "Mohair" and
"Shetland Fleck"
together. Very simple and
quick to make.

"Sheba" cardigan – it's easier than it looks. By cleverly slipping sts. only one colour is used on any one row. Worn with a skirt and top by "Gerard" and charm bracelet from "Butler and Wilson". Zebra print coat by "Horatio Lovely" from Patricia Roberts, Covent Garden.

MATERIALS 8 28 gram hanks of "Woollybear Real Shetland" in main colour and 15 25 gram balls of "Woollybear 100% Mohair" in contrast colour● a pair each of size 5 mm, size 3 mm and size 3¾ mm Aero knitting needles● 5 buttons.●

TENSION 13 stitches and 14 rows to view or 28 rows worked to 5 centimetres (2 inches) over the patterns using size 5 mm needles.● If you cannot obtain the correct tension using the size needles suggested, use larger or smaller ones accordingly.●

ABBREVIATIONS K., knit● p., purl● st., stitch● tog., together● dec., decrease (by working 2 sts. tog.)● inc., increase (by working twice into same st.)● single rib is k.1 and p.1 alternately● m., main colour● c., contrast colour● sl., slip● y.f., yarn forward● y.b., yarn back● garter st. is k. plain on every row● stocking stitch is k. on the right side and p. on the wrong side● up 1, pick up the loop, which lies between the needles, slip it onto left hand needle, then k. into back of it●

MEASUREMENTS The measurements are given in centimetres followed by inches in brackets.● Underarms 117.5 (47)● Length 60 (24)● Sleeve Length 42-5(17).●

BACK With size 3 mm needles and m. cast on 126 sts. and work 16 rows in single rib. Change to size 5 mm needles and work in pattern as follows: For easier working m. and c. are worked on separate rows; for every 4 rows worked only 2 will be apparent on the finished work. Similarly only 2 pattern rows are shown in the chart for each 4 worked. Do not pull colours not in use tightly across the back of the work.

1st row: With m., *k.5, sl.4, k.3, sl.2, k.2, sl.4, k.7, sl.4, k.2, sl.2, k.4, sl.3; repeat from * to end.

2nd row: With m., *sl.3, y.b., k.4, y.f., sl.2, y.b., k.2, y.f., sl.4, y.b., k.7, y.f., sl.4, y.b., k.2, y.f., sl.2, y.b., k.3, y.f., sl.4, y.b., k.5 y.f.; repeat from * to end.

3rd row: With c., *sl.5, k.4, sl.3, k.2, sl.2, k.4, sl.7, k.4, sl.2, k.2, sl.4, k.3; repeat from * to end.

4th row: With c. *k.3, y.f., sl.4, y.b., k.2, y.f., sl.2, y.b., k.4, y.f., sl.7, y.b., k.4, y.f., sl.2, y.b., k.2, y.f., sl.3, y.b., k.4, y.f., sl.5 y.b.; repeat from * to end.

5th row: With m. *sl.1, k.4, sl.4, k.3, sl.2, k.1, sl.3, k.3, sl.5, k.3, sl.3, k.2, sl.2, k.4, sl.2; repeat from * to end.

6th row: With m. *sl.2, y.b., k.4, y.f., sl.2, y.b., k.2, y.f., sl.3, y.b., k.3, y.f., sl.5, y.b., k.3, y.f., sl.3, y.b., k.1, y.f., sl.2, y.b., k.3, y.f., sl.4, y.b., k.4, y.f., sl.1; repeat from * to end.

7th row: With c., *k.1, sl.4, k.4, sl.3, k.2, sl.1, k.3, sl.3, k.5, sl.3, k.3, sl.2, k.2, sl.4, k.2; repeat from * to end.

8th row: With c. *k.2, y.f., sl.4, y.b., k.2, y.f., sl.2, y.b., k.3, y.f., sl.3, y.b., k.5, y.f., sl.3, y.b., k.3, y.f., sl.1, y.b., k.2, y.f., sl.3, y.b., k.4, y.f., sl.4, y.b., k.1; repeat from * to end.

The last 8 rows set the position and show how the garter stitch pattern is worked from the chart, alternating m. and c. for each pair of rows. Odd numbered rows are worked from right to left and even numbered rows from left to right.

Continuing in pattern as set, and given in the chart, work the **9**th to **88**th pattern rows. Working the extra sts. into the pattern as they occur, inc. 1 st. at each end of the next row and the 13 following 8th rows. On 154 sts. pattern 7 rows. Mark each end of the last row with coloured threads.

Continuing in pattern, work 96 rows more. To slope the shoulders: Cast off 7 sts. at the beginning of the next 16 rows. — 42 sts. Break off c.

Change to size 3 mm. needles and with m. only work as follows: Decrease row: K.2, *k.2tog., k.3; repeat from * to end. — 34 sts. K.3 rows, then cast off using a size larger needle.

LEFT FRONT First work the pocket back as follows: With size 3¾ mm needles and m. cast on 35 sts. and work 36 rows in stocking stitch, then leave these sts. on a stitch-holder until required.

With size 3 mm needles and m. cast on 65 sts. and work 16 rows in single rib. Change to size 5 mm needles, join in c. and work in pattern as follows, noting the information given for the back.***

1st row: With m., *k.5, sl.4, k.3, sl.2, k.2, sl.4*, k.7, sl.4, k.2, sl.2, k.4, sl.3; repeat from * to *, then k.3.

2nd row: With m., k.3,* y.f., sl.4, y.b., k.2, y.f., sl.2, y.b., k.3, y.f., sl.4, y.b., k.5*, y.f., sl.3, y.b., k.4, y.f., sl.2, y.b., k.2, y.f., sl.4, y.b., k.7; repeat from * to *.

3rd row: With c., *sl.5, k.4, sl.3, k.2, sl.2, k.4*, sl.7, k.4, sl.2, k.2, sl.4, k.3; repeat from * to *, sl.3.

4th row: With c., sl.1, *y.b., k.4, y.f., sl.2, y.b., k.2, y.f., sl.3, y.b., k.4, y.f., sl.5*, y.b., k.3, y.f., sl.4, y.b., k.2, y.f., sl.2, y.b., k.4, y.f., sl.7; repeat from * to *.

The last 4 rows set the position of the pattern given in the chart. Work the 5th to 72nd rows from the chart.

Pocket row: Pattern 15, slip next 35 sts. onto a stitch-holder and in their place, pattern across the 35 sts. of pocket back, pattern to end.

Work the 74th to 88th rows from the chart. ****To shape the side seam: Working the extra sts. into the pattern as they occur, inc. 1 st. at the beginning of the next row and the 13 following 8th rows — 79 sts.

Pattern 7 rows, marking the end of the last

of these rows with a coloured thread to denote armhole.

To slope the front edge: Continuing in pattern, dec. 1 st. at the end of the next row and the 22 following 4th rows.

On 56 sts. pattern 7 rows.

To slope the shoulder: Cast off 7 sts. at the beginning of the next row and the 6 following alternate rows. On 7 sts. work 1 row, then cast off.

The pocket top: With right side of work facing rejoin m. to the 35 sts. left on stitch-holder at front of work and using size 3 mm needles k.6 rows, then cast off. ****

Frontband: With right side of work facing rejoin m. at left front shoulder and using size 3 mm needles, pick up and k. 50 sts. down to first front edge decrease, then 90 sts. down to cast on edge. On 140 sts. k.3 rows, then cast off using a size larger needle.

RIGHT FRONT Work as given for left front until *** is reached.

1st and 2nd rows: With m., *k.6, sl.4, k.2, sl.2, k.4, sl.3, k.5, sl.4, k.3, sl.2, k.2, sl.4, k.7, sl.4, k.2, sl.2, k.4, sl.3**, turn and work from ** back to *, with m. to wrong side of work, when slipping sts.

3rd and 4th rows: With c., *sl.6, k.4, sl.2, k.2, sl.4, k.3, k.5, k.4, sl.3, k.2, sl.2, k.4, sl.7, k.4, sl.2, k.2, sl.4, k.3**, turn and work from ** back to *.

The last 4 rows set the position of the pattern given in the chart. Work the 5th to 72nd rows from the chart, then work the pocket row given for left front. Now work the 74th to 89th rows from the chart. Work as given for left front from **** to ****.

Frontband: With right side of work facing rejoin m. at cast on edge of right front and using size 3 mm needles pick up and k. 90

Continued on page 48●

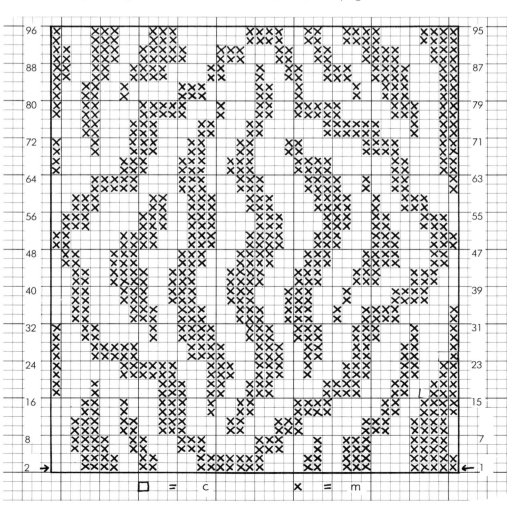

| | | | | = c | | | X | = m | | |

"Coco", the suit shape of the moment. Quick and easy to knit. Other good colourways are purple, navy, black or grey. 'Butler and Wilson' jewellery completes that chic French look.

MATERIALS For the Jacket: 8 50 gram hanks of "Patricia Roberts Shetland No. 2" in black marl or tweed plus in selected colour, 14 25 gram balls of either "Patricia Roberts" "Kid Mohair" or "Fine Cotton" and one 25 gram ball of either "Patricia Roberts Lurex No.1" or "Fine Cotton" for contrast● 2 large shoulder pads● 10 buttons● For the Skirt add 4 hanks of "Shetland No. 2" and 8 balls of either "Kid Mohair" or "Fine Cotton" and a waist length of elastic● A pair each of size 3¾mm and 4mm Aero knitting needles●

TENSION 9 stitches and 12 rows to 5 centimetres (2 inches) over the pattern using size 4mm needles and one strand of each of the 2 yarns recommended●
If you cannot obtain the correct tension using the size needles suggested use larger or smaller ones accordingly●

ABBREVIATIONS K., knit● p., purl● st., stitch● tog., together● dec., decrease (by working 2 sts. tog)● inc., increase (by working twice into same st.)● m., main colour – 1 strand each of the 2 main colour yarns● c., contrast colour – 1 strand each of "Shetland No. 2" and the contrast yarn● garter st. is k. plain on every row● sl., slip● p.s.s.o., pass sl. st. over●

NOTE The instructions are given for the small size. Where they vary, work the instructions given in the first brackets for the medium size or for the skirt only the instructions given in the second brackets for the large size●

MEASUREMENTS The measurements are given in centimetres followed by inches in brackets●
Jacket: Underarms 118 (47½) (125 [50])● Side seam 40 (16)● Length 65 (26)● Sleeve seam 40 (16)● All around at hem 99 (39½) (105 [42])●
Skirt: All around at widest part 90 [36] (95 [38]) (100 [40])● Length – 59 [23½]●

BACK With size 3¾mm needles and m. – 1 strand each of "Shetland No. 2" and either "Kid Mohair" or "Fine Cotton", cast on 88 (96) sts. by the thumb method and k.1 row (wrong side). Join in c. and with c. k.2 rows, with m. k.4 rows, with c. k.2 rows, with m. k.3 rows.
Change to size 4mm needles and p.1 row, then work in pattern as follows:
1st row: *K.2, p.2; repeat from * to end.
2nd row: *K.2, p.2; repeat from * to end.
3rd row: As 1st row.
4th row: *P.2, k.2; repeat from * to end.
5th row: *P.2, k.2; repeat from * to end.
6th row: As 4th row.
The last 6 rows form the pattern; repeat them twice more.
Continuing in pattern as set and working the extra sts. into the pattern as they occur, inc. 1 st. at each end of the next row and the 7 following 8th rows.
On 104 (112) sts. pattern 13 rows.
To shape the armholes: Cast off 4 sts. at the beginning of the next 2 rows, then dec. 1 st. at each end of the next row and the 10 following alternate rows. On 74 (82) sts. pattern 17 rows.
Inc. 1 st. at each end of the next row and the following 6th row. On 78 (86) sts. pattern 5 rows.
To slope the shoulders: Cast off 7 sts. at the beginning of the next 6 rows and 5 (7) sts. on the 2 following rows. Cast off the remaining 26 (30) sts.

LEFT FRONT First work the large pocket back: With size 4mm needles and m. cast on 20 sts. and work 30 rows in pattern as given for back, then leave these sts. on a stitch-holder until required.
Small pocket: Work thus: With size 4mm needles and m. cast on 16 sts. and work 18 rows in pattern as for back, then leave these sts. on a stitch-holder until required.
With size 3¾mm needles and m. cast on 49 (53) sts. by the thumb method and k.1 row (wrong side).
While working in garter st. stripes of 2 rows c., 4 rows m., 2 rows c., 2 rows m., dec. 1 st. at the end of the first row and the 4 following alternate rows. – 44 (48) sts.
Change to size 4mm needles and continuing with m. only k.1 row and p.1 row, then pattern 18 rows as for back. Inc. 1 st. at the beginning – side seam edge on the next row and the following 8th row.
On 46 (50) sts. work 3 rows.
Pocket row: Pattern 14, slip next 20 sts. onto stitch-holder at front of work and in their place pattern across the 20 sts. of pocket back, pattern 12 (16).
Work 3 rows.
Inc. 1 st. at the beginning of the next row and the 5 following 8th rows. On 52 (56) sts. pattern 13 rows.
To shape the armhole: Cast off 4 sts. at the beginning of the next row, then dec. 1 st. at the same edge on the 6 following alternate rows. On 42 (46) sts. work 1 row.
Pocket row: Dec., pattern 12, slip next 16 sts. onto a stitch-holder at front of work and in their place, pattern across the 16 sts. of the small pocket back, pattern 12 (16).
Work 1 row straight, then dec. 1 st. at the armhole edge on the next row and the 3 following alternate rows.
**On 37 (41) sts. pattern 8 rows.
To shape the neck: Cast off 5 (7) sts. at the beginning of the next row, then dec. 1 st. at the neck edge on each of the next 8 rows. – 24 (26) sts.
Inc. 1 st. at the beginning – armhole edge – of the next row and the following 6th row. On 26 (28) sts. pattern 5 rows.
To slope the shoulder: Cast off 7 sts. at the beginning of the next row and the following alternate row, then 6 (7) sts. on the next alternate row. On 6 (7) sts. work 1 row, then cast off.
Pocket tops Alike: With right side of work facing rejoin m. to the sts. on stitch-holder and k.2 rows in m., k.2 rows in c., k.2 rows in m., k.2 rows in c., then k.1 row in m. Cast off loosely k. wise in m.
Frontband: With right side of work facing rejoin m. and using size 3¾mm needles, pick up and k. 92 sts. from front edge and k. 1 row.
Increasing 1 st. at each end of every right side row, k.2 rows in c., k.4 rows in m., k.2 rows in c., then k.1 row in m. – 102 sts. Cast off k.wise loosely.

RIGHT FRONT Work the large pocket back as for left front.
With size 3¾mm needles and m. cast on 49 (53) sts. by the thumb method and k.1 row (wrong side).
Now, while working in garter st. stripes of 2 rows c., 4 rows m., 2 rows c., 2 rows m., dec. 1 st. at the beginning of the first row and the 4 following alternate rows. – 44 (48) sts.
Change to size 4mm needles and continuing with m. only k.1 row and p.1 row, then work 18 rows in pattern as for back.
Inc. 1 st. at the beginning – side seam edge – on the next row and the following 8th row. On 46 (50) sts. work 3 rows.
Pocket row: Pattern 12 (16), slip next 20 sts. onto stitch-holder at front of work and in their place pattern across the 20 sts. of pocket back, pattern 14.
On 46 (50) sts. work 3 rows.
Inc. 1 st. at the end of the next row and the 5 following 8th rows. On 52 (56) sts. pattern 14 rows.

To shape the armhole: Cast off 4 sts. at the beginning of the next row, then dec. 1 st. at the same edge on the 10 following alternate rows.
Now work as given for left front from ** to end, then work the pocket top.
Frontband: With right side of work facing rejoin m. and using size 3¾mm needles pick up and k. 92 sts. from front edge and k.1 row.
Increasing 1 st. at each end of every right side row, k.2 rows in c., then 1 row in m.
1st Buttonhole row (wrong side): With m. k.2, *cast off 2, k. next 15 sts.; repeat from * 4 times more, cast off 2, k. next st.
2nd Buttonhole row: Inc. in first st., k.1, turn, cast on 2 over those cast off, turn, k.16; repeat from * ending last repeat k.1, inc.
With m. k.1 row.
Still increasing 1 st. at each end of right side rows, with c. k.2 rows, with m. k.1 row – 102 sts. With m. cast off loosely k.wise.
Neckband: First join shoulder seams. With right side of work facing rejoin m. and using size 3¾mm needles pick up and k. 23 sts. from right front neck edge, 30 sts. from back neck edge and 23 sts. from left front neck edge.
On 76 sts. k.1 row. Increasing 1 st. at each end of right side rows, k.2 rows in c., k.4 rows in m., k.2 rows in c., then k.1 row in m. – 86 sts. With m. cast off loosely k.wise.

SLEEVES: Left sleeve: **With size 3¾mm needles and m. cast on 28 (32) sts. by the thumb method and k.1 row – wrong side row. Now while decreasing 1 st. at the beginning of each right side row, k.2 rows in c., k.2 rows in m., k.2 rows in c., k.2 rows in m. – 24 (28) sts.
Mark shaped end of last row with a coloured thread.
Change to size 4mm needles and continuing with m. only, k.1 row and p.1 row. Now pattern 18 rows as for back.** Then mark the last st. with a coloured thread and leave these sts. until required.
***W**ith size 3¾mm needles and m. cast on 16 sts. by the thumb method and k.1 row, with c. k. 2 rows, with m. k.2 rows, with c. k.2 rows, with m. k.2 rows.
Change to size 4mm needles and with m. only k.1 row and p.1 row, then pattern 18 rows as for back.*
Next row: Pattern across these 16 sts., then onto the same needle, pattern across the 24 (28) sts. on spare needle.
****O**n 40 (44) sts. pattern 3 rows.
Inc. 1 st. at each end of the next row and the 9 following 6th rows. On 60 (64) sts, pattern 11 rows.
To shape the sleevetop: Cast off 4 sts. at the beginning of the next 2 rows, then dec. 1 st. at each end of the next row and the 15 following alternate rows. On 20 (24) sts. work 1 row.
Dec. 1 st. at each end of the next 6 rows. Cast off 3 sts. at the beginning of the 2 following rows, then cast off the remaining 2 (6) sts.
Slit edging: With right side of work facing rejoin m. and using size 3¾mm needles pick up and k. 13 sts. between the marking threads. Increasing 1 st. at cuff edge on each right side row, with m. k.1 row, with c. k.2 rows, with m. k.2 rows, with c. k.2 rows, with m. k.1. – 17 sts. With m. cast off loosely k. wise.
Right sleeve: Work from * to * on left sleeve, then leave these 16 sts. on a spare needle until required. Now work from ** to ** but decreasing at end instead of beginning of right side rows.
Continued on page 103●

Continued on page 103●

JADE

MATERIALS Either 33 25 gram balls of "Woollybear 100% Mohair" or 16 50 gram hanks of "Woollybear Shetland Fleck" or 23 50 gram balls of "Woollybear Cotton Crepe" ● a medium sized cable needle● a pair each of size 3¾ mm and 3¼ mm Aero knitting needles●

TENSION and **NOTE** All as for "Zeta"●

MEASUREMENTS The measurements are given in centimetres followed by inches in brackets●

Underarms (excluding underarm pieces) 104 (41½)● Length 61 (24½)● Sleeve Seam 45 (18)●

BACK As given for "Zeta"●

LEFT FRONT With size 3¼ mm needles cast on 60 sts, and work 17 rows in single rib.
Increase row: Rib 1, *up 1, rib 2: repeat from * ending last repeat rib 1.—90 sts.
Work as given for right half back of "Zeta" until 100 rows have been worked in pattern, then work as given for the left half front of the sweater from ** to end.
Frontband: With size 3¼ mm needles cast on 12 sts. and work 118 rows in single rib Inc. 1 st. at each end of the next row and the following 15 alternate rows. On 44 sts. rib 59 rows, then cast off in rib.
Pocket back: With size 4 mm needles cast on 30 sts. and work 40 rows in single rib, then cast off in rib.

RIGHT FRONT Work as given for left front until the increase row has been worked, then as for right half front of "Zeta" to end. Then work the frontband and pocket back as for left front.

SLEEVES and insets● As given for "Zeta"●

MAKING UP Join shoulder seams continuing seams down centre of sleeves. Join centre back seam. Join underarm seams on sleeves up to marking threads. Join side seams, up to marking threads inserting pockets backs above welt ribbing and neatly sew them in place on back of fronts. Sew underarm pieces in place, so that the row ends up to the marking threads are sewn to the side seams and those above the marking threads are sewn to the free row ends of the sleeves. Join cast off edges of front bands. Fold front bands in half lengthways and pin in place, so that first front edge increases on frontbands are in line with the first front edge decreases on fronts, then sew in position. ●

CLAUDE

MATERIALS 8 50 gram hanks of "Woollybear Shetland Fleck" in main colour and 18 balls of "Woollybear 100% Mohair" in contrast colour a pair each of size 3¼ mm and 3¾ mm Aero knitting needles, a medium sized cable needle● 5 buttons●

TENSION 16 stitches and 18 rows to 5 centimetres (2 inches) over the cabled patchwork and 12 stitches and 18 rows to 5 centimetres (2 inches) over the moss st. parts of the yoke, all using size 3¾ mm needles●

ABBREVIATIONS K., knit● p., purl● st., stitch● tog., together● dec., decrease (by working 2 sts. tog.)● inc., increase (by working twice into same st.)● single rib is k.1 and p.1 alternately● r.s., right side● w.s., wrong side● up 1, pick up the loop which lies between the needles, slip it onto left hand needle, then k. into back of it● k.1b., k.1 through back of st.● p.1b., p.1 through back of st.● cable 8, slip 4 sts. onto cable needle and leave at front off work, k.4, then k.4 from cable needle● cable 12, slip next 6 sts. onto cable needle and leave at front of work, k.6, then k.6 from cable needle● cable 4b., cable 4 back thus, slip next 2 sts. onto cable needle at back of work, k.2, then k.2 from cable needle● cable 4f., cable 4 front, thus, slip next 2 sts. onto cable needle at front of work, k.2, then k.2 from cable needle● cr.4f., cross 4 front, slip next 2 sts. onto cable needle at front of work, with c. k.2, with m. k.2 from cable needle● cr.4b., cross 4 back, slip next 2 sts. onto cable needle and leave at back of work, with m. k.3, with c. k.2 from cable needle● cr.3lt., cross 3 left, slip next 2 sts. onto cable needle at front of work, with c. k.1, with m. k.2 from cable needle● cr.3rt., cross 3 right, slip next st. onto cable needle at back of work, with m. k.2, with c. k.1 from cable needle● cr.5lt., cross 5 left, slip next 2 sts. onto cable needle at front of work, with m. k. into front of 2nd and 3rd sts. on left hand needle, with c. k. into back of first st., allowing all 3 loops to fall from left hand needle together, with m. k.2 from cable needle● cr.5rt., cross 5 right, as cr.5lt., but leaving sts. on cable needle at back of work● y.r.n., yarn round needle● s.s.k., slip 1, k.1, pass slip st. over● 3 from 1, k.1, y.r.n., k.1 all into same st.● m., main colour● c., contrast colour● cable 5f., slip next 2 sts. onto cable needle at front of work, k.3, then k.2 from cable needle● cable 5b., slip next 3 sts. onto cable needle at back of work, k.2, then k.3 from cable needle●

MEASUREMENTS The measurements are given in centimetres followed by inches in brackets●
Underarms 105 (42)● Side seam 40 (16)● Length 60 (24)● Sleeve seam 42.5 (17)●

NOTE Instructions in brackets are worked the number of times stated after the brackets.

BACK With size 3¼ mm needles and m. cast on 106 sts. and work 24 rows in single rib. Change to size 3¾ mm needles and work in pattern as follows:
***Use separate balls of m. for each section of the pattern and one ball of c. on each side of centre cable panel, so that m. is not taken across the back of the work behind c. ***.
Increase row: With m. p.1, k.5, **up 1, k.3, up 1, with c. (k.3, up 1) 7 times; with m. k.2, up 1, k.2, with c. (k.2, up 1, k.1) 3 times; with m. k.2, with c. up 1, k.3**; with m. up 1, k.8; repeat from ** to ** with m. k.2, up 1, k.5, p.1. – 136 sts.
Foundation row: With m. k.1, p.8, **with c. k.4; with m. p.2, with c. k.12, with m. p.5, with c. (k.1, p.1) 14 times**; with m. p.14; repeat from ** to **, with m. p.10, k.1.
Now work in pattern as follows:
1st row: With m. p.1, k.6, **cable 4b., with c. (p.1, k.1) 14 times; cr.5rt. – see

abbreviations, with c. k.2, (y.r.n., s.s.k.) 5 times; with m. k.2, with c. k.4**; with m. k.10; repeat from ** to **, with m. k.8, p.1.
2nd row: With m. k.1, p.8, **with c. k.4, with m. p.2, with c. k.12, with m. p.2, with c. p.1b., with m. p.2, with c. (k.1, p.1) 14 times**; with m. p.14; repeat from ** to **, with m. p.10, k.1.
The last 2 rows set the position of the pattern given in the chart for the "Amelia" pattern on pages 2 and 3, but using m. instead of a. and c. for each of the 6 other contrasts. Work the 3rd to 72nd rows from the chart as set, then work the first 42 rows again, marking each end of the last row with coloured threads.
Decrease row: With m. p.1, k.7, (k.2tog., k.2) 13 times, k.2tog., k.12, k.2tog., (k.2, k.2tog.) 13 times, k.7, p.1. – 108 sts.
Now work in moss st. with cable panels in m. as follows:
1st row (wrong side): K.1, p.9, (k.1, p.1) 18 times, k.1, p.13, (k.1, p.1) 19 times, k.1, p.8, k.1.
2nd row (right side): P.1, k.9, (p.1, k.1) 18 times, p.1, k.13, (p.1, k.1) 19 times, p.1, k.8, p.1.
Now work in rose pattern as follows, with the cable panels as set before continuing at centre and each end of rows. Do not take m. across the back of the contrast colour. Use separate balls of m. at each side of flowers and leaves.
Foundation row (wrong side): With m. k.1, p.9, k.1, with c. p.1, with m. (k.1, p.1) 16 times, with c. p.1, with m. p.1, k.1, p.13, k.1, p.1, k.1, with c. p.1, with m. (k.1, p.1) 16 times, with c. p.1, with m. p.1, k.1, p.8, k.1.
1st row (right side): With m. p.1, cable 8, k.1, p.1, with c. 3 from 1, (p.1, k.1) 16 times, with c. 3 from 1, with m. k.1, p.1, k.13, p.1, k.1, p.1, with c. 3 from 1, with m. (p.1, k.1) 16 times, with c. 3 from 1, with m. k.1, p.1, cable 8, p.1.
2nd row: With m. k.1, p.9, k.1, with c. p.3, with m. p.2tog.b, (k.1, p.1) 14 times, p.2tog., with c. p.3, with m. p.1, k.1, p.13, k.1, p.1, k.1, with c. p.3, with m. p.2tog., (k.1, p.1) 14 times, p.2tog.b., with c. p.3, with m. p.1, k.1, p.8, k.1.
The last 3 rows set the position of the rose and leaf motifs given in the chart, noting that the details for working the leaves on specific rows are given in the small chart. Now work the 3rd to 48th rows from the charts as set, working 12 st. cables at the centre on the 7th, 25th and 43rd pattern rows and 8 st. cables at each end of the 13th, 25th and 37th rows.
With m. only work 4 rows in moss st. with cable panels as set, cabling the 8 st. cable groups at each end of the first of these rows.
Change to size 3¼ mm needles and work 10 rows in single rib.
To slope the shoulders: Cast off 7 sts. at the beginning of the next 10 rows. Cast off the remaining 38 sts.

LEFT FRONT With size 3¼ mm needles and m. cast on 61 sts. and work 24 rows in single rib.
Change to size 3¾ mm. needles and work as follows. Use separate balls of yarn for each section of the pattern as for back.
Increase row: With m. p.1, k.5, up 1, k.3, up 1, with c. (k.3, up 1) 7 times; with m. k.2, up 1, k.2, with c. (k.2, up 1, k.1) 3 times; with m. k.2, with c. up 1, k.3, with m. k.13. – 75 sts.
Now work in pattern as follows: **F**oundation row (wrong side): With m. k.1, p.12; with c. k.4; with m. p.2, with c. k.12; with m. p.5; with c. (k.1, p.1) 14 times; with m. p.10, k.1.
Now work from the chart as follows, noting

"Claude" jacket is knitted
in black "Shetland Fleck"
with "Redcurrant" mohair.

Flecked wool pinafore
skirt and viscose shirt by
"Un Après-Midi de Chien"
all from Patricia Roberts,
Covent Garden.

CLAUDE

that the cable 4b.s at the end of the 1st, 5th and 69th rows are replaced by k.3.

1st row: With m. p.1, k.6, cable 4b., with c. (p.1, k.1) 14 times; cr.5rt. – see abbreviations; with c. k.2, (y.r.n., s.s.k.) 5 times; with m. k,2, with c. k.4, with m. k.13.

2nd row: With m. k.1, p.12, with c. k.4; with m. p.2; with c. k.12; with m. p.2; with c. p.1b.; with m. p.2; with c. (k.1, p.1) 14 times; with m. p.10, k.1.

Work the 3rd to 72nd rows from the chart as set, then work the first 42 rows again, marking the end of the last row with a coloured thread.

Decrease row: With m. p.1, k.7, (k.2tog., k.2) 13 times, k.2tog., k.13. – 61 sts.

Now work in moss st. with cable panels as follows:

1st row (wrong side): With m. k.1, p.12, (k.1, p.1) 19 times, k.1, p.8, k.1.

2nd row (right side): P.1, k.9, (p.1, k.1) 18 times, p.1, k.14.

Now work in rose pattern, with cable panels at each end as before, as follows: Do not take m. across back of contrast colour; use separate balls of m. at each side of flower and leaves.

Foundation row (wrong side): With m. k.1, p.12, k.1, p.1, k.1, with c. p.1, with m. (k.1, p.1) 16 times, with c. p.1, with m. p.1, k.1, p.8, k.1.

1st row: With m. p.1, cable 8, k.1, p.1, with c. 3 from 1, (p.1, k.1) 16 times, with c. 3 from 1, with m. k.1, p.1, k.14.

The last 2 rows set the position of the rose and leaf motifs, work the 2nd to 10th rows from the chart as set, working the 12 st. cable on the 7th of these rows. Continuing in pattern from chart with cable panels as set, work as follows.

Decrease row: Pattern until 15 remain, with m. p.2tog., work to end as set.

Pattern 3 rows.

Repeat the last 4 rows 8 times, then work the first 2 rows again.

With m. only work 4 rows in moss st. with cable panels as set, decreasing 1 st. as before on the 3rd of these rows. – 50 sts.

Change to size 3¼ mm needles and work in single rib with cabled front band as follows:

1st row: *K.1, p.1; repeat from * until 16 remain, k.1, p.2tog., k.13.

2nd row: K.1, p.12, *k.1, p.1; repeat from * to end.

Continuing in rib with cabled front band as set, dec. 1 st. as before on the following 3rd row. On 48 sts. work 5 rows as set.

To slope the shoulder: Cast off 7 sts. at the beginning of the next row and the 3 following alternate rows, then 6 sts. on the following alternate row. – 14 sts.

On 14 sts. continue the cabled band as follows:

1st row (wrong side): K.1, p.12, k.1,

2nd row: All k.

Work 21 rows more as set, cabling the 12 sts. on the 6th of these rows. Cast off.

The pocket back: With size 3¾ mm needles and c. cast on 44 sts. and work 48 rows in moss st., then cast off.

RIGHT FRONT With size 3¼ mm needles and m. cast on 61 sts. and work 4 rows in single rib.

1st Buttonhole row: Rib 5, cast off 4, rib to end.

2nd Buttonhole row: Rib until 5 remain, turn, cast on 4, turn, rib to end.

Rib 18 rows.

Change to size 3¾ mm needles.

Increase row: With m. k.14, up 1, with c. (k.3, up 1) 7 times; with m. k.2, up 1; k.2; with c. (k.2, up 1, k.1) 3 times; with m. k.2; with c. up 1, k.3, with m. k.2, up 1, k.5, p.1. – 75 sts.

Now work in pattern as follows: **Foundation**

row: With m. k.1, p.8, with c. k.4; with m. p.2; with c. k.12; with m. p.5; with c. (k.1, p.1) 14 times, with m. p.14, k.1.

1st pattern and buttonhole row: With m. k.5, cast off 4, k. next st., cable 4b, with c. (p.1, k.1) 14 times; cr.5rt.; with c. k.2, (y.r.n., s.s.k.) 5 times; with m. k.2, with c. k.4, with m. k.8, p.1.

2nd pattern and buttonhole row: With m. k.1, p.8, with c. k.4, with m. p.2, with c. k.12; with m. p.2; with c. p.1b., with m. p.2, with c. (k.1, p.1) 14 times, with m. p.6, turn, cast on 4 over those cast off, p.4, k.1.

Now work the 3rd to 72nd rows from the chart as set, ignoring the cable 4b.s on the chart at the beginning of the 33rd, 37th and 41st rows, but working buttonholes as before on the 37th and 38th rows.

Work the first 42 rows again, with buttonholes on the 1st and 2nd 37th and 38th rows. Mark the beginning of the last row with a coloured thread.

Decrease row: With m. k.13, k.2tog., (k.2, k.2tog.) 13 times, k.7, p.1. – 61 sts.

Now work in moss st. with cable panels as follows:

1st row (wrong side): With m. k.1, p.8, (k.1, p.1) 19 times, k.1, p.12, k.1.

2nd row: K.14, p.1, (k.1, p.1) 18 times, k.9, p.1.

Now work in rose pattern with cable panels as follows:

Foundation row (wrong side): With m. k.1, p.9, k.1, with c. p.1, with m. (k.1, p.1) 16 times, with c. p.1, with m. p.1, k.1, p.13, k.1.

1st row: With m. k.13, p.1, k.1, p.1, with c. 3 from 1, with m. (p.1, k.1) 16 times, with c. 3 from 1, with m. k.1, p.1, cable 8, p.1.

The last 2 rows set the position of the rose and leaf motifs, work the 2nd to 10th rows from the chart, cabling the 12 st. group on the 7th of these rows. Continuing in pattern with cable panels as set, work as follows:

Decrease row: Work 13 sts. as set, p.2tog., pattern to end.

Pattern 3 rows.

Repeat the last 4 rows 8 times, then the first 2 rows again.

With m. only work 4 rows in moss st., with cable panels as set, decreasing 1 st. as before on the 3rd of these rows. – 50 sts.

Change to size 3¼ mm needles and work in single rib with cabled front band as follows:

1st row: K.13, p.2tog., k.1, *p.1, k.1; repeat from * to end.

2nd row: *P.1, k.1; repeat from * until 13 remain, p.12, k.1.

Continuing in rib with cabled front band as set, dec. 1 st. as before on the following 3rd row. On 48 sts. work 6 rows as set.

To slope the shoulder: Cast off 7 sts. at the beginning of the next row and the 3 following alternate rows, then 6 sts. on the following alternate row. – 14 sts.

Continue the cabled band as follows: 1st row (right side): All k.

2nd row: K.1, p.12, k.1

Work 21 rows more, cabling the 12 sts. on the 5th of these rows. Cast off.

The pocket back: As for left front.

SIDES Both alike● With size 3¼ mm needles and m. cast on 24 sts. and work 24 rows in single rib. Change to size 3¾ mm needles.

Increase row: With c. k.2, up 1, with m. k.5, with c. (up 1, k.2) 3 times, up 1, with m. k.5, with c. (up 1, k.2) 3 times – 32 sts.

Foundation row: With c. k.9 with m. p.5, with c. k.10, with m.p.5, with c. k.3.

Now work in cable pattern as follows:

1st row: With c. k.3. with m. k.1. (y.r.n., k.2tog) twice, c. k.10, with m. cable 5f., with c. k.9.

2nd row: With c. k.7, k.2tog, with m. p.5, with c. k.1, up 1, k.7, k.2tog, with m.p.5, with

c. k.1, up 1, k.2.

The last 2 rows set the position of the cable pattern given in the chart for the "Amelia" pattern using m for a. and c. for the other contrasts; work the 3rd to 64th rows from the chart, then the first 41 rows again.

Now divide the sts. for the armhole: Pattern 10 as set and leave these sts. on a stitch-holder until required for second point; cast off 12, work to end and continue on these 10 sts. for first point.

The first point: Work 8 rows in pattern, decreasing 1 st. at inner edge on each row. Take the 2 remaining sts. tog. and fasten off.

The second point: With right side of work facing rejoin yarn to inner edge of sts. left on stitch-holder and work as given for first point to end.

SLEEVES Both alike● With size 3¼ mm needles and m. cast on 63 sts. and work 24 rows in single rib.

Change to size 2¾ mm needles and work in pattern as follows, noting the information given for back.

Increase row: *With c. (k.1, up 1) 14 times, with m. k.2, with c. (k.1, up 1) 6 times, with m. k.2*; with c. (k.1, up 1) twice, with m. (k.1, up 1) 7 times; repeat from * to *, with c. k.2. – 114 sts.

Foundation row: With c. k.2, *with m. p.2, with c. k.12, with m. p.5, with c. (k.1, p.1) 14 times*, with m. p.14, with c. k.4; repeat from * to *.

1st row: *With c. (p.1, k.1) 14 times, cr.5rt. – see abbreviations, with c. k.2, (y.r.n., s.s.k.) 5 times, with m. k.2*, with c. k.4, with m. k.10, cable 4b.; repeat from * to *, with c. k.2.

The last row sets the position of the pattern given in the chart for the back, but beginning and ending 11 sts. from each end of each row. Work the 2nd to 72nd rows from the chart, then the 1st to 52nd rows again.

To shape the sleevetop; Cast off 6 sts. at the beginning of the next 2 rows, then dec. 1 st. at each end of the next row and the 3 following alternate rows.

On 94 sts. work 1 row.

Decrease row: With m. k.1, then (k.6, k.2tog.) 5 times, k.12, (k.2tog., k.6) 5 times, k.1 more. – 84 sts.

Now work in single rib at sides with cable panel at centre as follows.

Next row (wrong side): With m. (p.1, k.1) 18 times, p.12, (k.1, p.1) 18 times.

Continuing in rib with cable panel at centre, dec. 1 st. at each end of the next row and the 5 following alternate rows. Work 1 row straight, then dec. 1 st. at each end of the next 8 rows. – 56 sts.

Cast off 3 sts. st the beginning of the next 4 rows, 4 sts. on the 6 following rows and 5 sts. on the 2 following rows. Cast off the remaining 10 sts.

MAKING UP Do not press. Join shoulder seams. Join sleeve seams. Neatly sew side pieces up to marking threads on back. Sew one row end edge of each pocket back to front edges of side pieces 2.5 cms (1 inch) above ribbing. Sew fronts to side pieces, neatly catching pocket backs in place on wrong side of fronts. Set in sleeves. Join cast off edges of front bands, then sew bands in place at back neck edge. Sew on buttons. ●

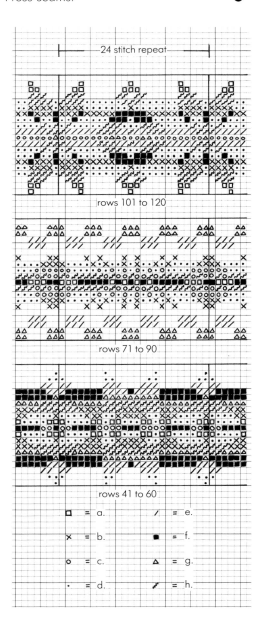

MATERIALS 7 (7) (9) 28 gram hanks of "Woollybear Real Shetland" in main colour, 1 hank in each of a., c., e., f and g. and 1 (1) (2) hanks in each of the 3 other contrast colours● a pair each of size 3 mm and 2¾ mm Aero knitting needles●

TENSION 17 stitches and 18 rows to 5 centimetres [2 inches] over the Fair Isle pattern using size 2¾ mm needles●
If you cannot obtain the correct tension using the size needles suggested, use larger or smaller ones accordingly●

ABBREVIATIONS K., knit● p., purl● st., stitch● tog., together● dec., decrease (by working 2 sts. tog.)● inc., increase (by working twice into same st.)● single rib is k.1 and p.1 alternately● s.s., stocking stitch is k. on the right side and p. on the wrong side● m., main colour● a., first contrast● b., second contrast● c., third contrast● d., fourth contrast● e., fifth contrast● f., sixth contrast● g., seventh contrast● h., eighth contrast● up 1, pick up the loop which lies between the needles, slip it onto left hand needle, then k. into back of it● k.1 down, k. into st. below next st. on left hand needle●

NOTE The instructions are given for the small womans size, followed by the medium womans size in first brackets and the medium mans size in the second brackets●

MEASUREMENTS The measurements are given in centimetres followed by inches in square brackets● Underarms 99 [39½] (105.5 [42¼]) (112.5 [45])● Side seam 35 [14]● Length 55 [22] (55 [22]) (63 [25])● Sleeve seam 41 [16½] (41 [16½]) (49 [19½])●

BACK With size 2¾ mm needles and m. cast on 141 (151) (161) sts. and work 11 rows in single rib.
Increase row: Rib 3, *up 1, rib 5; repeat from * ending last repeat rib 3. — 169 (181) (193) sts.
Change to size 3 mm needles and work in pattern as follows. The Fair Isle bands are worked entirely in s.s. so only the colour details are given on these; take care not to pull colours not in use tightly across the back of the work.
1st row: With m. k.1 down, *p.1, k.1 down; repeat from * to end.
2nd row: With m. p.1, *k.1, p.1; repeat from * to end.
3rd to **10**th rows: Repeat 1st and 2nd rows 4 times.
11th row: For Fair Isle 1a., *3m., 1a.; repeat from * to end.
12th row: 2a., *1m., 3a.; repeat from * ending last repeat 2a.
13th row: As 11th row.
14th row: All m.
15th row: 3m., *1b., 5m.; repeat from * ending last repeat 3m.
16th row: 2m., *3b., 3m.; repeat from * ending last repeat 2m.
17th row: 1c., *5b., 1c.; repeat from * to end.
18th row: 1b., *1c., 3b., 1c., 1b.; repeat from * to end.
19th row: 2g., *1c., 1g., 1c., 3g.; repeat from * ending last repeat 2g.
20th row: 3g., *1c., 5g.; repeat from * ending last repeat 3g.
21st to **29**th rows: Work 19th row back to 11th row.
30th row: All m.
31st to **40**th rows: As 1st to 10th rows.
41st row: 1d. (6m., 1d.) (1d.), 7m., * 1d., 7m.; repeat from *, ending last repeat 1d. (6m.) (1d.).
42nd row: 2d. (5m., 3d.) (2d.), *6m., 2d., 5m., 2d., 6m., 3d.; repeat from * ending last repeat 2d. (3d., 5m.) (2d.).
43rd row: 1m. (4m., 2e., 1m.) (1m.), *2e., 5m., 3e., 3m., 3e., 5m., 2e., 1m.; repeat from

* ending last repeat 1m. (1m., 2e., 4m.) (1m.).
44th to **60**th rows: The last 3 rows set the position of the Fair Isle pattern, now work these rows from the chart as set.
61st to **70**th rows: As 1st to 10th rows.
71st row: 2g., *3m., 3g.; repeat from * ending last repeat 2g.
72nd row: As 71st row.
73rd row: 2m., *3e., 3m.; repeat from * ending last repeat 2m.
74th row: As 73rd row.
75th row: All m.
76th row: 1b. (1b., 4m., 2b.) (1b.), *4m., 1b., 1m., 1b., 3m., 1b., 1m., 1b., 3m., 1b., 1m., 1b., 4m., 2b.; repeat from * ending last repeat 1b. (2b., 4m., 1b.) (1b.).
77th to **90**th rows: Work from chart as set.
91st to **100**th rows: As 1st to 10th rows.
101st row: 4m. (2m., 1a., 7m.) (4m.), *1a., 7m.; repeat from * ending last repeat 4(2) (4)m.
102nd row: 3m. (2m., 2a., 5m.) (3m.), *2a., 6m., 3a., 6m., 2a., 5m.; repeat from * ending last repeat 3m. (5m., 2a., 2m.) (3m.).
103rd to **120**th rows: Work from chart as set.
The last 120 rows form the pattern. Mark each end of the last row with coloured threads to denote armholes.**
Work the first 68 (68) (98) rows again.
To slope the shoulders: Cast off 55 (60) (65) sts. at the beginning of the next 2 rows. — 59 (61) (63) sts.
Change to size 2¾ mm needles and with m., work 10 rows in single rib, then cast off in rib.

FRONT Crew necked version● Work as given for back until ** is reached.
Work the first 29 (29) (59) rows again.
Now divide the sts. for the neck: Next row: P.65 (70) (75) and leave these sts. on a spare needle until required for right front shoulder, p.39 (41) (43) and leave these sts. on a spare needle until required for neckband, p. to end and continue on these 65 (70) (75) sts. for the left front shoulder.
Left front shoulder: To shape the neck: Maintaining the continuity of the pattern, dec. 1 st. at the neck edge on each of the next 10 rows. On 55 (60) (65) sts. pattern 28 rows, then cast off.
Right front shoulder: With right side of work facing rejoin yarn to inner edge of sts. left on spare needle and work to end of row, then work as given for left front shoulder to end.
Neckband: With right side of work facing rejoin m. at left front shoulder and using size 2¾ mm needles pick up and k. 34 sts. from left front neck edge, k. across the 39 (41) (43) sts. at centre front, then pick up and k. 34 sts. from right front neck edge.
On 107 (109) (111) sts. work 9 rows in single rib, then cast off in rib.

FRONT Vee necked version● Work as given for back until ** is reached.
Work 1 row in pattern, then divide the sts. for the neck as follows: Next row: Pattern 84 (90) and leave these sts. on a spare needle until required for right front shoulder, p.2tog., pattern to end and continue on these 84 (90) (96) sts. for the left front shoulder.
Left front shoulder: To slope the neck: Dec. 1 st. at the end of the next row and at the same edge on the 28 (29) (30) following alternate (alternate) (third) rows. On 55 (60) (65) sts. pattern 9 (7) (5) rows. Cast off the remaining 55 (60) (65) sts.
Right front shoulder: With right side of work facing rejoin yarn to inner edge of sts. left on spare needle and work to end of row, then work as given for left front shoulder to end.
Neckband: With right side of work facing rejoin m. at left front shoulder and using size 2¾ mm needles pick up and k.56 (58) (80)

sts. from left front neck edge and 56 (58) (80) sts. from right front neck edge. — 112 (116) (160) sts.
Work 1 row in single rib.
Next row: Rib to within 2 sts. of centre, slip 1, k.1, pass slip st. over, k.2 tog., rib to end. **R**epeat the last 2 rows 3 times more. On 104 (108) (152) sts. rib 1 row, then cast off.

SLEEVES Both alike● With size 2¾ mm needles and m. cast on 65 (65) (73) sts. and work 21 rows in single rib.
Increase row: Rib 1, *up 1, rib 2; repeat from * to end. — 97 (97) (109) sts.
Change to size 3 mm needles and work 20 (20) (50) rows in pattern as given for first (first) (second) size given for back and beginning with the 1st (1st) (91st) pattern row.
Maintaining the continuity of the pattern, and working the extra sts. into the pattern as they occur, inc. 1 st. at each end of the next row and the 11 following 8th rows.
On 121 (121) (133) sts. pattern 21 rows, ending with the 10th pattern rows. Cast off.

MAKING UP Pin out to size and press lightly on the wrong side with a warm iron over a damp cloth. Join shoulder seams. Join side seams up to marking threads. Join sleeve seams up to the 120th pattern row. Set in sleeves, so that the 10 free row ends at top of sleeves are sewn to the row ends above the marking threads on back and front. Press seams. ●

rows 101 to 120

rows 71 to 90

rows 41 to 60

□ = a.	╱ = e.
✕ = b.	■ = f.
○ = c.	△ = g.
· = d.	╱ = h.

24 stitch repeat

Fairisle sweater may be knitted in a crew necked or vee necked version. The sweater on the right is knitted in the man's size.

Back to school: College jacket, viscose shirts and tartan trousers, all by "Un Après-Midi de Chien". Pinstripe jacket by "New York".

JULES and JIM

Knitted in a combination of Shetland and Chenille, these Fair-Isles are easy to knit. The man's sweater "Jim" may also be knitted with a crew neck. It looks good on a woman too.

MATERIALS 6 50 gram hanks of "Patricia Roberts Shetland No. 2" in main colour and 2 hanks in contrast colour a., plus 2 50 gram balls of "Patricia Roberts Chenille" in contrasts d., f., g., and b. and 1 ball in contrasts h.,e. and c.● A pair each of size 3mm and 3¾mm Aero knitting needles; 6 buttons●

TENSION 13 stitches and 14 rows to 5 centimetres (2 inches) over the Fair Isle pattern●
If you cannot obtain the correct tension using the size needles suggested use larger or smaller ones accordingly●

ABBREVIATIONS K., knit● p., purl● st., stitch● tog., together● inc., increase (by working twice into same st.)● dec., decrease (by working 2 sts. tog.)● single rib is k.1 and p.1 alternately● up1, pick up the loop, which lies between the needles, slip it onto left hand needle, then k. into the back of it● s.s, stocking stitch is k. on the right side and p. on the wrong side● sl., slip● p.s.s.o., pass sl. st. over● m., main colour● a., first contrast● b., second contrast● c., third contrast● d., fourth contrast● e., fifth contrast● f., sixth contrast● g., seventh contrast● h., eigth contrast●

MEASUREMENTS The measurements are given in centimetres followed by inches in brackets●
Underarms 101 (40½)● Side seam 35 (14)● Length 61 (24½)● Sleeve seam 43 (17)●

SPECIAL NOTE When knitting with Chenille, it is essential to check ones tension before commencing work and if necessary change needle sizes accordingly.

BACK With size 3mm needles and m. cast on 127 sts. and work 22 rows in single rib.
1st. dec. row: Rib 12, * sl.1, k.2tog., p.s.s.o., rib 17; repeat from * ending last repeat rib 12. – 115 sts.
Rib 9 rows.
2nd. dec. row: Rib 11, * sl.1, k.2tog., p.s.s.o., rib 15; repeat from * ending last repeat rib 11. – 103 sts.
Rib 6 rows.
Increase row: Rib 1, * up1, rib 4; repeat from * ending last repeat rib 2. – 129 sts.
Change to size 3¾mm needles and k.1 row and p. 1 row.
Work in pattern as follows. Take care not to pull colours not in use tightly across the back of the work. The pattern is worked in stocking stitch so only the colour details are given.
1st. row: 1m., * 3c., 2m., 2c., 1m., 2c., 2m., 3c., 1m.; repeat from * to end.
2nd. row: 1c., * 3m., 1c., 1m., 2c., 1m., 2c., 1m., 1c., 3m., 1c.; repeat from * to end.
The last 2 rows set the position of the pattern given in the chart. Work the 3rd. to 64th. rows from the chart.
To shape the armholes: Cast off 3 sts. at the beginning of the next 2 rows, then dec. 1 st. at each end of the next 9 rows.
On 105 sts. pattern 59 rows.
To slope the shoulder: Cast off 15 sts. at the beginning of the next 4 rows. – 45 sts.
Change to 3mm needles and with m. work 8 rows in single rib, then cast off.

LEFT FRONT With size 3mm needles and m. cast on 64 sts. and work 22 rows in single rib.
1st. decrease row: Rib 11, * sl.1, k.2tog., p.s.s.o., rib 17; repeat from * ending last repeat rib 10. – 58 sts.
Rib 9 rows.
2nd. decrease row: Rib 10, * sl.1, k.2tog., p.s.s.o., rib 15; repeat from * ending last repeat rib 9. – 52 sts.
Rib 6 rows.
Increase row: Rib 2, * up1, rib 4; repeat from * ending last repeat rib 2. – 65 sts.
Change to size 3¾mm needles and k.1 row and p.1 row, then work 64 rows in pattern as

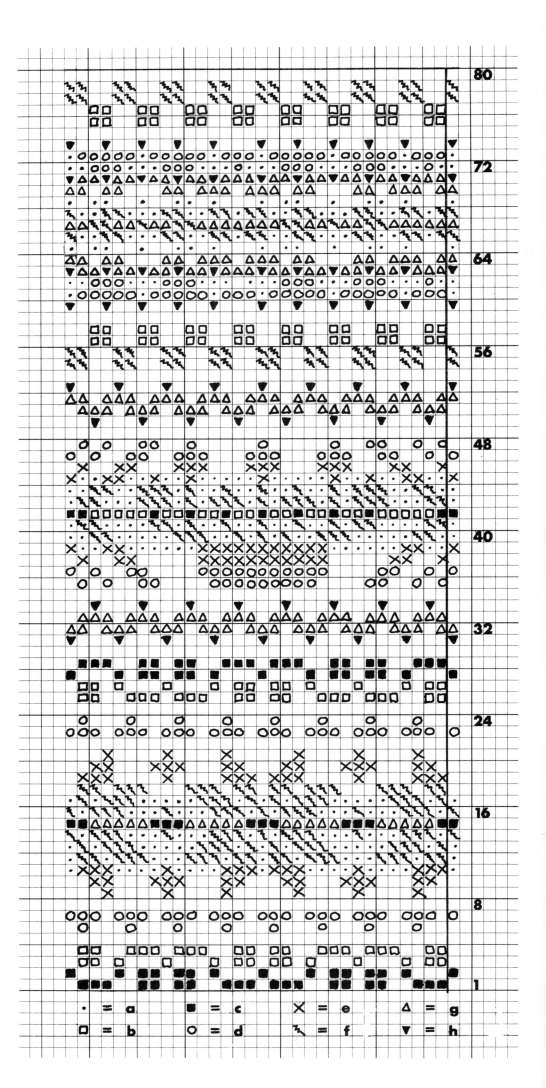

• = **a**	■ = **c**	✕ = **e**	△ = **g**
▢ = **b**	○ = **d**	⚡ = **f**	▼ = **h**

given for back.

Work 1 extra row here, when working right front.

To shape the armhole: Cast off 3 sts. at the beginning of the next row. Work 1 row back to armhole edge.

Dec. 1 st. at the armhole edge on each of the next 9 rows.

On 53 sts. pattern 36 rows.

To shape the neck: Cast off 7 sts. at the beginning of the next row, then dec. 1 st. at the neck edge on each of the next 16 rows.

On 30 sts. pattern 6 rows.

To slope the shoulder: Cast off 15 sts. at the beginning of the next row. On 15 sts. work 1 row, then cast off.

Neckband: With right side of work facing rejoin m. and using size 3mm needles pick up and k. 34 sts. from neck edge. Work 9 rows in single rib, then cast off.

Buttonband: With size 3mm needles and m. cast on 10 sts. and work 160 rows in single rib, then cast off in rib.

RIGHT FRONT Work as given for left front, noting the variation in the rows before shaping the armhole.

Neckband: As given for left front.

Buttonhole band: With size 3mm needles and m. cast on 10 sts. and work 4 rows in single rib.

1st. Buttonhole row: Rib 4, cast off 2, rib to end.

2nd. Buttonhole row: Rib 4 turn, cast on 2 over those cast off, turn, rib to end.

Rib 28 rows.

Repeat the last 30 rows 4 times, then work the 2 buttonhole rows again.

Rib 4 rows, then cast off.

SLEEVES With size 3mm needles and m. cast on 44 sts. and work 31 rows in single rib.

Increase row: Rib 2, * up1, rib 2; repeat from * to end. – 65 sts.

Change to size 3¾mm needles and k. 1 row. Now beginning with the 50th. pattern row (wrong side row) work the 50th. to 80th. pattern rows.

Continuing in pattern as set, inc. 1 st. at each end of the next row and the 14 following 4th. rows.

On 95 sts. pattern 7 rows.

To shape the sleevetop: Cast off 3 sts. at the beginning of the next 2 rows, then dec. 1 st. at each end of the next row and the 5 following alternate rows.

On 77 sts. work 1 row. Dec. 1 st. at each end of the next 18 rows. – 41 sts.

Cast off 4 sts. at the beginning of the next 4 rows, 6 sts. on the 2 following rows. – 12 sts.

Next row: (K.2tog.) 3 times, k.1, (k.2tog.) 3 times. Cast off remaining 7 sts.

MAKING UP Do not press. Join shoulder seams. Set in sleeves. Join sleeve and side seams. Neatly sew front bands in place. Sew on buttons. ●

MATERIALS 7 50 gram hanks of "Patricia Roberts Shetland N0. 2" in main colour and 2 hanks in contrast colour a. plus 2 50 gram balls of "Patricia Roberts Chenille" in contrasts f., d, g., b and e. and 1 ball in contrasts c. and h. ● A pair each of size 3mm and 3¾mm Aero Knitting needles●

TENSION 13 stitches and 14 rows to 5 centimetres (2 inches) over the Fair Isle pattern●

If you cannot obtain the correct tension using the size needles suggested use larger or smaller ones accordingly●

ABBREVIATIONS K., knit● p., purl● st., stitch● tog., together● dec., decrease (by working 2 sts. tog.)● inc., increase (by working twice into same st.)● single rib is k.1, p.1 alternately● up1, pick up the loop which lies between the needles, slip it onto left hand needle, then k. into back of it● s.s., stocking sitch is k. on the right side and p. on the wrong side● sl., slip● p.s.s.o., pass sl. st. over● m., main colour● a., first contrast● b., second contrast● c., third contrast● d., fourth contrast● e., fifth contrast● f., sixth contrast● g., seventh contrast● h., eighth contrast●

MEASUREMENTS The measurements are given in centimetres followed by inches in brackets●

Underarms 123 (49¼) ● Side seam 49 (19¾) ● Length 68 (27¼) ● Sleeve seam 49 (19½)●

SPECIAL NOTE When knitting with Chenille it is essential to check ones tension before commencing work and if necessary change needle sizes accordingly●

BACK With size 3mm needles and m. cast on 129 sts. and work 31 rows in single rib.

Increase row: Rib 1, * up1, rib 4; repeat from * to end. – 161 sts.

Change to size 3¾mm needles and k. 1 row and p. 1 row.

Work in pattern as follows: Take care not to pull colours not in use tightly across the back of the work. The pattern is worked in stocking stitch so only the colour details are given.

1st. row: 1m., * 3c, 2m., 2c., 1m., 2c., 2m., 3c., 1m.; repeat from * to end.

2nd. rows: 1c., * 3m., 1c., 1m., 2c., 1m., 2c., 1m., 1c., 3m., 1c.; repeat from * to end.

The last 2 rows set the position of the pattern given in the chart, work the 3rd. to 80th. rows from the chart, then work the first 8 rows again. Mark each end of the last row with coloured threads to mark armholes.

Pattern 72 rows.

To slope the shoulders: Cast off 28 sts. at the beginning of the next 4 rows.

Change to size 3mm needles and work 10 rows in single rib. Cast off in rib.

FRONT Vee necked version: Work as given for back until the 80 pattern rows have been worked, then work first 3 rows again.

Now divide the sts. for the neck: Next row:

Pattern 80 and leave these sts. on a spare needle until required for right half front, p.1 and leave this st. on safety pin until required for neckband, pattern to end and continue on these sts. for the left half front.

Left half front: To slope the neck:

Continuing in pattern as set, dec. 1 st. at the neck edge on the next row and the following 3rd. rows.

Mark the end of the last row with a coloured thread to denote armhole.

Dec. 1 st. at the neck edge on the 22 following 3rd. rows.

On 56 sts. pattern 6 rows, ending at armhole edge.

To slope the shoulder: Cast off 28 sts. at the beginning of the next row. On 28 sts. work 1 row, then cast off.

Right half front: With right side of work facing, rejoin yarn to inner edge of sts. left on spare needle to end of row, then work as given for left half front to end.

Neckband: With right side of work facing rejoin m. at left front shoulder and using size 3mm needles pick up and k.70 sts. from left front neck edge, k.1 st. from safety pin, then pick up and k.70 sts. from right front neck edge. – 141 sts.

Next row: P.1, * k.1, p.1; repeat from * to end.

Next row: Rib as set to within 2 sts. of centre st., sl.1, k.1, p.s.s.o., k.1, k.2tog., rib to end.

Next row: Rib to within 2 sts. of centre st., sl.1, k.1, p.s.s.o., p.1, k.2tog., rib to end.

Repeat the last 2 rows 3 times, then cast off.

FRONT Crew necked version: Work as given for back until the armholes have been marked.

Pattern 45 rows.

Now divide the sts. for the neck: Next row: Pattern 72 and leave these sts. on a spare needle until required for right front shoulder, cast off 17, pattern to end and continue on these 72 sts. for the left front shoulder.

Left front shoulder: To shape the neck: Dec. 1 st. at the neck edge on each of the next 16 rows.

On 56 sts. pattern 10 rows.

To slope the shoulder: Cast off 28 sts. at the beginning of the next row. On 28 sts. work 1 row, then cast off.

Right front shoulder: With right side of work facing rejoin yarn to inner edge of sts. left on spare needle and work to end row, then work as given for left front shoulder to end.

Neckband: With right side of work facing rejoin m. at left front shoulder and using size 3mm needles, pick up and k. 30 sts. from left front neck edge, 16 sts. from centre front neck edge and 30 sts. from right front neck edge. – 76 sts.

Work 9 rows in single rib, then cast off in rib.

SLEEVES With size 3mm needles and m. cast on 52 sts. and work 23 rows in single rib.

Increase row: Rib 2, * up1, rib 4; repeat from * ending last repeat rib 2.

Change to size 3¾mm needles and on 65 sts. k.1 row, then work in pattern as follows, beginning with the 50th. row.

50th. row (wrong side): 2m., * 1h., 3m.; repeat from * ending last repeat 2m. instead of 3.

The last row sets the position of the pattern, now work the 51st. to 58th. rows from the chart.

Continuing in pattern and working the extra sts. into the pattern as they occur, inc. 1 st. at each end of the next row and the 26 following 4th. rows.

On 119 sts. work 3 rows, then cast off.

MAKING UP Do not press. Join shoulder seams. Set in sleeves, between the marking threads on back and front. Join sleeve and side seams. ●

MATERIALS One colour version● either 8 (9) (20) (21) 28 gram hanks of "Woollybear Real Shetland" or 11 (12) (27) (28) 25 gram balls of "Woollybear Fine Cotton"● Multicolour version● either 7 (8) (17) (18) 28 gram hanks of "Woollybear Real Shetland" or 10 (11) (25) (26) balls of "Woollybear Fine Cotton" in main colour, 1 (2) (4) (4) hanks or balls of the same yarn in the contrast colours indicated by red and blue on the chart, 1 (1) (2) (2) in the contrast indicated by green and 1 hank or ball in the contrast indicated by yellow●
Either version● a pair each of size 2¼ mm and 2¾ mm Aero knitting needles● a fine cable needle● 1 button●

TENSION 42 stitches and 84 rows – 1 repeat of the cabled diamond pattern to 10 centimetres (4 inches) in width and 19 centimetres (7½ inches) in depth, using size 2¾ mm needles.
If you cannot obtain the correct tension using the size needles suggested, use larger or smaller ones accordingly●

ABBREVIATIONS K., knit● p., purl● st., stitch● tog., together● dec., decrease (by working 2 sts. tog.)● inc., increase (by working twice into same st.)● 3 from 1, k. into the front, then the back, then the front again of same st.● sl., slip● p.s.s.o., pass sl. st. over● s.s.k., sl.1, k.1, p.s.s.o.● c.8b., cable 8 back, slip next 4 sts. onto cable needle and leave at back of work, k.4, then k.4 from cable needle● c.8f., as c.8b., but leaving sts. on cable needle at front of work● up 1, pick up the loop which lies between the needles and slip it onto left hand needle, then k. into back of it● y.r.n., yarn round needle● c.6f., cable 6 front, slip next 3 sts. onto cable needle and leave at front of work, k.3, then k.3 from cable needle● c.10f., cable 10 front, slip next 5 sts. onto cable needle and leave at front of work, k.5, then k.5 from cable needle● 2 from 2, k.2tog., then p. the same 2 sts. tog. again●

MEASUREMENTS The measurements are given in centimetres followed by inches in brackets●
Sizes Child's (3 years) [Child's (5 years)] [Woman's] [Man's] Underarms 80 (32) [80 (32)] [120 (48)] [120 (48)]. Side seam 20 (8) [25 (10)] [40 (16)] [42.5 (17)] Length 35 (14) [41 (16½)] [60 (24)] [62.5 (25)]. Sleeve seam 20 (8) [25 (10)] [40 (16)] [45 (18)]●

NOTE The instructions are given for the first size, where they vary, work the figures in the first brackets for the second size, the figures in the second brackets for the third size and the figures in the third brackets for the fourth size●
Instructions in square brackets are worked the number of times stated after the brackets.

MULTICOLOUR Sweater. The written instructions are given for the one colour sweater. The multicolour one is worked in the same way, but with contrast colours as shown in the chart. Use separate small balls of contrast colours for each section of the pattern and use separate balls of m. at each side of the larger motifs – like the boats.

BACK With size 2¼ mm needles cast on 114 (114) (170) (170) sts. and work 23 (23) (35) (35) rows in single rib.
Increase row: Rib 2, *up 1, rib 2; repeat from * to end. 170 (170) (254) (254) sts.
Change to size 2¾ mm needles and work in pattern as follows; for the multicolour version see the chart for the colour details.
1st row: K.1, *p.2, k.4, p.4, k.4, p.1, p.2tog., k.7, 3 from 1, p.2tog., p.2, [k.3, p.3] 4 times, k.3, p.1, p.2tog., k.7, 3 from 1, p.2tog., p.1, k.4, p.4, k.4, p.2; repeat from * until 1 remains, k.1.

2nd row: K.3, *p.4, k.4, p.4, k.2, p.10, k.2, [p.3, k.3] 5 times, p.10, k.2, p.4, k.4, p.4, k.4; repeat from * ending last repeat k.3.
3rd row: K.3, *p.4, k.4, p.4, k.2tog., k.8, 3 from 1, p.1, p.2tog., p.2, [k.3, p.3] 4 times, k.2, k.2tog., k.8, 3 from 1, k.1, s.s.k., p.4, k.4, p.4, k.4; repeat from * ending last repeat k.3.
4th row: K.1, p.2, *k.4, p.4, k.4, p.16, [k.3, p.3] 4 times, k.3, p.13, k.4, p.4, k.4, p.4; repeat from * ending last repeat p.2, k.1.
5th row: K.3, *p.4, k.4, p.3, p.2tog., c.8b., 3 from 1, k.3, p.2tog., p.2, [k.3, p.3] 4 times, k.2tog., c.8b., 3 from 1, k.3, p.2tog., p.3, k.4, p.4, k.4; repeat from * ending last repeat k.3.
6th row: K.1, p.2, *k.4, p.4, k.4, p.15, [k.3, p.3] 4 times, k.3, p.14, k.4, p.4, k.4, p.2; repeat from * ending last repeat p.2, k.1.
The last 6 rows set the position of the pattern given in the chart; work the 7th to 34th rows from the chart as set.
35th row: Inc. in first st., *sl.1, k.2tog., p.s.s.o., k.5, up 1, k.1, p.3, k.18, p.3, up 1, k.1, c.8f., sl.1, k.2tog., p.s.s.o., k.5, up 1, p.3, [k.2, p.4] 3 times, k.2, p.2, up 1, p.1, c.8f.; repeat from * ending last repeat c.6f., k.1, k.2tog.
36th, 38th, 40th, 42nd, 44th, 46th and 48th rows: Work from chart as set.
37th row: Inc., k.1, *sl.1, k.2tog., p.s.s.o., k.3, up 1, k.2, p.3, k.18, p.3, k.2, up 1, k.8, sl.1, k.2tog., p.s.s.o., k.3, up 1, k.1, p.1, k.1, p.1, k.1, k.20, turn, k.20, turn, k.20, p.1, k.1, p.1, up 1, k.8; repeat from * ending last repeat k.6, k.2tog.
39th row: Inc., k.2, *sl.1, k.2tog., p.s.s.o., k.1, up 1, k.1, p.7, k.14, p.7, k.1, up 1, k.8, sl.1, k.2tog., p.s.s.o., k.1, up 1, p.1, k.1, p.1, k.1, p.1, k.21, turn, k.21, turn, k.21, p.1, k.1, p.1, k.1 up 1, k.8; repeat from * ending last repeat k.5, k.2tog.
41st row: Inc., k.2, *sl.1, k.2tog., p.s.s.o., up 1, k.11, c.8f., k.1, p.11, up 1, k.7, sl.1, k.2tog., p.s.s.o., up 1, k.1, p.1, k.1, p.1, k.22, turn, k.22, turn, k.22, p.1, k.1, p.1, k.1, p.1, up 1, k.7; repeat from * ending last repeat k.4, k.2tog.
43rd row: Inc., k.4, * s.s.k., k.1, p.7, k.14, p.7, k.1, k.2tog., 3 from 1, k.7, s.s.k., p.1, k.1, p.1, k.23, turn, k.23, turn, k.23, p.1, k.1, p.1, k.1, p.2tog., 3 from 1, k.7; repeat from * ending last repeat k.2, k.2tog.
45th row: Inc., k.5, *s.s.k., k.2, p.3, k.18, p.3, k.2, k.2tog., k.1, 3 from 1, k.8, s.s.k., k.1, p.1, k.1, p.1, k.17, [p.1, k.1] 3 times, p.1, k.2tog., k.1, 3 from 1, k.8; repeat from * ending last repeat k.2, k.2tog.
47th row: Inc., c.6f., *s.s.k., k.1, p.3, k.18, p.3, k.1, k.2tog., k.3, 3 from 1, c.8f., s.s.k., p.1, k.1, p.1, k.2, [p.3, k.2] 3 times, [p.1, k.1] 3 times, p.2tog., k.3, 3 from 1, c.8f.; repeat from * ending last repeat k.1, k.2tog. instead of c.8f.
49th row: Inc., k.7, *p.2tog., k.5, k.14, p.5, p.2tog., k.5, 3 from 1, k.8, p.2tog., k.1, p.1, [k.2, p.3] 3 times, k.2, p.1, k.1, p.1, k.1, k.2tog., k.5, 3 from 1, k.8; repeat from * ending last repeat k.2tog. instead of k.8.
51st row: K.1, *inc., k.7, p.2tog., p.6, k.1, c.8f., k.1, p.6, p.2tog., k.7, inc., inc., k.7, s.s.k., p.1, k.17, p.1, k.1, p.1, k.1, p.2tog., k.7, inc.; repeat from * until 1 remains, k.1.
Now work the 52nd to 124th (152nd) (168th) (168th) rows from the chart, but increasing 1 st. at the beginning and decreasing 1 st. at the end of the 119th to 133rd, odd numbered, rows as for 35th to 49th rows.
Mark each end of the 68th (90th) (146th) (156th) rows with marking threads.
Work the first nil (nil) (58) (68) pattern rows.

To slope the shoulders: Continuing in pattern as set, cast off 11 (11) (18) (18) sts. at the beginning of the next 10 rows.
Cast off the remaining 60 (60) (74) (74) sts.

"Martinique" sweater may be knitted in one colour or multicolour, for a man, woman or child.

FRONT Work as given for the back until 32 (32) (48) (48) rows have been worked in pattern.

Now divide the sts. for the pockets. Next row: Pattern 32 (28) (43) (33), *then pattern 32 (36) (42) (52) sts. and leave these on a stitch-holder until required for pocket back*, pattern 42 (42) (84) (84); repeat from * to *, pattern to end.

Pocket backs (both alike): With wrong side of work facing rejoin yarn and beginning with a p. row s.s. 50 (50) (74) (74) rows.

With wrong side of work facing rejoin yarn to front and work as follows: Next row: Pattern 32 (28) (43) (33), then pattern across the 32 (36) (42) (52) sts. of one pocket back, pattern 42 (42) (84) (84), then pattern across the 32 (36) (42) (52) sts. of other pocket back, pattern to end.

Now continue in pattern as given for back until 83 (111) (151) (153) rows have been worked in pattern from the beginning and the armholes have been marked.

Now divide the sts. for the neck: Next row: Pattern 81 (81) (122) (122) and leave these sts. on a spare needle until required for right front shoulder; pattern 8 (8) (10) (10) and leave these sts. on a safety pin until required for buttonhole band, pattern to end and continue on these 81 (81) (122) (122) sts. for the left front shoulder.

Left front shoulder: Pattern 21 (21) (37) (37) rows.

To shape the neck: Cast off 14 sts. at the beginning of the next row, then dec. 1 st. at the neck edge on each of the next 12 (12) (18) (18) rows.

On 55 (55) (90) (90) sts. pattern 6 (6) (18) (26) rows.

To slope the shoulder: Cast off 11 (11) (18) (18) sts. at the beginning of the next row and the 3 following alternate rows. On 11 (11) (18) (18) sts. work 1 row, then cast off.

Right front shoulder: With right side of work facing rejoin yarn to inner edge of sts. left on spare needle and work to end of row, then work as given for left front shoulder to end.

Buttonhole band: With right side of work facing rejoin yarn to the 8 (8) (10) (10) sts. left on safety pin at centre front and using size 2¼ mm needles work as follows:

Increase row: K.4 (4) (5) (5), up 1, k.4 (4) (5) (5). – 9 (9) (11) (11) sts.

Beginning wrong side rows with p.1 and right side rows with k.1, rib 13 (13) (25) (25) rows.

1st Buttonhole row: Rib 3, cast off 3 (3) (5) (5), rib to end.

2nd Buttonhole row: Rib 3, turn, cast on 3 (3) (5) (5), turn, rib to end.

Rib 6 (6) (10) (10) rows, then cast off in rib.

Buttonband: With size 2¼ mm needles cast on 9 (9) (11) (11) sts. and work 22 (22) (38) (38) rows in single rib as for buttonhole band, then cast off in rib.

SLEEVES Both alike● With size 2¼ mm needles cast on 58 (58) (72) (72) sts. and work 23 (23) (35) (35) rows in single rib.

Increase row: Rib 2 (2) (3) (3), *up 1, rib 2; repeat from * ending last repeat rib 2 (2) (3) (3). – 86 (86) (106) (106) sts.

Change to size 2¾ mm needles.

For the first 2 sizes: Work 4 (6) rows in pattern as given for back.

For the third and fourth sizes: Work in pattern as follows:

1st row: K.1, p.4, k.4, p.2; work from * on first pattern row given for back until 11 remain, p.2 more, then k.4, p.4, k.1.

2nd row: K.5, p.4, k.4, work from * on 2nd pattern row until 9 remain, k.4, p.4, k.1.

The last 2 rows set the position of the repeat pattern given for back and in the chart, work the 3rd to 18th pattern rows from the chart.

□ = k. on the right side and p. on the wrong side.	⋋ = k.2tog.
⌃ = p. on the right side and k. on the wrong side.	⋌ = s.s.k.
∿∿∿ = see written instructions.	⋏ = p.2tog.

O = y.r.n.   ⌄ = 3 from 1   ⤳⤨ = c. 8 f.
V = up 1   ✕ = 2 from 2   ⤳⤨ = c. 8 b.
⌄ = inc.   = c. 6 f.
   = c. 10 f.

⋀ = sl.1, k.2 tog., p.s.s.o..

For all sizes: Working the extra sts. into the pattern as they occur, inc. 1 st. at each end of the next row and the 20 (20) (31) (31) following 3rd (4th) (4th) (4th) rows.
On 128 (128) (170) (170) sts. work 3 (3) (3) (23) rows, then cast off.
COLLAR With size 2¼ mm needles cast on 120 (120) (170) (186) sts. and work 4 rows in single rib.
Decrease row: Rib 2, sl.1, k.2tog., p.s.s.o., rib until 5 remain, sl.1, k.2tog., p.s.s.o., rib 2.
Rib 5 rows.
Repeat the last 6 rows once (once) (3) (3) times more. Cast off the remaining 112 (112) (154) (170) sts. in rib.
MAKING UP Pin out to size and press lightly on the wrong side with a cool iron over a dry cloth. Join shoulder seams. Sew cast off edges of sleeves to the row ends between the marking threads on back and front. Join sleeve and side seams. Neatly sew cast off edge of collar in place. Sew buttonhole band to right front edge on children's and women's garments and left front edge on man's. Sew cast off edge of buttonband in place behind base of buttonhole band, then sew one row and edge to appropriate front edge. Neatly join row ends of pocket backs. Sew on button. ●

MARTINIQUE

SHORT MULTI-COLOUR SWEATER

MATERIALS For the woman's size only: 22 25 gram balls of "Patricia Roberts Fine Cotton" in main colour, 4 balls in the contrast colour indicated by red in the chart, 3 balls in the contrast indicated by blue, 2 balls in that indicated by green and 1 in the contrast indicated by yellow. A pair each of size 2¼mm and 2¾mm Aero knitting needles and a fine cable needle●

TENSION AND ABBREVIATIONS As main pattern●

MEASUREMENTS These are given for the woman's size only in centimetres followed by inches in brackets.
Underarms 120 (48)● Side seam 31 (12¼)●
Length 51 (20½)● Sleeve seam 40 (16)●

BACK Work as given for woman's size (3rd. size) of main pattern, until the 168 pattern rows have been worked, but marking each end of the 104th. row with coloured threads to denote armholes. Then work the first 16 pattern rows again.
To slope the shoulders: Cast off 18 sts. at the beginning of the next 10 rows.
Cast off the remaining 74 sts.

FRONT Work as given for front of main pattern until 109 rows have been worked in pattern, but marking each end of the 104th. row with coloured threads.
Now divide the stitches for the neck and continue to end as given for main pattern.

SLEEVES, COLLAR AND MAKING UP As given for woman's size on main pattern. ●

Cotton "Martinique" sweaters; left in one colour, and right the short multicolour version.

FLORA

MATERIALS Either 15 25 gram balls of "Woollybear Fine Cotton", or 13 25 gram balls of "Woollybear Pure Silk"● a pair of size 3 mm Aero knitting needles●

TENSION 13 stitches and 22 rows to 5 centimetres (2 inches) over the rose lace pattern, using size 3 mm needles●
If you cannot obtain the correct tension using the size needles suggested, use larger or smaller ones accordingly●

ABBREVIATIONS K., knit● p., purl● st., stitch● tog., together● dec., decrease (by working 2 sts. tog.)● inc., increase (by working twice into the same st.)● sl., slip● p.s.s.o., pass sl. st. over● m.b., make bobble thus, on a wrong side row, p.1, y.r.n., p.1 all into same st., turn, p.3, turn, pick up the loop originally worked into and slip it onto left hand needle, pass 2nd, 3rd and 4th sts. on left hand needle over this st., then knit this st., making sure the bobble is in the right side of work● y.r.n., yarn round needle● s.s.k., sl.1 k.1, p.s.s.o.● 3 from 1, k.1, p.1, k.1 all into same st.●

NOTE Instructions in brackets are worked the number of times stated after the brackets●

MEASUREMENTS The measurements are given in centimetres followed by inches in brackets●
Underarms 112 (45)● Side seam 31 (12½)● Length 50 (20) Sleeve seam 28 (11)●

BACK With size 3 mm needles cast on 146 sts. by the thumb method and work as follows:
1st edging row: K.2, *cast off 4, k. next st.; repeat from * to end.
2nd edging row: K.2, *turn, cast on 3 over those cast off, turn, k.2; repeat from * to end.
*** On 122 sts. k.2. rows. Now work in rose lace as follows:
1st row: K.1, *y.r.n., s.s.k.; repeat from * until 1 remains, k.1.
2nd row: All k.
3rd row: K.1, *s.s.k., y.r.n.; repeat from * until 1 remains, k.1.
4th row: All k.
5th row: as 1st row.
6th row: K.1, *m.b. – see abbreviations, k.7; repeat from * until 1 remains, k.1.
7th row: As 3rd row.
8th row: K.1, *for the leaf p.1, then k.39; repeat from * until 1 remains, k.1.
When counting stitches, while working leaves, count the stitches for each leaf as one stitch.
9th row: K.3, *(y.r.n., s.s.k.) 18 times, k.1, then for leaf 3 from 1, then k.2; repeat from * ending last repeat k.1.
10th row: K.1, *for the leaf p.3, k.39; repeat from * ending last repeat k.1 more.
11th row: K.2, *(y.r.n., s.s.k.) 7 times, k.11, (s.s.k., y.r.n.) 6 times, k.1, then for the leaf k.1, y.r.n., k.1, y.r.n., k.1, then k.1 more; repeat from * to end.
12th row: K.1, for the leaf p.5, then k.13, p.1, k.4, p.1, k.4, p.1, k.15; repeat from * until 1 remains, k.1 more.
13th row: K.2, *(s.s.k., y.r.n.) 6 times, k.14, (s.s.k., y.r.n.) 5 times, k.2, then for the leaf k.2, y.r.n., k.1, y.r.n., k.2, then k.1; repeat from * to end.
14th row: K.1, *then for the leaf p.7, then k.3, m.b., k.8, p.1, k.12, p.1, k.9, m.b., k.3; repeat from * ending last repeat k.4.
15th row: K.1, *(s.s.k., y.r.n.) 6 times, k.16, (s.s.k., y.r.n.) 5 times, k.1, then for the leaf, k.3, y.r.n., k.1, y.r.n., k.3; repeat from * until 1 remains, k.1.
16th row: K.1, *for the leaf p.9, then, k.39; repeat from * ending last repeat k.40.
17th row: K.3, *(y.r.n., s.s.k.) 5 times, k.16, (y.r.n., s.s.k.) 5 times, k.1, then for the leaf k.3, sl.1, k.2tog., p.s.s.o., k.3, then k.2;

repeat from * ending last repeat k.1.

18th row: K.1, *for the leaf p.2, p.3tog., p.2, then k.39; repeat from * ending last repeat K.40.

19th row: K.1, *(s.s.k., y.r.n.) 6 times, k.14, (s.s.k., y.r.n.) 6 times, k.1, then for the leaf, k.1, sl.1, k.2tog., p.s.s.o., k.1; repeat from * until 1 remains, k.1.

20th row: K.1, *for the leaf p.3tog., then k.13, p.1, k.5, p.4, k.2, p.1, k.13; repeat from * ending last repeat k.14 – 122 sts.

21st row: K.1, (y.r.n., s.s.k.) 6 times, *k.3, (p.1, k.1) 3 times, p.1, k.8, (y.r.n., s.s.k.) 11 times; repeat from * ending last repeat by working instructions in last brackets 5 times, then k.1.

22nd row: K.1, *m.b., k.7, m.b., k.2, p.1, k.4, p.1, (k.1, p.1) 4 times, k.3, p.1, k.3, m.b., k.7; repeat from * ending last repeat, k.1 more.

23rd row: K.1 *(s.s.k., y.r.n.) 4 times, k.5, p.1, (k.1, p.1) 5 times, k.6, (s.s.k., y.r.n.) 5 times; repeat from * ending last repeat k.1.

24th row: K.10, *p.1, k.4, (p.1, k.1) twice, p.2, (k.1, p.1) twice, k.2, p.1, k.5, p.1, k.16; repeat from * ending last repeat k.8.

25th row: K.1, *(y.r.n., s.s.k.) twice, k.9, (p.1, k.1) 6 times, p.1, k.8, (y.r.n., s.s.k.) 3 times; repeat from * until 1 remains, k.1.

26th row: K.14, *p.3, (k.1, p.1) 4 times, k.2, p.1, k.7, p.1, k.18; repeat from * ending last repeat k.6.

27th row: K.1, *(s.s.k., y.r.n.) twice, k.7, (p.1, k.1) 7 times, p.1, k.8, (s.s.k., y.r.n.) 3 times; repeat from * until 1 remains, k.1.

28th row: K.13, *p.1, k.1, p.2, k.1, (p.1, k.1) 3 times, p.2, k.1, p.2, k.1, p.1, k.22; repeat from * ending last repeat k.11.

29th row: K.1, *(y.r.n., s.s.k.) twice, k.7, (p.1, k.1) 8 times, p.1, k.6, (y.r.n., s.s.k.) 3 times; repeat from * ending last repeat k.1.

30th row: K.5, *m.b., k.7, p.2, (k.1, p.1) twice, k.1, p.4, k.1, p.1, k.2, p.1, k.1, p.1, k.6, m.b., k.7; repeat from * ending last repeat k.4.

31st row: K.1, *(s.s.k., y.r.n.) twice, k.5, (p.1, k.1) 8 times, p.1, k.8, (s.s.k., y.r.n.) 3 times; repeat from * ending last repeat k.1.

32nd row: K.14, *(p.1, k.1) twice, p.2, k.1, p.8, k.1, p.1, k.3, p.1, k.19; repeat from * ending last repeat k.7.

33rd row: K.1, *y.r.n., (s.s.k., y.r.n.) twice, k.4, (p.1, k.1) 3 times, (y.r.n., s.s.k.) twice, p.1, k.1, p.1, k.3, p.1, k.7, s.s.k., (y.r.n., s.s.k.) 3 times; repeat from * until 1 remains, k.1.

34th row: K.14,* p.1, k.1, p.2, k.1, p.3, k.5, p.1, k.1, p.2, k.4, p.1, k.18; repeat from * ending last repeat k.6.

35th row: K.1, *(s.s.k., y.r.n.) twice, k.5, p.1, k.1, p.1, k.2, (y.r.n., s.s.k.) 4 times, k.1, p.1, k.8, (s.s.k., y.r.n.) 4 times; repeat from * until 1 remains, k.1.

36th row: K.14, *p.2, k.1, p.1, k.11, p.2, k.23; repeat from * ending last repeat k.11.

37th row: K.1, *(y.r.n., s.s.k.) twice, k.5, p.1, k.1, p.1, k.3, (y.r.n., s.s.k.) 4 times, p.1, k.1, p.1, k.6, (y.r.n., s.s.k.) 4 times; repeat from * until 1 remains, k.1.

38th row: K.1, *m.b., k.7, m.b., k.4, p.2, k.1, p.1, k.9, p.1, k.1, p.3, k.9; repeat from * until 1 remains, k.1.

39th row: K.1, *(s.s.k., y.r.n.) twice, k.9, p.1, k.2, (y.r.n., s.s.k.) 3 times, (k.1, p.1) twice, k.4, (s.s.k., y.r.n.) 5 times; repeat from * until 1 remains, k.1.

40th row: K.12, *p.1, k.4, p.1, k.1, p.1, k.5, p.1, k.1, p.2, k.1, p.1, k.3, p.1, k.17; repeat from * ending last repeat k.7.

41st row: K.1, *(y.r.n., s.s.k.) 4 times, k.13, p.1, k.1, p.1, k.4, (y.r.n., s.s.k.) 6 times; repeat from * ending last repeat k.1.

42nd row: K.17, *(p.1, k.1) 4 times, p.1, k.4, p.2, k.25; repeat from * ending last repeat k.10.

43rd row: K.1, *(s.s.k., y.r.n.) 5 times, k.5,

(p.1, k.1) 3 times, p.1, k.4, (s.s.k., y.r.n.) 7 times; repeat from * until 1 remains, k.1.

44th row: K.21, *(p.1, k.1) twice, p.1, k.35; repeat from * ending last repeat k.16.

45th row: K.1, *(y.r.n., s.s.k.) 5 times, k.16, (y.r.n., s.s.k.) 7 times; repeat from * until 1 remains, k.1.

46th row: K.5, *m.b., k.7, m.b., k.23, m.b., k.7; repeat from * ending last repeat k.4.

47th row: K.1, *s.s.k., (y.r.n., s.s.k.) 5 times, k.14, (y.r.n., s.s.k.) 7 times, y.r.n.; repeat from * until 1 remains, k.1.

48th row: All k.

49th row: K.1, *(y.r.n., s.s.k.) 6 times, k.12, (y.r.n., s.s.k.) 8 times, repeat from * until 1 remains, k.1.

50th row: K.22, *p.2, k.1, p.3, k.34; repeat from * ending last repeat k.14.

51st to **55**th rows: As 3rd to 7th rows.

56th row: All k.

57th to **61**st rows: As 1st to 5th rows.

62nd row: K.5, *m.b., k.7; repeat from * ending last repeat k.4.

63rd row: As 3rd row.

64th row: K.21, *for the leaf p.1, then k.39; repeat from * ending last repeat k.20.

65th row: K.1, *(y.r.n., s.s.k.) 9 times, k.1, for the leaf 3 from 1, then k.2, (y.r.n., s.s.k.) 9 times; repeat from * until 1 remains, k.1.

66th row: K.21, *for the leaf p.3, then k.39; repeat from * ending last repeat k.20.

67th row: K.7, *(s.s.k., y.r.n.) 6 times, k.1, for the leaf k.1, y.r.n., k.1, y.r.n., k.1, then k.1 more, (y.r.n., s.s.k.) 7 times, k.11; repeat from * ending last repeat k.6.

68th row: K.5, *p.1, k.15, for the leaf p.5, then k.13, p.1, k.4, p.1, k.4; repeat from * ending last repeat k.1 instead of k.4.

69th row: K.8, *(s.s.k., y.r.n.) 5 times, k.2, then for the leaf k.2, y.r.n., k.1, y.r.n., k.2, then k.1 more, (s.s.k., y.r.n.) 6 times, k.14; repeat from * ending last repeat k.8.

70th row: K.7, *p.1, k.1, m.b., k.7, m.b., k.3, for the leaf p.7, then k.3, p.1, k.8, p.1, k.12; repeat from * ending last repeat k.7.

71st row: K.9, *(s.s.k., y.r.n.) 5 times, k.1, then for the leaf k.3, y.r.n., k.1, y.r.n., k.3, then (s.s.k., y.r.n.) 6 times, k.16; repeat from * ending last repeat k.9.

72nd row: K.21, *for the leaf p.9, then k.39; repeat from *, ending last repeat k.20.

73rd row: K.9, *(y.r.n., s.s.k.) 5 times, k.1, then for the leaf k.3, sl.1, k.2tog., p.s.s.o., k.3, then k.2, (y.r.n., s.s.k.) 5 times, k.16; repeat from * ending last repeat k.9.

74th row: K.21, *for the leaf p.2, sl.1, p.2tog., p.s.s.o., p.2, then k.39; repeat from * ending last repeat k.20.

75th row: K.7, *(s.s.k., y.r.n.) 6 times, k.1, then for the leaf, k.1, sl.1, k.2tog., p.s.s.o., k.1, then (s.s.k., y.r.n.) 6 times, k.14; repeat from * ending last repeat k.9.

76th row: K.1, *p.4, k.2, p.1, k.13, for the leaf sl.1, p.2tog., p.s.s.o., this completes the leaf, then k.13, p.1, k.5; repeat from * ending last repeat k.6.

77th row: K.2, *p.1, k.8, (y.r.n., s.s.k.) 11 times, k.3, (p.1, k.1) 3 times; repeat from * to end.

78th row: K.1, *p.1, (k.1, p.1,) twice, k.3, p.1, k.3, m.b., k.7, m.b., k.10, p.1, k.4, (p.1, k.1) twice; repeat from * until 1 remains, k.1 more.

79th row: K.2, *p.1, k.1, p.1, k.6, (s.s.k., y.r.n.) 9 times, k.5, (p.1, k.1) 4 times; repeat from * to end.

80th row: K.2, *p.1, k.1, p.1, k.2, p.1, k.4, p.2, k.21, (p.1, k.1) twice, p.2, k.1; repeat from * to end.

81st row: K.2, *p.1, (k.1, p.1) twice, k.8, (y.r.n., s.s.k.) 5 times, k.9, (p.1, k.1) 4 times; repeat from * to end.

82nd row: K.2, *p.1, k.1, p.1, k.2, p.1, k.7, p.1, k.18, p.3, k.1, (p.1, k.1) twice; repeat from * to end.

83rd row: K.2, *p.1, (k.1, p.1) twice, k.8, (s.s.k., y.r.n.) 5 times, k.7, (p.1, k.1) 5 times; repeat from * to end.

84th row: K.2, *p.1, k.1, p.2, k.1, p.2, k.1, p.1, k.22, p.1, k.1, p.2, k.1, (p.1, k.1) twice; repeat from * to end.

85th row: K.2, *p.1, (k.1, p.1) 3 times, k.6, (y.r.n., s.s.k.) 5 times, k.7, (p.1, k.1) 5 times; repeat from * to end.

86th row: K.1, *p.3, k.1, p.1, k.2, p.1, k.1, p.1, k.6, m.b., k.7, m.b., k.7, p.2, (k.1, p.1) 3 times; repeat from * until 1 remains, k.1.

87th row: K.2, *then k.2 more, p.1, k.1, p.1, k.8, (s.s.k., y.r.n.) 5 times, k.5, (p.1, k.1) 6 times; repeat from * to end.

88th row: K.1, *p.8, k.1, p.1, k.3, p.1, k.19, (p.1, k.1) twice, p.2, k.1; repeat from * until 1 remains, k.1 more.

Now shape the body as follows:

89th row: Inc. in first st., *k.1, p.1, k.3, p.1, k.7, (s.s.k., y.r.n.) 6 times, k.4, (p.1, k.1) 3 times, (y.r.n., s.s.k.) twice, p.1*; repeat from * to * until 1 remains, inc.

90th row: K.1, p.2, *k.5, p.1, k.1, p.2, k.23, p.2, k.1, p.1, k.1, p.3; repeat from * until 1 remains, k.1.

91st row: K.2, *y.r.n., s.s.k., k.1, p.1, k.8, (s.s.k., y.r.n.) 6 times, k.5, p.1, k.1, p.1, k.2, (y.r.n., s.s.k.) 3 times; repeat from * until 2 remain, k.2.

92nd row: K.10, *p.2, k.23, p.2, k.1, p.1, k.11; repeat from * ending last repeat k.5.

93rd row: Inc. in first st., *(y.r.n., s.s.k.) twice, p.1, k.1, p.1, k.6, (y.r.n., s.s.k.) 6 times, k.5, p.1, k.1, p.1, k.3, (y.r.n., s.s.k.) twice; repeat from * until 3 remain, y.r.n., s.s.k., inc.

94th row: K.9, *p.1, k.1, p.2, k.10, m.b., k.12, p.2, k.1, p.1, k.9; repeat from * ending last repeat k.6.

95th row: K.1, (y.r.n., s.s.k.) twice, *(k.1, p.1) twice, k.4, (s.s.k., y.r.n.) 7 times, k.9, p.1, k.2, (y.r.n., s.s.k.) 3 times; repeat from * until 1 remains, k.1.

96th row: K.7, *p.1, k.1, p.2, p.1, k.3, p.1, k.17, p.1, k.2, (p.1, k.1) twice, p.1, k.5; repeat from * ending last repeat k.4.

97th row: Inc. in first st., k.3, *p.1, k.1, p.1, k.4, (y.r.n., s.s.k.) 10 times, k.7, p.1, k.5; repeat from * until 2 remain, p.1, inc.

98th row: K.2, *(p.1, k.1) 3 times, p.1, k.4, p.2, k.27; repeat from * until 6 remain, (p.1, k.1) 3 times.

99th row: (K.1, p.1) 3 times, k.4, *(s.s.k., y.r.n.) 12 times, k.5, (p.1, k.1) 3 times, p.1, k.4; repeat from * ending last repeat k.4.

100th row: K.4, *p.1, (k.1, p.1) twice, k.35; repeat from * until 4 remain, (p.1, k.1) twice.

101st row: Inc., k.9, *(y.r.n., s.s.k.) 12 times, k.16; repeat from * ending last repeat k.13, inc.

102nd row: K.13, *p.1, (k.7, m.b.) 3 times, k.15; repeat from * ending last repeat k.12.

103rd row: K.10, *(y.r.n., s.s.k.) 13 times, k.14; repeat from * to end.

104th row: All k.

105th row: Inc., k.8, *(y.r.n., s.s.k.) 14 times, k.12; repeat from * until 1 remains, inc.

106th row: K.7, *p.6, k.34; repeat from * until 5 remain, p.4, k.1.

107th row: K.2, *s.s.k., y.r.n.; repeat from * until 2 remain, k.2.

108th row: All k.

109th row: Inc. in first st., k.1, *y.r.n., s.s.k.; repeat from * until 1 remains, k.1, inc.

110th row: K.3, *m.b., k.7; repeat from * ending last repeat k.2.

111th row: K.1, *s.s.k., y.r.n.; repeat from * until 1 remains, k.1.

112th row: All k.

The last 112 rows form the pattern; now continue in pattern as follows:

1st row: Inc., *y.r.n., s.s.k.; repeat from * until 1 remains, inc.

2nd row: All k.

3rd to 5th rows: As 107th to 109th rows.

6th row: K.1, *m.b., k.7; repeat from * ending last repeat k.8.

7th row: K.1, *s.s.k., y.r.n.; repeat from * until 1 remains, k.1.

8th row: K.9, *p.1, for the leaf, then k.39; repeat from * ending last repeat k.8.

9th row: Inc., (y.r.n., s.s.k.) 3 times, *k.1, for the leaf 3 from 1, then k.2, (y.r.n., s.s.k.) 18 times; repeat from * ending last repeat by working the instructions in brackets 3 times, then inc. in last st.

10th row: K.10, *p.3, for the leaf, then k.39; repeat from * ending last repeat k.9.

11th row: K.2, (s.s.k., y.r.n.) 3 times, k.1, for the leaf k.1, y.r.n., k.1, y.r.n., k.1, *then k.1, (y.r.n., s.s.k.) 7 times, k.11, (s.s.k., y.r.n.) 6 times, k.1, for the leaf k.1, y.r.n., k.1, y.r.n., k.1; repeat from * until 10 remain, k.1, (y.r.n., s.s.k.) 4 times, k.1.

12th row: K.10, for the leaf p.5, then *k.13, p.1, k.4, p.1, k.4, p.1, k.15; for the leaf p.5, then repeat from * until 9 remain, k.9.

The last 12 rows set the position of the next repeat of the pattern. Continuing in pattern as set and working the extra sts. into the pattern as they occur, inc. 1 st. at each end of the next row and the 3 following 4th rows. – 148 sts. **

Pattern 1 row marking each end with coloured threads. Work should now measure 31 centimetres (12½ inches) from beginning. Pattern 72 rows more.

To slope the shoulders: Cast off 8 sts. at the beginning of the next 12 rows. Cast off the remaining 52 sts.

FRONT Work as given for the back until ** is reached.

Now divide the sts. for the neck: Next row: Marking the first st. with a coloured thread, pattern 72 sts. and leave these sts. on a spare needle until required for right front shoulder, cast off 4, pattern to end, marking last st. with a coloured thread and continue on these 72 sts. for the left front shoulder.

Left front shoulder: To shape the neck: Continuing in pattern as set dec. 1st. at neck edge on each of the next 10 rows. On 62 sts. pattern 2 rows. Dec. 1st. at neck edge on the next row and the 13 following 4th rows. On 48 sts. pattern 7 rows.

To slope the shoulder: Cast off 8 sts. at the beginning of the next row and the 4 following alternate rows. On 8 sts. work 1 row, then cast off.

Right front shoulder: With right side of work facing rejoin yarn to inner edge of sts. left on spare needle and work to end of row, then work as given for left front shoulder to end.

Neck edging: Join right shoulder seam. With right side of work facing rejoin yarn at left front shoulder and using size 3 mm. needles pick up and k. 53 sts. from left front neck edge, 4 sts. from those cast off at centre front, 53 sts. from right front neck edge, then 48 sts. from back neck edge. – 158 sts.

K.3 rows.

Next row: K.2, *cast off 2, k. next st.; repeat from * to end.

Next row: K.2, * turn, cast on 3 over those cast off, turn, k.2; repeat from * to end.

Cast off row: K.2tog., *(k.1, pass first st. on right hand needle over 2nd st.) 3 times, k.2tog., pass first st. on right hand needle over 2nd st.; repeat from * to end.

SLEEVES Both alike. With size 3 mm. needles cast on 74 sts. by the thumb method, then work the 2 edging rows given for back. –

---

62 sts.

***K2 rows then work in pattern as follows:

1st to 5th rows: As for back.

6th row: k.3, *m.b., k.7; repeat from * ending last repeat with m. k.2.

7th row: As 3rd row.

8th row: K.11, p.1, k.39, p.1, k.10.

9th row: K.1, (y.r.n., s.s.k.) 4 times, k.1, 3 from 1, k.2, (y.r.n., s.s.k.) 18 times, k.1, 3 from 1, k.2, (y.r.n., s.s.k.) 4 times, k.1.

10th row: K.11, p.3, k.39, p.3, k.10.

11th row: K.1, (s.s.k., y.r.n.) 4 times, k.2, y.r.n., k.1, y.r.n., k.2, (y.r.n., s.s.k.) 7 times, k.11, (s.s.k., y.r.n.) 6 times, k.2, y.r.n., k.1, y.r.n., k.2, (y.r.n., s.s.k.) 4 times, k.2.

12th row: K.11, p.5, k.13, p.1, k.4, p.1, k.4, p.1, k.15, p.5, k.10.

The last 12 rows set the position of the pattern given for the back, work the 13th to 16th rows as set.

Continuing in pattern, and working the extra sts. into the pattern as they occur, inc. 1 st. at each end of the next row and the 12 following 8th rows. On 88 sts. pattern 7 rows, then cast off.

MAKING UP Do not press. Join left shoulder seam, Neatly sew cast off edges of sleeves to row ends of back and front, between the marking threads. Join sleeve and side seams. ●

BLANCHE

MATERIALS Either 17 25 gram balls of "Woollybear Lambswool" or 12 28 gram hanks of "Woollybear Shetland", or 21 25 gram balls of "Woollybear Cashmere"● a pair each of size 3 mm and 2¾ mm Aero knitting needles●

TENSION and **NOTE** As for "Flora"●

ABBREVIATIONS As for "Flora", plus single rib is k.1 and p.1 alternately●

BACK With size 2¾ mm needles cast on 144 sts and work 55 rows in single rib.

Decrease Row: Rib 8, *k.2tog., rib 4; repeat from * ending last repeat rib 8. – 122 sts.

Change to size 3 mm needles and work as given for back of "Flora" sweater from *** to end.

FRONT Work as given for back until ** is reached on back of "Flora" pattern then work as given for front of "Flora" until the right front shoulder has been worked.

The neck inset: With size 2¾ mm needles and m. cast on 10 sts. and work 2 rows in single rib.

Continuing in rib inc. 1st. at each end of the next 70 rows.

On 150 sts. work 20 rows.

Cast on the 64 sts. for the back neckband at the beginning of the next row. On 214 sts. work 17 rows in single rib, then cast off loosely.

SLEEVES Both alike● With size 2¾ mm needles cast on 74 sts. and work 55 rows in single rib.

Decrease row: Rib 3, *k.2tog. rib 4; repeat from * ending last repeat rib 3. – 62 sts.

Change to size 3 mm needles and work as given for "Flora" sweater from *** to end.

MAKING UP Do not press. Join shoulder seams. Join the last 18 row ends of back neckband to those at opposite edge. Sew inset and back neckband in place. Neatly sew cast off edges of sleeves to row ends of back and front between the marking threads. Join sleeve and side seams. ●

Far left and centre right, sweater and cardigan in cashmere and angora available as made up garments only. Centre left, "Jane" to knit in lambswool. Left, "Greta" to knit yourself in lambswool or cashmere.

CANDY

MATERIALS 22 25 gram balls of "Patricia Roberts Lambswool No. 1" in main colour plus either "Patricia Roberts Kid Mohair" or "Angora" 3 balls in contrast a. green and 2 balls in each of the 5 other contrast colours●

A pair each of size 2¼mm and 2¾mm Aero knitting needles● a fine cable needle●

TENSION 13 stitches and 26 rows – 13 rows to view – to 5 centimetres (2 inches) over the fisherman's rib, using size 2¾mm needles.●

If you cannot obtain the correct tension using the size needles suggested, use larger or smaller ones accordingly●

ABBREVIATIONS K., knit● p., purl● st., stitch● tog., together● dec., decrease (by working 2 sts. tog)● inc., increase (by working twice into same st.)● inc.k.p., increase by knitting first into front, then purling into back of st.● inc.p.k., increase by purling first into front then knitting into back of st.● k. or p1b., k. or p.1 into back of st.● up 1, pick up the loop, which lies between the needles, slip it onto the left hand needle, then k. into back of it● k.1down, k.1 working into st. below next st. on left hand needle● y.r.n., yarn round needle● sl., slip● p.s.s.o., pass slip st. over● s.c., start circle thus, with appropriate contrast colour k.1, (y.r.n., k.1) 3 times all into next st., turn, p.7, turn, k.7● f.rib, fisherman's rib – k.1 down and p.1 alternately● s.s.k., sl.1, k.1, p.s.s.o.● app., appropriate● cont., contrast● cr.6b., cross 6 back, slip next 3 sts. onto cable needle at back of work, with appropriate cont., k.3, with m. or other cont. k.3 from cable needle● cr.6f., cross 6 front, sl. next 3 sts. onto cable needle at front of work, with m. or other cont. k.3, with app. cont. k.3 from cable needle● cr.5b., cross 5 back, sl. next 2 sts. onto cable needle at back of work, with app. cont. k.3, with m. or other cont. k.2 from cable needle● cr.5f., cross 5 front, thus, sl. next 3 sts. onto cable needle at front of work, with m. or other cont. k.2, with app. cont. k.3 from cable needle● cr.4b., cross 4 back, sl. next st. onto cable needle at back of work, with app. cont. k.3, with m. or other contrast k. st. from cable needle● cr.4f., with m. or other cont. k. into back of 4th st. on left hand needle, with app. cont. k. first 3 sts. allowing all 4 sts. to fall from left hand needle tog.● r.s., right side● w.s., wrong side● ex.r., extra rows thus, p. app. number of sts., turn, k. across them, turn, p. them again● 3 from 1, with app. cont. k.1, y.r.n., k.1 all into 1 st., turn, p.3, turn, k.3● 6 into 3, with m. k.1, sl. next 3 sts. onto right hand needle, pass 2nd of these sts. over first st., (pass this st. back to other needle, pass 2nd st. over this st.) 3 times, k. this st., then k.1 more● cr.7, sl. next 3 sts.onto cable needle at front of work, sl.1 and leave this st. on a safety pin at back of work, with e. k.3, with b. k.1 from safety pin, with e. k.3 from cable needle● m., main colour● a., first contrast● b., second contrast● c., third contrast● d., fourth contrast● e., fifth contrast●

MEASUREMENTS The measurements are given in centimetres followed by inches in brackets●
Underarms: 114 (45½)●Side seam: 48 (19)● Length: 73 (29)● Sleeve seam: 42.5 (17)●

BACK With size 2¾mm needles and m. cast on 169 sts. by the thumb method, then k. 1 row.
Now work in pattern as follows:
1st Picot row: With a. k.3, *turn, p.1, turn, k.2, turn, p.3, turn, k.6; repeat from * ending last repeat k.4.
2nd Cluster row: With a. p.1, *slip next 3 sts. onto cable needle; wrap a. round the 3 sts. 4 times, bring yarn to front of work, then slip the sts. back onto left hand needle and p. across the 3 sts. p.1; repeat from * to end.
3rd row: With m. k.2, *with a. (k.1b., p.3) 6 times, k.1b., join in a separate small ball of m., with m. k.3; repeat from * ending last repeat k.2.
4th row: With m. p.1, *still with m. k.1, (with a. p.1b., k.3), 6 times, p.1b., with m. k.1, p.1; repeat from * to end.
5th row: With m. p.1, *inc. k.p., with a. k.1b., p.2tog., p.1, (k.1b., p.3) 4 times, k.1b., p.1, p.2tog., k.1b., with m. inc.p.k. – see abbreviations, p.1; repeat from * to end.
6th row: With m. p.1, *k.1, p.1, with m.a. p.1b., k.2, (p.1b., k.3) 4 times, p.1b., k.2, p.1b., with m. p.1, k.1, p.1; repeat from * to end, but using separate small balls of a. for each section of the pattern.
7th row: With m. p.1, *k.1, inc.p.k., with a. k.1b., p.2, k.1b., p.2tog., p.1, k.1b., p.3, k.1b., p.3, k.1b., p.2tog., k.1b., p.2, k.1b., with m. inc.k.p., k.1, p.1; repeat from * to end.
8th row: With m. p.1, *k.1, p.1, k.1, with a. (p.1b., k.2) twice, (p.1b., k.3) twice, (p.1b., k.2) twice, with m. (k.1, p.1) twice; repeat from * to end.
9th row: With m. p.1, *k.1, p.1, inc.k.p., with a. (k.1b., p.2) twice, k.1b., p.2tog., p.1, k.1b., p.1, p.2tog., k.1b., (p.2, k.1b.) twice, with m. inc. p.k., p.1, k.1, p.1; repeat from * to end.
10th row: With m. p.1, *(k.1, p.1) twice, with a. (p.1b., k.2) 6 times, p.1b., with m. (p.1, k.1) twice, p.1; repeat from * to end.
11th row: With m. p..1, *k.1, p.1, k.1, inc.p.k., with a k.1b., p.2tog., (k.1b., p.2) 4 times, k.1b., p.2tog., k.1b., with m. inc.k.p., (k.1, p.1) twice; repeat from * to end.
12th row: With m. p.1, *k.1, (p.1, k.1) twice, with a. p.1b., k.1, (p.1b., k.2) 4 times, p.1b., k.1, p.1b., with m. (k.1, p.1) 3 times: repeat from * to end.
13th row: With m. p.1, *(k.1, p.1) twice, inc.k.p., with a. k.1b., p.1, k.1b., p.2tog., (k.1b., p.2) twice, k.1b., p.2tog., k.1b., p.1, k.1b., with m. inc.k.p., (p.1, k.1) twice, p.1; repeat from * to end.
14th row: With m. p.1, *(k.1, p.1) 3 times, with a. (p.1b., k.1) twice, (p.1b., k.2) twice, (p.1b., k.1) twice, p.1b., with m. (p.1, k.1) 3 times, p.1; repeat from * to end.
15th row: With m. p.1, *k.1, (p.1, k.1) twice, inc.p.k., with a. (k.1b., p.1) twice, (k.1b., p.2tog.) twice, (k.1b., p.1) twice, k.1b., with m. inc.k.p., (k.1, p.1) 3 times; repeat from * to end.
16th row: With m. p.1, *k.1, (p.1, k.1) 3 times, with a. (p.1b., k.1) 6 times, p.1b., with m. (k.1, p.1) 4 times; repeat from * to end.
17th row: With m. p.1, *continue with one ball of m. (k.1, p.1) 3 times, inc. k.p., with a. (k.2tog.b.) 3 times, k.1b., (k.2tog.) 3 times, with m. inc.p.k., (p.1, k.1) 3 times, p.1; repeat from * to end. – 145 sts.
18th row: With m. k.1, *(p.2, k.2) twice, slip next 7 sts. onto cable needle, wrap a. around these 7 sts. 7 times, bring a. to front of work, slip 7 sts. back onto left hand needle and p .3, p.2tog., p.2 across these sts., break off a., with m. (k.2, p.2) twice, inc.p.k.; repeat from * ending last repeat k.1, instead of inc. – 144 sts.
Darn in ends finishing with a back st.
Change to size 2¼mm needles.
1st double rib row: P.1, *k.2, p.2; repeat from * ending last repeat p.1.
2nd rib row: K.1, *p.2, k.2; repeat from * ending last repeat k.1.
Repeat these 2 rows 16 times more, then work the first row again.
Increase row: Rib 18 * up 1, rib 36; repeat from * ending last repeat, rib 18. – 148 sts.

Change to size 2¾mm needles and work in fisherman's rib as follows:
1st row: * P.1, k.1 down; repeat from * to end.
2nd row: * P.1, k.1 down; repeat from * to end.
The last 2 rows form the fisherman's rib pattern; repeat them once more.
Now continuing in fisherman's rib for all the parts in main colour work as follows. Use separate small balls of contrasts for the motifs and separate balls of m. at each side of the motifs so that the colours not in use are not pulled tightly across back of work.
1st row: fisherman's rib 41, s.s.k., with a. s.c. – see abbreviations, with m. k.2tog., f.rib to end.
2nd row: With m. f.rib 103, with a. p.3, with m. p.1, with a. p.3; with m. f.rib to end.
3rd row: With m. f.rib 39, with a. and m. cr.6b., with m. k.1 down, with m. and a. cr.6f., with m. f.rib to end.
4th row: With m. f.rib 100, and a. p.3, with m. k.1 down, (p.1, k.1 down) 3 times, with a. p.3, with m. f.rib to end.
5th row: With m. f.rib 36, with a. and m. cr.6b., with m. f.rib 7, with m. and a. cr.5f., with m. f.rib to end.
6th row: With m. f.rib 98, with a. p.3, with m. f.rib 12, with a. p.3, with m. f.rib to end.
Tthe last 6 rows set the position of the pattern given in the chart; note that the parts in m. are in f.rib throughout.
Work the 7th to 120th rows from the chart.
Exchanging green with pink, orange with yellow and purple with blue on the next repeat of the pattern, work 60 rows. Mark each end of the last row with coloured threads to denote armholes. **
Pattern 120 rows, working the next repeat of the pattern in the original colours.
To slope the shoulders: Cast off 8 sts. at the beginning of the next 12 rows. Cast off the remaining 52 sts.

FRONT Work as given for back until ** is reached.
Pattern 87 rows more.
Now divide the sts. for the neck: Next row: Pattern 67 and leave these sts. on a spare needle until required for right front shoulder, cast off 14, pattern to end and continue these 67 sts. for the left front shoulder.
Left front shoulder: To shape the neck: Dec. 1 st. at the neck edge on each of the next 18 rows. On 49 sts. pattern 14 rows.
To slope the shoulder: Cast off 8 sts. at the beginning of the next row and the 4 following alternate rows.
On 9 sts. work 1 row, then cast off.
Right front shoulder: With right side of work facing rejoin yarn to inner edge of sts. left on spare needle and work to end of row, then, continuing from chart as set, work as given for left front shoulder to end.
Neckband: first join right shoulder seam. With right side of work facing with size 2¼mm needles and m. pick up and k. 36 sts. from left front neck edge, 18 sts. from centre front, 36 sts. from right front neck edge and 64 sts. from back neck edge – 154 sts.
Work 20 rows on double rib, then cast off in rib.

SLEEVES Both alike: With size 2¾mm needles and m. cast on 85 sts. and using m. throughout work as given for back, until the 18 edging pattern rows have been worked, noting that there will be 73 sts. after the 17th row and 72 sts. after the 18th row.
Change to size 2¼mm size needles and work 24 rows in double rib as given for back.**
Change to size 2¾mm needles and work 6 rows in fisherman's rib – k.1 down and p.1 alternately.

Continuing in fisherman's rib and working the extra sts. into the rib as they occur inc. 1 st. at each end of next row and the 13 following 12th rows. On 100 sts. pattern 5 rows.
To shape the sleeve top: Dec 1 st. at each end of the next row and the 27 following alternate rows. On 44 sts. work 1 row.
Dec 1 st. at each end of the next 10 rows then cast off 3 sts. at the beginning of the next 4 rows. Cast off the remaining 12 sts.
MAKING UP Do not press. Neatly join left shoulder seam. Set in sleeves. Join sleeve and side seams. Fold neckband in half to wrong side and catch in place. ●

MATERIALS 27 25 gram balls of either "Patricia Roberts Lambswood No 1", "Cashmere" or "Fine Cotton" ●
A pair each of size 2¼mm and 2¾mm Aero knitting needles ●
TENSION As given for "Candy" ●
ABBREVIATIONS As given for "Candy" but noting that all the sts. are worked in one colour ●
MEASUREMENTS As given for "Candy" ●
BACK AND FRONT Work exactly as given for "Candy" but in one colour only and omitting neckband ●
SLEEVES Work as given for "Candy" ●

COLLAR Front: Work as given for back of "Candy" until the 18 edging pattern rows have been worked – but all in one colour.
Change to size 2¼mm needles and work 24 rows in double rib as given for back, then cast off in rib ●
Back: Work as given for sleeves until ** is reached. Cast off in rib.
MAKING UP Do not press. Join shoulder seams. Set in sleeves. Join sleeve and side seams. Join row end edges of back and front collar. Sew cast off edges of collar in place at back and front neck edges.

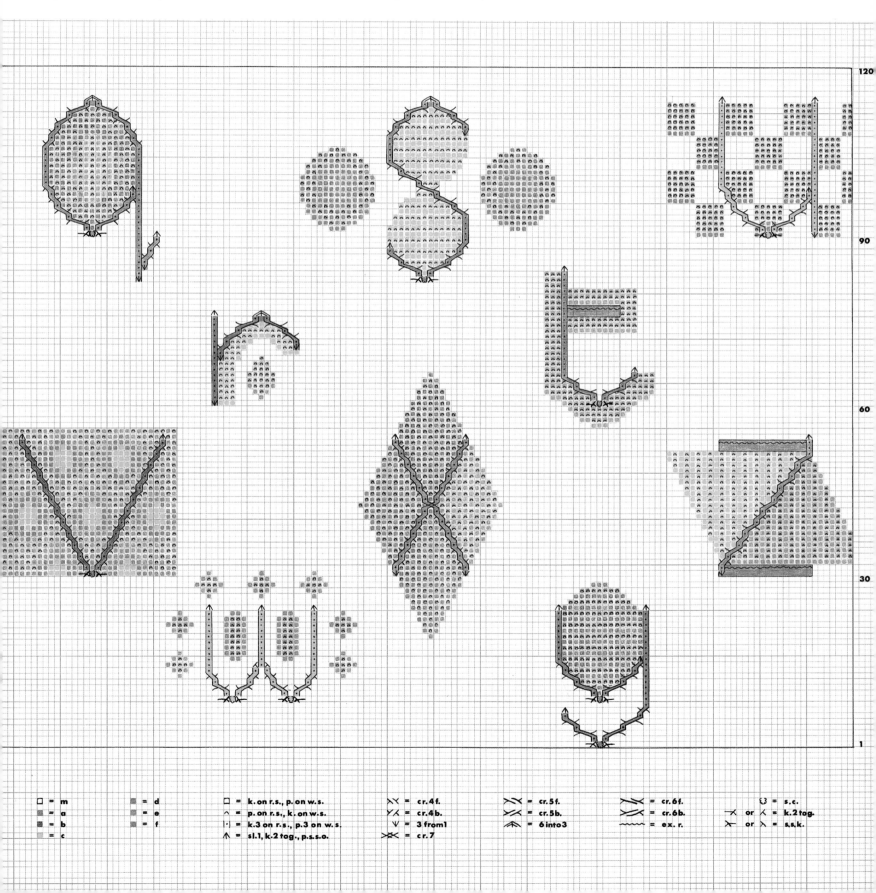

□ = m	▣ = d	□ = k. on r.s., p. on w.s.	⤬ = cr.4 f.	⤬ = cr.5 f.	⤬ = cr.6 f.	⑬ = s.c.			
▦ = a	▪ = e	∧ = p. on r.s., k. on w.s.	⤰ = cr.4 b.	⤬ = cr.5 b.	⤬ = cr.6 b.	⤼ or ⤳ = k.2 tog.			
▨ = b	▣ = f	|·| = k.3 on r.s., p.3 on w.s.	∨ = 3 from1	⤮ = cr.7	∿ = ex. r.	⤫ or ⤬ = s.s.k.			
▥ = c		∧ = sl.1, k.2 tog., p.s.s.o.	⤬ = cr.7	▲ = 6 into3					

"Plain Jane", left,
a classic easy to knit
sweater, in our especially
soft lambswool. For a man
use rugged shetland
tweed.

"Candy", right, with its
intricate stitchcraft,
combined with a delicate
scalloped edging looks
great worn with a 'Liberty
Print Varuna Wool' skirt.

MATERIALS Either 16 50 gram balls of "Patricia Roberts Lambswool No 2"●
Or 16 50 gram hanks of "Patricia Roberts Shetland No 2" in plain, flecked or marled colours●
Or 24 25 gram balls of "Patricia Roberts Lurex" — see picture. Note that the lurex is used double throughout●
A pair each of size 2¾ and size 3¼mm Aero knitting needles; a medium sized cable needle●

TENSION Using size 3¼mm needles, the tension over one repeat of the 48 stitches and 84 row pattern will measure 13.5cms (5½ inches) in width and 21cms (8½ inches) in depth●
If you cannot obtain the correct tension using the size needles suggested, use larger or smaller ones accordingly●

ABBREVIATIONS K., knit● p., purl● st., stitch● tog., together● dec., decrease (by working 2 sts. tog.) inc., increase (by working twice into same st.)● double rib is k.2 and p.2 alternately● c.6, cable 6 thus, slip next 3 sts. onto cable needle at front of work, k.3, then k.3 from cable needle● c.9b., cable 9 back, thus, slip next 6 sts. onto cable needle at back of work, k.3, then from cable k.3, then p.3● c.9f., cable 9 front thus, slip next 3 sts. onto cable needle at front of work, p.3, k.3, then k.3 from cable● single rib is k.1 and p.1 alternately● up 1, pick up the loop which lies between the needles, slip it onto left hand needle, then k. into back of it●

MEASUREMENTS The measurements are given in centimetres followed by inches in brackets.
Underarms: 108 (44)● Side seams: 39 (15½)● Length: 64 (25½)● Sleeve seam — woman's: 44 (17¾)● man's: 47 (18¾)

NOTE The instructions are given for the woman's size. Where they vary, work the instructions in the bracket for the man's size.
Special Note: When using "Lurex" 2 strands are used throughout.

BACK With size 2¾mm needles cast on 146 sts. and work 31 rows in double rib, beginning right side rows with k.2 and wrong side rows with p.2.
Increase row: Rib 2, *up 1, rib 3; repeat from * to end. – 194 sts.
Change to size 3¼mm needles and work in pattern as follows:
1st row: K.1, *(p.1, k.1, p.1) 11 times, k.6, (p.1, k.1, p.1) 3 times; repeat from * until 1 st. remains, k.1.
2nd row: K.1, *(k.1, p.1, k.1) 3 times, p.6, (k.1, p.1, k.1) 11 times; repeat from * until 1 st. remains, k.1 more.
3rd and **4**th rows: As 1st and 2nd rows.
5th row: K.1, *(p.1, k.1, p.1) 11 times, c.6, (p.1, k.1, p.1) 3 times; repeat from * until 1 remains, k.1.
6th row: As 2nd row.
7th row: K.1, *(p.1, k.1, p.1) 9 times, c.9b., c.9f., p.1, k.l, p.1; repeat from * until 1 remains, k.1.
8th row: K.1, *k.1, p.1, k.1, p.6, k.2, p.2, k.2, p.6, (k.1, p.1, k.1) 9 times; repeat from * ending k.1 more.
9th row: K.1. *(p.1, k.1, p.1) 9 times, k.6, p.2, k.2, p.2, k.6, p.1, k.1, p.1; repeat from * until 1 remains, k.1.
10th and **11**th rows: As 8th and 9th rows.
12th row: K.1, *k.1. p.1, k.1, p.18, (k.1, p.1, k.1) 9 times; repeat from * until 1 remains, k.1 more.
13the row: K.1, *(p.1, k.1, p.1) 8 times, c.9b., k.6, c.9f.; repeat from * until 1 remains, k.1.
14th row: K.1, p.24, (k.1, p.1, k.1) 8 times; repeat from * until 1 remains, k.1 more.
15 row: K.1, *(p.1, k.1, p.1) 8 times, k.6, p.2, k.2, p.4, k.2, p.2, k.6; repeat from * until 1

remains, k.1 more.
16th row: K.1, *p.6., k.2, p.2, k.4, p.2, k.2, p.6, (k.1, p.1, k.1) 8 times; repeat from * until 1 remains, k.1 more.
17th and **18**th rows: As 15th and 16th rows.
19th row: K.1, *(p.1, k.1, p.1) 8 times, k.24; repeat from * until 1 remains, k.1 more.
20th row: K.1, *p.24, (k.1, p.1, k.1) 8 times; repeat from * until 1 remains, k.1 more.
21st row: As 19th row.
22nd row: K.1, *(p.1, k.4, p.1) 4 times, (k.1, p.1, k.1) 8 times; repeat from * until 1 remains, k.1 more.
23rd row: K.1, *(p.1, k.1, p.1) 8 times, (k.1, p.4, k.1) 4 times; repeat from * until 1 remains, k.1 more.
24th and **25**th rows: As 22nd and 23rd rows.
26th row: K.1, p.30, *(k.1, p.1, k.1) 4 times, p.36; repeat from * ending last repeat p.6, k.1.
27th row: K.7, *(p.1, k.1, p.1) 4 times, k.36; repeat from * ending last repeat k.31.
28th row: As 26th row.
29th row: K.1, *k.6, (p.1, k.1, p.1) 4 times, k.6, (p.2, k.2, p.2) 4 times; repeat from * until 1 remains, k.1.
30th row: K.1, *(k.2, p.2, k.2) 4 times, p.6, (k.1, p.1, k.1) 4 times, p.6; repeat from * until 1 remains, k.1.
31st and **32**nd rows: As 29th and 30th rows.
33rd row: K.1, *c.9f., p.1, k.1, p.2, k.1, p.1, c.9b., k.24; repeat from * ending last repeat k.25.
34th row: K.1, p.33, *k.1, p.1, k.2, p.1, k.1, p.42; repeat from * ending last repeat p.9, k.1.
35th row: K.10, *p.1, k.1, p.2, p.1, k.1, k.42; repeat from * ending k.34.
36th row: K.1, *p.1, (k.4, p.2) 4 times, k.2, p.6, k.1, p.1, k.2, p.1, k.1, p.6, k.2, p.1; repeat from * until 1 remains, k.1.
37th row: K.2, *p.2, k.6, p.1, k.1, p.2, k.1, p.1, k.6, p.2, (k.2, p.4) 4 times, k.2; repeat from * to end.
38th row: As 36th row.
39th row: K.2, *p.2, c.9f., c.9b., p.2, (k.2, p.4) 4 times, k.2; repeat from * to end.
40th row: K.1, p. until 1 remains, k.1.
41st row: K.10, *c.6, k.42; repeat from * ending last repeat k.34.
42nd row: K.1, p. until 1 remains, k.1
43rd row: K.1, p.2, *k.2, p.5, k.6, p.5, (k.2, p.4) 5 times; repeat from * ending last repeat p.2, k.1 instead of p.4.
44th row: K.3, *(p.2, k.4) 5 times, k.1 more, p.6, k.5, p.2, k.4; repeat from * ending last repeat k.3.
45th and **46**th rows: As 43rd and 44th rows.
47th and **48**th rows: As 41st and 42nd rows.
49th row: K.4, *c.9b., c.9f., k.30; repeat from * ending last repeat k.28.
50th to **53**rd rows: Work 36th and 37th rows twice.
54th: K.1, p.33, *k.1, p.1, k.2, p.1, k.1, p.42; repeat from * ending last repeat p.9, k.1.
55th row: K.1, *c.9b., p.1, k.1, p.2, k.1, p.1, c.9f., k.24; repeat from * until 1 remains, k.1 more.
56th row: As 26th row.
57th to **60**th rows: As 29th to 32nd rows.
61st row: As 27th row.
62nd row: As 26th row.
63rd row: As 19th row.
64th to **67**th rows: As 22nd to 25th rows.
68th row: As 20th row.
69th and **70**th rows: As 19th and 20th rows.
71st to **74**th rows: As 15th to 18th rows.
75th row: K.1, *(p.1, k.1, p.1) 8 times, c.9f., K.6, c.9b.; repeat from * until 1 remains, k.1.
76th row: As 12th row.
77th row: K.1, *(p.1, k.1, p.1) 9 times, k.18,

p.1, k.1, p.1; repeat from * until 1 remains, k.1.
78th to **80**th rows: As 8th to 10th rows.
81st row: K.1, *(p.1, k.1, p.1) 9 times, c.9f., c.9b., p.1, k.1, p.1; repeat from * until 1 remains, k.1.
82nd row: As 2nd row.
83rd row: As 5th row.
84th row: As 2nd row.
These 84 rows form the pattern. Work the first 38 rows again, marking each end of the last row with coloured threads.**
Pattern 92 rows more.
To slope the shoulders: Cast off 17 sts. at the beginning of the next 8 rows. — 58 sts.
Change to size 2¾mm needles and work 20 rows in single rib. Cast off in rib.

FRONT Work as given for back until ** is reached.
Pattern 65 rows more.
Now divide the sts. for the neck: Next row: Pattern 84 and leave these sts. on a spare needle until required for right front shoulder, cast off 26, pattern to end and continue on these 84 sts. for the left front shoulder.
Left front shoulder: To shape the neck:
Dec. 1 st. at neck edge on each of the next 16 rows. On 68 sts. pattern 10 rows.
To slope the shoulder: Cast off 17 sts. at the beginning of the next row and the 2 following alternate rows. On 17 sts. work 1 row, then cast off.
Right front shoulder: With right side of work facing rejoin yarn to inner edge of sts. left on spare needle and work to end of row, then work as given for left front shoulder to end.
Neckband: With right side of work facing rejoin yarn and using size 2¾mm needles pick up and k. 32 sts. from left front neck edge, 26 sts. from centre front and 32 sts. from right front neck edge.
On 90 sts. work 19 rows in single rib, then cast off in rib.

SLEEVES Alike: First join shoulder seams. With right side of work facing rejoin yarn at one marking thread and using size 3¼mm needles pick up and k. 194 sts. from the row ends between the marking threads and work 16 rows in pattern as given for back.
Continuing in pattern as set, dec. 1 st. at each end of the next row and the 49 (34) following alternate (4th) rows. On 94 (124) sts. pattern 1 (3) row(s).
Change to size 2¾mm needles.
Decrease row: K.1, *p.1, k.2 tog., repeat from * to end. — 63 (83) sts.
Work 61 (31) rows in single rib, then cast off in rib.

MAKING UP Do not press. Join sleeve and side seams. Fold neckband in half to wrong side and slip st. in place. ●

"Plain Jane" may also be knitted for a man in "Shetland Tweed No. 2".

MATERIALS 11 25 gram balls of either "Woollybear Lambswool" or 14 "Woollybear Cashmere" in main colour● 5 20 gram balls of "Woollybear Angora" in first contrast and 2 balls in each of the 4 other contrast colours● a pair each of size 3 mm and 3¾ mm Aero knitting needles●

TENSION 36 stitches and 32 rows – 1 repeat of the diamond pattern – to 12.5 centimetres (5 inches) in both width and depth, using size 3¾ mm needles●

If you cannot obtain the correct tension using the size needles suggested use larger or smaller needles accordingly●

ABBREVIATIONS K., knit● p., purl;● st., stitch● tog., together● dec., decrease (by working 2 sts. tog.)● inc., increase (by working twice into same st.)● m., main colour● a., first contrast● b., second contrast● c., third contrast● d., fourth contrast● e., fifth contrast● y.r.n., yarn round needle● sl., slip● up 1, pick up the loop which lies between the needles, slip it onto left hand needle, then p. into back of it● 3 from 1, with m. k.1, y.r.n., k.1 all into same st.● c.b., complete bobble thus, on wrong side rows, with m. k.3, bring yarn forward, then slip these 3 sts. back onto left hand needle, pick up the loop into which the 3 from 1 on previous row was worked, slip it onto left hand needle, pass the 3 sts. in m. over this st., then with a. or d. as appropriate p. this st.● 5 from 1, k.1, y.r.n., k.1, y.r.n., k.1 all into next st.● 4 over 1, pass 2nd, 3rd, 4th and 5th sts. on left hand needle over first st., then with m. p. this st.● m.b., with e. k.1, y.r.n., k.1, y.r.n., k.1, all into next st., turn, k.5, turn, p.5, turn, k.5, turn, pick up the loop originally worked into and slip it onto left hand needle, then pass the 5 sts. in e. over this loop, then slip it onto right hand needle● w.s., wrong side● double rib is k.2 and p.2 alternately● s.s., stocking stitch is k. on the right side and p. on the wrong side●

MEASUREMENTS The measurements are given in centimetres followed by inches in brackets●
Underarms 115 (46)● Side seam 36 (14½)● Length 57.5 (23)● Sleeve seam 37.5 (15)●

BACK With size 3 mm and m. cast on 126 sts. and work 23 rows in double rib, beginning right side rows with p.2 and wrong side rows with k.2.
Now divide the sts. for the panels: Next row: k.2, (p.1, up 1) 6 times, p.14, (up 1, p.1) 11 times, p.13 more, (up 1, p.1) 6 times, inc. k.wise in next st., then leave these 77 sts. on a spare needle until required for left half back, inc. k.wise in next st., p.2, k.2, p.4, up 1, p.2, up 1, p.4, k.2, p.2, inc. k.wise in next st. and leave these 24 sts. on a stitch-holder until required for centre panel; inc. k.wise in next st., (p.1, up 1) 6 times, p.14, (up 1, p.1) 11 times, p.13 more, (up 1, p.1) 6 times, k.2 and continue on these 77 sts. for the right half back.
Right half back: Change to size 3¾ mm needles and work in pattern as follows: This is worked entirely in s.s., except where indicated, so only the colour details are given. Use separate balls of a. for each vertical zig-zag. Use a separate ball of m. at each side of large motifs like the hearts. Do not weave in the yarns and take care not to pull colours not in use tightly across the back of the work.
1st row: With m. p.2, then k. 2b., 2m., 2b., 2m., 2b., 3m., turn, p.3m., 2b., 3m., 2b., 1m., 2b., turn, k.1b., 2m., 2b., 2m., 3b., 3m., 1a., 9m., 1a., 25c., turn, p.25c., turn, k.2c., (1m., 3c.) 5 times, 1m., 2c., 1a., 9m., 1a., 3m., 2b., 2m., 2b., 3m., 1b., turn, p.1b., 3m., 2b., 2m., 2b., 3m., turn, k. 3m., 2b., 2m., 2b., 2m., 2b., p.2m.

2nd row: With m. k.2, then p.2b., 2m., 3b., 1m., 1b., 3m., 3a., 7m., 3a., 3m., (1c., 3m.) 5 times, 3a., 7m., 3a., 3m., 2b., 2m., 2b., 2m., 1b., with m. k.2.
3rd row: With m. p.2, then k.1b., 2m., 2b., 2m., 2b., 2m., turn, p.2m., 1b., 2m., 2b., 3m., 1b., turn, k.2b., 2m., 2b., 5m., 2a., with m. 3 from 1, 2a., 5m., 2a., with m. 3 from 1, 2a., 21m., turn, p.21m., turn, k.21m., 2a., with m. 3 from 1, 2a., 5m., 2a., with m. 3 from 1, 2a., 4m., 2b., 3m., 2b., turn, p.2b., 3m., 2b., 4m., turn, k.4m., 2b., 4m., 1b., with m. p.2.
4th row: With m. k.2, then p.1a., 3m., 2b., 4m., 3a., with m. c.b., 3a., 3m., 3a., with m. c.b., 3a., 19m., 3a., with m. c.b., 3a., 3m., 3a., with m. c.b., 3a., 3m., 2b., 3m., with m. k.2.
The last 4 rows set the pattern and show how the turning rows are worked on every odd numbered row; note that the turning rows are shown over 3 rows of the chart. Now work the **5**th to 96th rows from the chart, marking the end of the 80th pattern row with a coloured thread to denote armhole. The chart is on previous page.
Work the first 36 rows again.
For the shoulder: Cast off 56 sts. at the beginning of the next row. On 21 sts. work 1 row, then leave these sts. on a stitch-holder until required.
Left half back: With right side of work facing rejoin yarn to inner edge of 77 sts. left on spare needle and using size 3¾ mm needles work the 96 pattern rows as given for right half back, marking the beginning of the 80th row with a coloured thread to denote armhole.
Work the first 37 pattern rows again.
For the shoulder: Cast off 56 sts. at the beginning of the next row. Leave the remaining 21 sts. on a stitch-holder until required.
Centre panel: With right side of work facing rejoin m. to the 24 sts. at centre back and using size 3 mm needles work in cable pattern as follows:
1st row: P.2, k.2, p.2, k.12, p.2, k.2, p.2.
2nd row: K.2, p.2, k.2, p.12, k.2, p.2, k.2.
3rd to 8th rows: Repeat 1st and 2nd rows 3 times.
9th row: P.2, k.2, p.2, cable 12, p.2, k.2, p.2.
10th row: As 2nd row.
11th to 18th rows: Repeat 1st and 2nd rows 4 times.
The last 18 rows form the pattern; repeat them 10 times more, then work the first 12 rows again.
Neckband: Slip the 21 sts. of left half back, the 24 sts. of centre panel and the 21 sts. of right half back onto a size 3 mm needle and work as follows:
Next row: (K.2, p.2) 4 times, k.2tog., k.1, p.2tog., across sts. of right half back, then p.2tog., k.2, p.2, k.2, p.1, p.2tog., k.2, p.2tog., p.1, k.2, p.2, k.2, p.2tog. across centre panel, then p.2tog., k.1, k.2tog., (p.2, k.2) 4 times across left half back.
Now work 19 rows in double rib, beginning right side rows with k.2 and wrong side rows with p.2. Cast off in rib.
FRONT Work as given for the back, reading left half front for right half back and right half front for left half back, until 91 rows have been worked in pattern on left half front.
***Maintaining the continuity of the 96 row repeat pattern, dec. 1 st. at the beginning of the next (wrong side) row and the 20 following alternate rows. – 56 sts. Cast off.
Right half front: With right side of work facing rejoin yarn to inner edge of 77 sts. left on spare needle and using size 3¾ mm needles work as given for left half back until 91 rows have been worked in pattern.
***Maintaining the continuity of the 96 row

repeat pattern, dec. 1 st. at the end of the next (wrong side) row and the 20 following alternate rows. On 56 sts. work 1 row. Cast off the remaining 56 sts.
Centre panel: Work as given for centre panel on back, until the 18 pattern rows have been worked 7 times, then work the first 4 rows again.
Continuing in cable rib and working the extra sts. into the double rib pattern as they occur, inc. 1 st. at each end of the next 34 rows. – 92 sts. Cast on 4 sts. at the beginning of the next 2 rows.
On 100 sts. work 14 rows in double rib with centre cable as set.
Next row: Rib 44 as set, then k.2, p.2tog., p.1, k.2, p.1, p.2tog., k.2 across the cable, rib to end as set.
On 98 sts. work 5 rows in doubled rib, then cast off in rib.
SLEEVES Both alike● With size 3 mm needles and m. cast on 56 sts. and work 35 rows in double rib.
Increase row: P.2, *up 1, p.1; repeat from * ending last repeat, p.2. – 109 sts.
Change to 3¾ mm needles and work in pattern as follows, noting information given for back.
1st row: K.2b., 2m., 2b., 2m., 2b., 3m., turn, p.3m., 2b., 3m., 2b., 1m., 2b., turn, k.1b., 2m., 2b., 2m., 3b., 3m., then 1a., 9m., 1a., 25c., turn, p.25c., turn, k.2c., (1m., 3c.) 5 times, 1m., 2c., then 1a., 9m., 1a., 3m., 2b., 2m., 2b., 3m., 2b., 2m., 2b., 2m., 2b., 3m., turn, p.3m., 2b., 3m., 2b., 1m., 2b., 3m., 2b., 2m., 2b., 3m., turn, k.3m., (2b., 2m) 4 times, 3b., 3m., 1a., 9m., 1a., 13c., turn, p.13c., turn, k.2c., (1m., 3c.) twice, 1m., 2c.
2nd row: P. (1c., 3m.) 3 times, 3a., 7m., 3a., 3m., 2b., 2m., 2b., 2m., 2b., 2m., 3b., 1m., 1b., 3m., 3a., 7m., 3a., (3m., 1c.) 5 times, 3m., 3a., 7m., 3a., 3m., 2b., 2m., 2b., 2m., 1b.
The last 2 rows set the position of the pattern given in the chart. Work the 3rd to 64th rows from the chart as set.
Change to size 3 mm needles; break off m., join in d. and e. and work in chequers as follows:
1st row: With d., inc. in first st., then k.3, *with e. k.5, with d. k.5; repeat from * ending last repeat with e. k.5.
2nd row: *With e. k.1, p.1, k.1, p.1, k.1, with d., p.1, k.1, p.1, k.1, p.1; repeat from * to end.
3rd row: *With d., p.1, k.1, p.1, k.1, p.1; with e. k.1, p.1, k.1, p.1; k.1; repeat from * to end.
4th and 5th rows: As 2nd and 3rd rows.
6th row: As 2nd row.
7th row; *With e. k.5, with d. k.5; repeat from * to end.
8th row: *With d. k.1, p.1, k.1, p.1, k.1, with e. p.1, k.1, p.1, k.1, p.1; repeat from * to end.
9th row: *With e. p.1, k.1, p.1, k.1, p.1, with d. k.1, p.1, k.1, p.1, k.1.
10th and 11th rows: As 8th and 9th rows.
12th row: As 8th row.
Cast off loosely.
MAKING UP Do not press. Neatly sew centre back panel in place. Sew centre front panel in place, so that the first increases on centre panel are in line with the first front edge decreases. Join shoulder seams, continuing seam across neckband. Sew cast off edges of sleeves to the row ends between the marking threads on back and front. Join sleeve and side seams.

"Kelly" right, luxurious sweater in "Cashmere" or "Lambswool", with Zebra print trousers by "Horatio Lovely" and striped shirt by "Kamikaze".

Left "Grandpa" tweed trousers and jacket by "Un Après-Midi de Chien".

LUCKY

MATERIALS 30 25 gram balls of
"Woollybear 100% Mohair" in main colour,
8 balls in first contrast; 2 balls in second and
third contrasts, 3 balls in fourth contrast and
2 balls in fifth contrast● a pair each of size
3 mm and 3¾ mm Aero knitting needles● a
medium cable needle● 6 buttons●
TENSION 36 stitches and 32 rows —
1 repeat of the diamond pattern to
15 centimetres (6 inches) in both width and
depth using size 3¾ mm needles●
If you cannot obtain the correct tension
using the size needles suggested use larger
or smaller ones accordingly●
ABBREVIATIONS As for "Kelly"●
MEASUREMENTS The measurements are
given in centimetres followed by inches in
brackets●
Underarms 135 (54)● Side seam 51 (20½)●
Length 76 (30½)● Sleeve seam – excluding
ribbing 35 (14)●
BACK Work as given for back of "Kelly"
until 96 rows have been worked in pattern
on right half back, marking the end of the
96th row instead of the 80th row with a
coloured thread to denote armhole.
Work the first 52 pattern rows again.
For the shoulder: Cast off 56 sts. at the
beginning of the next row.
On 21 sts. work 1 row, then leave these sts.
on a stitch-holder until required.
Left half back: Work as given for left half
back of "Kelly" until 96 rows have been
worked in pattern, but marking the beginning
of the 96th row instead of the 80th row with
coloured threads to denote armhole.
Work the first 53 pattern rows again.
For the shoulder: Cast off 56 sts. at the
beginning of the next row.
Leave the remaining 21 sts. on a
stitch-holder until required.
Centre panel: Work as for centre panel on
back of "Kelly" until the 18 cable pattern
rows have been worked 13 times in all, then
work the back neckband as for back of
"Kelly".
LEFT FRONT With size 3 mm (No. 11)
needles and m. cast on 54 sts. and work 23
rows in double rib, beginning right side rows

with p.2 and wrong side rows with k.2.
Increase row: P.2, (p.1, up 1) 6 times, p.14, (up 1, p.1) 11 times, p.13 more, (up 1, p.1) 6 times, p.2. – 77 sts.

Work as given for right half back until 33 rows have been worked in pattern.
Now work the pocket as follows: Next row: Pattern 21 and leave these sts. on a stitch-holder until required, pattern 35 and continue on these sts. for pocket back, slip the remaining 21 sts. onto a stitch-holder until required.

Pocket back: Join in d. and with d. only s.s. 60 rows.
With wrong side of work facing, onto the needle holding the 35 sts. of pocket back pattern as for 34th pattern row across the 21 sts. left on stitch-holder.
Next row: Pattern as for 35th row across these 56 sts., then onto the same needle the 21 sts. left on stitch-holder.
Work the 36th to 96th pattern rows. Mark the end of the last row with a coloured thread to show armhole.
Work the first 11 pattern rows again.
Now work as given for left half front of "Kelly" from *** to end.

Buttonband and half collar with size 3 mm needles and m. cast on 20 sts. and work 176 rows in double rib. Mark the end of the last row with a coloured thread. Inc. 1 st. at the beginning of the next row and at the same edge on each of the next 33 rows. – 54 sts. Cast on 4 sts. at the beginning of the next row. On 58 sts. work 15 rows in double rib, then cast off.

RIGHT FRONT Work as given for left front until the 96 pattern rows have been worked, but mark the beginning of the 96th row instead of the end with coloured thread.
Work the first 11 pattern rows again.
Now work as given for right half front of "Kelly" from *** to end.

Buttonholeband and half collar: With size 3 mm needles and m. cast on 20 sts. and work 6 rows in double rib.
1st Buttonhole row: Rib 7, cast off 6, rib to end.
2nd Buttonhole row: Rib 7, turn, cast on 6, turn, rib to end.
Rib 40 rows.
Repeat the last 42 rows 3 times, then work the 2 buttonhole rows again. Inc. 1 st. at the end of the next row and at the same edge on each of the next 33 rows. – 54 sts. Work 1 row straight.
Cast on 4 sts. at the beginning – the shaped edge – of the next row. On 58 sts. work 4 rows in double rib then work the 2 buttonhole rows again.
Rib 8 rows, then cast off.

SLEEVES Left sleeve● with size 3 mm needles and m. cast on 56 sts. and work 18 rows in double rib. Now divide the sts. for the thumb hole: **Next row:** Rib 28, cast off 8, rib to end.
Next row: Rib 20, turn, cast on 8 over those cast off, rib to end.
Work 63 rows in double rib, work 1 extra row here when working right sleeve.
Now work as given for sleeves of "Kelly" from the increase row to end.
Right sleeve● As for left sleeve, noting the variation in the rows, before working the increase row.

MAKING UP Do not press. Neatly sew centre back panel in place. Sew front bands in position so that the first increases on front bands are in line with first front edge decreases. Join shoulder seams. Sew cast off edges of sleeves to the row ends between the marking threads on back and fronts. Join sleeve and side seams. Join row ends of pocket backs. Sew on buttons.

●

□	=	m.
	=	a.
	=	b.
	=	c.
	=	d.
	=	e.
ʒ	=	turn.
∩	=	c.b.
∨	=	with m. 3 from 1.
^	=	k. on wrong side row.
ı	=	slip 1.
⊙	=	m.b.
◪	=	4 over 1.
←	=	p.5.
→	=	k.5.
⅋	=	5 from 1.

96
95
94
93
92
91
90
89
88
87
86
85
84
83
82
81
80
79
78
77
76
75
74
73
72
71
70
69
68
67
66
65
64
63
62
61
60
59
58
57
56
55
54
53
52
51
50
49
48
47
46
45
44
43
42
41
40
39
38
37
36
35
34
33
32
31
30
29
28
27
26
25
24
23
22
21
20
19
18
17
16
15
14
13
12
11
10
9
8
7
6
5
4
3
2

"Amelia" sweater knitted in pure mohair combined with real silk. Wear it as a headwrap with "Butler and Wilsons" new Baroque jewellery, available from their shop at 189 Fulham Road.

Pinafore by "Un Après-Midi de Chien". Coat by "Concetto". All from Patricia Roberts, Covent Garden.

MATERIALS Two 25 gram spools of "Woolybear Pure Silk" in each of 6 contrast colours, plus either 9 25 gram balls of "Woollybear 100% Mohair" in main colour and 3 balls in first contrast, or 6 50 gram balls of "Woollybear Cotton Crepe" in main colour and 2 balls in first contrast● a pair each of size 3¼ mm and 3¾ mm Aero knitting needles● both fine and medium sized cable needles●

TENSION 16 stitches and 18 rows to 5 centimetres (2 inches) over the cabled patchwork and 12 stitches and 18 rows to 5 centimetres (2 inches) over the moss st. parts of the yoke, all using size 3¾ mm. needles●
If you cannot obtain the correct tension using the size needles suggested use larger or smaller ones accordingly●

ABBREVIATIONS K., knit● p., purl● st., stitch● tog., together● dec., decrease (by working 2 sts. tog.)● inc., increase (by working twice into same st.)● single rib is k.1 and p.1 alternately● r.s., right side● w.s., wrong side● up 1; pick up the loop which lies between the needles, slip it onto left hand needle, then k. into back of it● k.1b., k.1 through back of st.● p.1b., p.1 through back of st.● cable 8, slip 4 sts. onto cable needle and leave at front of work, k.4, then k.4 from cable needle● cable 12, slip next 6 sts. onto cable needle and leave at front of work, k.6, then k.6 from cable needle● cable 4b., cable 4 back, thus slip next 2 sts. onto cable needle at back of work, with appropriately coloured thick yarn, k.2, then with appropriately coloured thick yarn, k.2, from cable needle● cable 4f., as cable 4b., but leaving sts. on cable needle at front of work● cr.4f., cross 4 front, slip next 2 sts. onto cable needle at front of work, with appropriate fine contrast k.2, then with appropriately coloured thick yarn k.2 from cable needle● cr.4b., cross 4 back, slip next 2 sts. onto cable needle at back of work, with appropriately coloured thick yarn k.2, then with appropriate fine contrast, k.2 from cable needle● cr.3lt., cross 3 left, slip next 2 sts. onto cable needle at front of work, with appropriate fine contrast k.1, then with appropriately coloured thick yarn k.2 from cable needle● cr.3rt., cross 3 right, slip next st. onto cable needle at back of work, with appropriately coloured thick yarn k.2, then with appropriate fine contrast k.1 from cable needle● cr.5lt., cross 5 left thus, slip next 2 sts. onto cable needle at front of work, with m. k. into front of 2nd and 3rd sts. on left hand needle, with g. k. into back of first st., allowing all 3 loops to fall from left hand needle together, with a. k.2 from cable needle● cr.5rt., cross 5 right thus, slip next 2 sts. onto a cable needle at back of work, with a. k. into front of 2nd and 3rd sts. on left hand needle, with e. k. into back of first st., allowing all 3 loops to fall from left hand needle together, with m. k.2 from cable needle● y.r.n., yarn round needle● s.s.k., slip 1, k.1, pass sl.st. over● 3 from 1, k.1, y.r.n., k.1. all into one st.● m., main colour – thick yarn● a., first contrast – thick yarn● the following contrasts are in fine yarn● b., second contrast● c., third contrast● d., fourth contrast● e., fifth contrast● f., sixth contrast● g., seventh contrast● cable 5f., slip next 2 sts. onto cable needle at front of work, with appropriate colour k.3, then with appropriate colour k.2 from cable needle● cable 5b., slip next 3 sts. onto cable needle at back of work, with appropriate colour k.2, then with appropriate colour k.3 from cable needle●

MEASUREMENTS The measurements are given in centimetres followed by inches in brackets●

Underarms 105 (42)● Side seam 29 (11½)● Length 46 (18½)● Sleeve seam 31 (12½)●

NOTE Instructions in brackets are worked the number of times stated after the brackets●

BACK & FRONT – Alike● With size 3¼ mm. needles and m. cast on 106 sts. and work 8 rows in single rib.
Change to size 3¾ mm needles and work as follows. Use separate balls of yarn for each section of the pattern, so that colours not in use are not taken across the back of the work. When breaking off yarns leave sufficiently long ends to darn in at completion.
Increase row: With m. p.1, k.5, **up 1, k.3, up 1; with b. (k.3, up 1) 7 times; with m. k.2. up 1; with a. k.2; with c. (k.2, up 1, k.1) 3 times; with a. k.2, with d. up 1, k.3**; with m. up 1, k.8; repeat from ** to **, with m. k.2, up 1, k.5, p.1. – 136 sts.
Foundation row (wrong side): With m. k.1, p.8; ** with d. k.4; with a. p.2; with c. k.12; with a. p.2; with m. p.3; with b. (k.1, p.1) 14 times**; with m. p.14; repeat from ** to **, with m. p.10, k.1.
Now work in pattern given in chart as follows:
1st row: With m. p.1, k.6, **cable 4b., with b. (p.1, k.1) 14 times; cr.5rt. – see abbreviations; with c. k.2, (y.r.n., s.s.k.) 5 times; with a. k.2, with d. k.4**; with m. k.10; repeat from ** to **, with m. k.8, p.1.
2nd row: With m. k.1, p.8; **with d. k.4, with a. p.2, with c. k.12; with m. p.2; with e. p.1b.; with a. p.2; with b. (k.1, p.1) 14 times**; with m. p.14; repeat from ** to **, with m. p.10, k.1.
3rd row: With m. p.1, k.10, ** with b. (p.1, k.1) 13 times; with a. and e. cr.4b., with e. k.1b., with m. and e. cr.4f.; with c. k.1, (y.r.n.,

s.s.k.) 4 times; with a. and d. cr.3rt., with d. k.4**, with m. k.14; repeat from ** to **, with m. k.8, p.1.
4th row: With m. k.1, p.8; **with d. k.5; with a. p.2; with c. k.9, with m. p.2, with e. p.1b., (k.1, p.1b.) twice, with a. p.2, with b. (k.1, p.1) 13 times**; with m. p.14; repeat from ** to **, with m. p.10, k.1.
The last 4 rows set the pattern given in the chart; work the 5th to 72nd rows from the chart as set, then work the first 16 rows again.
Decrease row: With m. k.2, (k.2, k.2tog.) 15 times, k.3, k.2tog., k.2, k.2tog., k.3, (k.2tog., k.2) 15 times, k.2 more. – 104 sts.
Now work in moss st. as follows: 1st row: *p.1, k.1; repeat from * end.
2nd row: *k.1, p.1; repeat from * to end.
Cast off 8 sts. at the beginning and end of the next two rows then leave the remaining 88 sts. on a spare needle, until required for yoke.

SLEEVES Both alike● With size 3¼ mm needles and m. cast on 63 sts. and work 16 rows in single rib.
Change to size 3¾ mm needles and work in pattern as follows, noting the information given for back.
Increase row: *With b. (k.1, up 1) 14 times, with m. k.2, up 1, with a. k.2, with c. (k.1, up 1) 6 times, with a. k.2*; with d. (k.1, up 1) twice, with m. (k.1, up 1) 7 times; repeat from * to *, with d. k.2. – 114 sts.
Foundation row: With d. k.2, *with a. p.2, with c. k.12, with a. p.2, with m. p.3, with b. (k.1, p.1) 14 times,* with m. p.14, with d. k.4; repeat from * to *.
1st row: *With b. (p.1, k.1) 14 times, cr.5rt. – see abbreviations, with c. k.2, (y.r.n., s.s.k) 5 times, with a. k.2,* with d. k.4, with m. k.10, cable 4b.; repeat from * to *, with d. k.2.

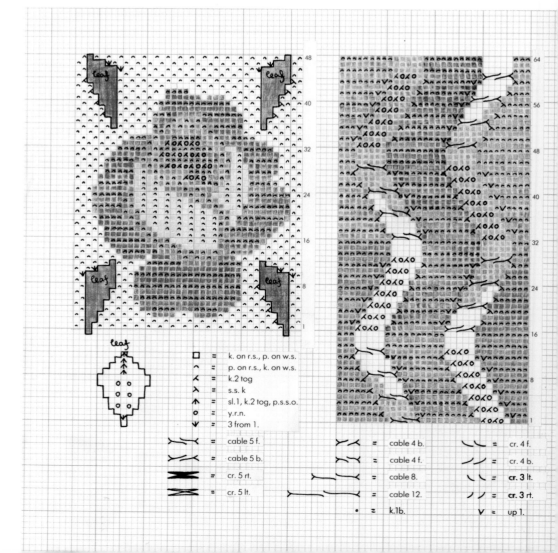

□	=	k. on r.s., p. on w.s.
	=	p. on r.s., k. on w.s.
⋋	=	k.2 tog
⋌	=	s.s. k
⋀	=	sl.1, k.2 tog, p.s.s.o.
○	=	y.r.n.
	=	3 from 1.

	=	cable 5 f.				=	cable 4 b.
	=	cable 5 b.				=	cable 4 f.
	=	cr. 5 rt.				=	cable 8.
	=	cr. 5 lt.				=	cable 12.
•	=	k.1b.			V	=	up 1.

leaf

The last row sets the position ot the pattern given in the chart for the back and front, but beginning and ending 11 sts. from each end of each row. Work the 2nd to 72nd rows, then the 1st to 16th again as set.

Decrease row: With m. k.21, (k.2tog., k.2) 7 times, k.2tog., k.3, k.2tog., k.2, k.2tog., k.3, (k.2tog., k.2) 7 times, k.2tog., k.21. — 96 sts.

With m. work 2 rows in moss st. as for back.

Next row: Cast off 20, moss st. 12, then leave these 13 sts. on a stitch-holder until required, moss st. 30, then moss st. 13 more and leave these 13 sts. on a stitch-holder until required, cast off the remaining 20 sts.

With right side of work facing rejoin a. to the 30 sts. left at centre and work as follows:

Next row: K.5, *up 1, k.4; repeat from * ending last repeat k.5.

On 36 sts. work 3 rows in single rib. Continuing in rib, dec. 1 st. at each end of the next row and the 9 following alternate rows, then dec. 1 st. at each end of the next 7 rows. Take the 2 remaining sts. tog. and fasten off.

BACK YOKE With right side of work facing rejoin m. to the inner edge of the 13 sts. left at left hand side of one ribbed sleeve point, and using size 3¾ mm needles moss st. as set across these sts. then onto the same needle moss st. across the 88 sts. of back left on spare needle, then moss st. across the 13 sts. left on stitch-holder at right hand side of other sleeve.

On 114 sts. work in rose pattern as follows:

Foundation row: With m. moss st. 2, *with c. p.1, with m. moss st. 32, with d. p.1, with m. moss st.4; repeat from * ending last repeat with m. moss st. 2 instead of 4.

1st row: With m. moss st 2, *with d. 3 from 1, with m. moss st.32, with c. 3 from 1, with

m. moss st 4; repeat from * ending last repeat moss st.2.

2nd row: With m. moss st. 2, *with c. p.3., with m. p.2tog. b, moss st. 28, p.2tog with d. p. 3, with m. moss st.4; repeat from * ending last repeat moss st. 2.

The last 3 rows set the position of the rose and leaf/motifs given in the chart. Use separate balls or lengths of m. at each side of leaf and rose motifs, so that colours not in use are not taken across the back of the work. Now work the 3rd to 48th rows as set.

Continuing with m. only work 2 rows in moss st., casting off 11 sts. at the beginning of each row. — 92 sts.**

Change to size 3¼ mm needles and work 2 rows in single rib. Continuing in rib, cast off 4 sts. at the beginning of the next 12 rows. — 44 sts. Rib 4 rows then cast off in rib.

FRONT YOKE Work as given tor back yoke until ** is reached.

Change to size 3¼ mm needles and work 1 row in single rib.

Now divide the sts. for the neck: Next row rib 34 and leave these sts on a spare needle until required for right shoulder, rib 24 and leave these sts. on a stitch-holder until required for the neckband, rib to end and continue on these 34 sts for left front shoulder.

Left front shoulder: To shape the neck and slope the shoulder: Next row: Cast off 4, rib until 2 remain, dec. Next row: Dec., rib to end.

Repeat the last 2 rows 4 times more. Cast off the remaining 4 sts.

Right front shoulder: with right side of work facing rejoin m. to inner edge of 34 sts. left on spare needle and rib to end of row. Then work as given for left front shoulder to end.

Neckband: With right side of work facing rejoin m. at left front shoulder and using size 3¼ mm needles pick up and k.16 sts from left front neck edge, rib across the 24 sts at centre front, then pick up and k. 16 sts from right front neck edge — 56 sts.

Work 3 rows in single rib, then cast off in rib.

SIDES Both alike: With size 3¼ mm needles and m. cast on 24 sts. and work 8 rows in single rib. Change to size 3¾ mm needles.

Increase row: With c. k.2, up 1, with m.k.5, with f. (up 1, k.2) 3 times, up 1, with a. k.5, with d. (up 1, k.2) 3 times. — 32 sts.

Foundation row: With d. k.9, with a. p.5, with f. k.10, with m. p.5, with c. k.3.

Now work in cable pattern as follows: 1st row: With c. k.3, with m. k.1, (y.r.n., k.2tog) twice, with f. k.10, with a. cable 5f., with d. k.9.

2nd row: With d. k.7, k.2tog., with a. p.5, with f. k.1, up 1, k.7, k.2tog., with m. p.5, with c. k.1, up 1, k.2.

The last 2 rows set the position of the cable pattern given in the chart. Work the 3rd to 64th rows from the chart, then the first 24 rows again.

Decrease row: With m. k.1, *k.2tog., k.2; repeat from * ending last repeat k.1. — 24 sts.

With m. work the 2 moss st. rows given for back, then cast off.

MAKING UP Do not press. Neatly sew side pieces to row end edges of back and front. Join shoulder seams. Join sleeve seams. Sew row ends of ribbing at top of sleeves to row ends of moss st. part of yoke, then sew cast off groups on sleeves to the sts. cast off on side pieces and at each side of back and front. ●

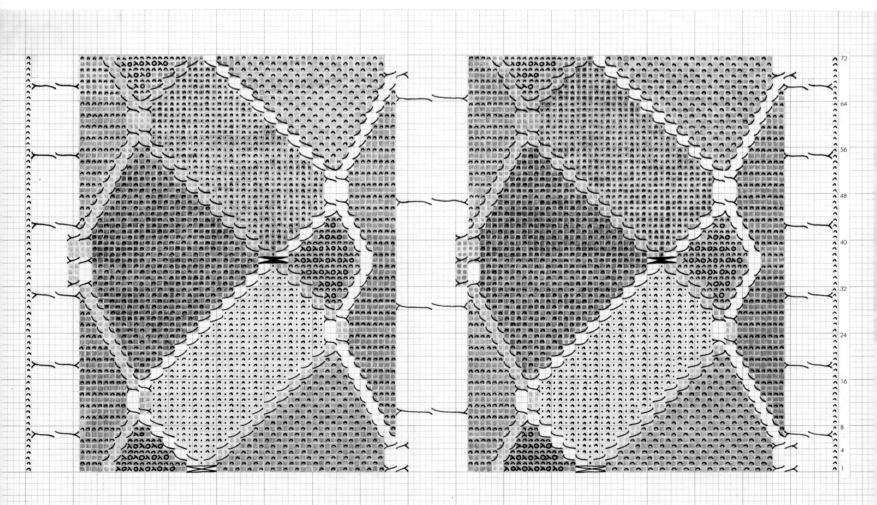

MATERIALS For the sweater: Either 20 25 gram balls of "Patricia Roberts 100% Mohair" in main colour, 5 balls in first contrast and 1 ball in each of the 4 other contrast colours●
Or 9 50 gram hanks of "Patricia Roberts Shetland No 2" in main colour, 2 hanks in first contrast and 1 hank in each of the 4 other contrast colours● pair of shoulder pads●
For the skirt: In one colour: 6 50 gram balls of "Patricia Roberts Lambswool No 2" for the shorter skirt● or 8 balls for the longer one● a waist length of elastic●
In two colours: 4 50 gram hanks of "Patricia Roberts Shetland No 2" in main colour and 2 hanks in contrast colour for the shorter skirt● or 6 hanks in main colour and 2 hanks in contrast colour for the longer one● a waist length of elastic●
For either garment: A pair each of size 3¼mm and 4mm Aero knitting needles●
TENSION 14 stitches and 14 rows to 5 centimetres (2 inches) over twisted rib using size 4mm needles●
If you cannot obtain the correct tension using the size needles suggested, use larger or smaller ones accordingly●
ABBREVIATIONS K., knit● p., purl● st., stitch● k.1b. or p.1b., k.1 or p1 through back of st.● tog., together● dec., decrease (by working 2 sts. tog)● inc., increase (by working twice into same st.)● single rib is k.1 and p.1 alternately● sl., slip● p.s.s.o., pass sl.st. over● m.h.b., make half bobble thus, with a. k.1, y.r.n., k.1 all into next st., turn, p.3, turn, k.3, cut off a. leaving an end 12 cms (5 inches) long●r.s., right side● w.s., wrong side● m., main colour ● a., first contrast● b., second contrast● c., third contrast● d., fourth contrast● e., fifth contrast● 3 into 1, using the colour used for the st. just knitted, sl.1, k.2tog., p.s.s.o.● 3 from 1, k.1, y.r.n., k.1 all into 1 st.● c.k., complete knot thus, p.3, then pass the first and second of these sts. over the third st. on right hand needle● tw. rib, twisted rib – k.1b. and p.1 alternately on right side rows and p.1b. and k.1 alternately on wrong side rows● y.r.n., yarn round needle●
MEASUREMENTS The measurements are given in centimetres followed by inches in brackets●
Sweater: Underarms 100 (40)● Sleeve seam 42.5 (17)● Side seam 45 (18)● Length 69 (27¾)●
Skirt: All round 100 (40)● Length – shorter 40 (16) – longer 51 (20½)●
BACK With size 3¼mm needles and m. cast on 121 sts. and work 11 rows in single rib.
Increase row: Rib 6, *inc., inc., rib 10; repeat from * ending last repeat rib 5. – 141 sts.
Change to size 4mm needles and work in pattern as follows.
1st row: With m. k.1b., *p.1, k.1b.; repeat from * to end.
2nd row: with m. p.lb., *k.1, p.1b.; repeat from * to end.
3rd and **4**th rows: As 1st and 2nd rows.
5th row: With m. tw.rib 10, *with a. m.h.b. – see abbreviations, with m. tw. rib 11; repeat from * ending last repeat tw.rib 10.
6th row: With m. tw.rib 10, *with a. p.3, with m. tw.rib 11; repeat from * ending last repeat tw.rib 10.
7th row: With m. tw.rib 10, *still with m. 3 into i, tw. rib 11; repeat from * ending last repeat tw.rib 10. Now knot the 2 ends of each bobble in a. firmly tog., then using wrong end of a bodkin darn ends into back of bobble once, then back st. through. Cut off ends.
8th row: With m. in tw.rib.

9th row: With m. tw.rib 57, knot in b., with b. k.1, with m. tw.rib 47, knot in a., with a. k.1, with m. tw. rib 35.
10th row: With m. tw.rib 35, with a. inc., with m. p.2tog., with m. rib 45, with b. inc., with m. rib 55.
11th row: With m. tw. rib 17 *knot in d., with d. k.1, with m. tw.rib 9, knot in another ball of d., with d. k.1, ** with m. tw. rib 26, k.2tog.b., with b. inc., p.1, with m. tw.rib 7*, using c. instead of d. and a. instead of b., repeat from * to *, then using e. instead of d. work from * to **, with m. tw.rib 17.
12th row: With m. tw. rib 17, *with e. inc., with m. k.2tog., tw.rib 5, k.2 tog., with e. inc. **, with m. tw.rib 7, with a. k.2, inc., with m. k.2tog., tw. rib 25*, using c. instead of e. and b. instead of a. repeat from * to *, then using d. instead of e. repeat from * to **, with m. tw.rib 17.
13th row: With m. tw.rib 4, with a. m.h.b., with m. tw.rib 12, *with contrast p.1, inc., with m. k.2tog.b., p.1, k.1b., p.1, k.2tog.b., with contrast inc., p.1, with m. tw.rib 12, with a. m.h.b.**, with m. tw.rib 11, k.2tog.b., with contrast inc., p.3, with m. tw.rib 7; repeat from * to *, ending last repeat at **, then with m. tw.rib 4.
14th row: With m. tw.rib 4, *with a. p.3, with m. tw. rib 12, with contrast p.1, k.1, inc., with m. k.2tog., p.1b., k.2tog., with contrast inc., k.1, p.1**, with m. tw.rib 7, with contrast k.4, inc., with m. k.2tog., with contrast k.10*; repeat from * to *, then from * to **, with m. tw.rib 12, with a. p.3, with m. tw.rib 4.
15th row: With m. tw.rib 4, 3 into 1, tw.rib 12, *with contrast p.1, k.1, p.1, inc., with m. 3 into 1, with contrast inc., p.1, k.1, p.1, with m. tw.rib 12, 3 into 1**, tw.rib 9, k.2tog.b., with contrast inc., p.5, tw.rib 7*; repeat from * to *, then from * to **, tw.rib 4. Fasten off bobbles as before.
16th row: With m. tw.rib 16, *inc., with contrast k.2tog., p.1, k.1, p.3, k.1, p.1. k.2tog., with m. inc.**, with m. tw.rib 5, p.6, with contrast p.1, inc., with m. k.2tog., tw.rib 20; repeat from *, then work from * to **, tw.rib 16.
The last 16 rows set the position of the pattern. Now continuing in the 64 row repeat pattern given in the chart, with the colours given in the colour sequence graph, work the 17th to 64th rows, then the 1st to 50th rows again.
To shape the armholes: Continuing in pattern as set, cast off 8 sts. at the beginning of the next 2 rows, then dec. 1 st. at each end of the next 10 rows. – 105 sts.**
If the dog motif is not to be worked, pattern 48 rows.
If the dog motif is to be worked: Pattern 2 rows. Then work the dog's ear as follows: With a. cast on 2 sts., inc. in both sts., turn, p.1, k.1, p.1, inc., turn, p.1, (k.1, p.1) twice, turn, p.1, (k.1, p.1) twice, then leave these 5 sts. on a safety pin.
Next row: Pattern 76 as set, with c. k.21 for the dog motif, with m. tw.rib 8.
The last row sets the position of the dog motif. Continuing in star and zig-zag pattern work the 2nd to 40th rows of the dog motif from the chart.
Pattern 6 rows as set.
For either version: To slope the shoulders: Cast off 8 sts. at the beginning of the next 8 rows. Cast off the remaining 41 sts.
FRONT If the dog motif is not to be worked: Work as given for back until ** is reached, then pattern 23 rows.
If the dog motif is to be worked, work as given for back until the 21st row of the dog motif has been worked.
For either version: Divide the sts. for the neck: Next row: Pattern 43 and leave these

sts. on a spare needle until required for right front shoulder, cast off 19, pattern to end and continue on these 43 sts. for the left front shoulder.
Left front shoulder: Continuing in pattern as set, dec. 1 st. at the neck edge on each of the next 11 rows. On 32 sts. pattern 13 rows.
To slope the shoulder: Cast off 8 sts. at the beginning of the next row and the 2 following alternate rows. On 8 sts. work 1 row, then cast off.
Right front shoulder: With right side of work facing rejoin yarn to inner edge of sts. left on spare needle and work to end of row, then work as given for left front shoulder to end.
Neckband: First join right shoulder seam. With right side of work facing rejoin m. and using size 3¼mm needles pick up and k. 32 sts. from left front neck edge, 14 sts. from centre front, 32 sts. from right front neck edge and 31 sts. from back neck edge. – 109 sts.
Work 7 rows in single rib. Cast off in rib using a size larger needle.
SLEEVES Both alike● With size 4mm needles and m. cast on 53 sts. and work 4 rows in tw.rib as for back.
5th row: with m. tw.rib 2, *with a. m.h.b., with m. tw.rib 11; repeat from * ending last repeat tw.rib 2.
6th row: With m. tw.rib 2, *with a. p.3, with m. tw.rib 11; repeat from * ending last repeat tw.rib 2.
7th row: With m. tw.rib 2, *3 into 1, tw.rib 11; repeat from * ending last repeat tw.rib 2.
8th row: With m. in tw.rib.
9th row: With m. tw.rib 49, with a. k.1, with m. tw.rib 3.
10th row: With m. tw.rib 3, with a. inc., with m. k.2tog., tw.rib to end.
11th row: With m. tw.rib 9, with c. k.1, with m. tw.rib 9, with c. k.1, with m. tw.rib 26, k.2tog.b., with a. inc., p.1, with m. tw.rib 3. The last 11 rows set the position of the pattern given in the charts. Work the **12**th to **16**th rows as set.**
Maintaining the continuity of the pattern and working the extra sts. into the pattern as they occur. inc. 1 st. at each end of the next row and the 15 following 4th rows.
On 85 sts. pattern 11 rows marking each end of the last row with coloured threads.
To shape the sleevetop: **D**ecrease row: With m. k.1b., p.1, sl.1, k.2tog., p.s.s.o., pattern until 5 remain, sl.1, k.2tog., p.s.s.o., p.1, k.1b.
Pattern 3 rows.
Repeat the last 4 rows 10 times, then work the decrease row again. On 37 sts. work 1 row.
Cast off 6 sts. at the beginning of the next 4 rows. Cast off the remaining 13 sts.
MAKING UP Do not press. Join left shoulder seam, continuing seam across neckband or collar. Join side seams. Join sleeve seams up to marking threads. Run gathering threads around outer edge of top half of sleevetops and gather in gently to fit into armhole. Pin, then sew in place. Remove gathering threads. Catch shoulder pads in place. Sew cast off sts. below dog's ear in place.
SKIRT Back and front alike: With size 4mm needles and m. cast on 141 sts and work 104 rows for shorter skirt or 136 rows for longer one, either all in m. or in m. with all contrasts in a. in pattern as given for back of sweater.
Change to size 3¼mm needles.
Decrease row: Rib 2, *sl.1, k.2tog., p.s.s.o., rib 4; repeat from * ending last repeat rib 3.
On 101 sts. work 11 rows in single rib, then cast off loosely in rib.
Making up: Join side seams. Join ends of elastic and secure with a herringbone casing on wrong side of waistband. ●

"Tinkerbell" may be knitted with or without the dog motif. Choose these subtle shades or bright ones as in the children's version.

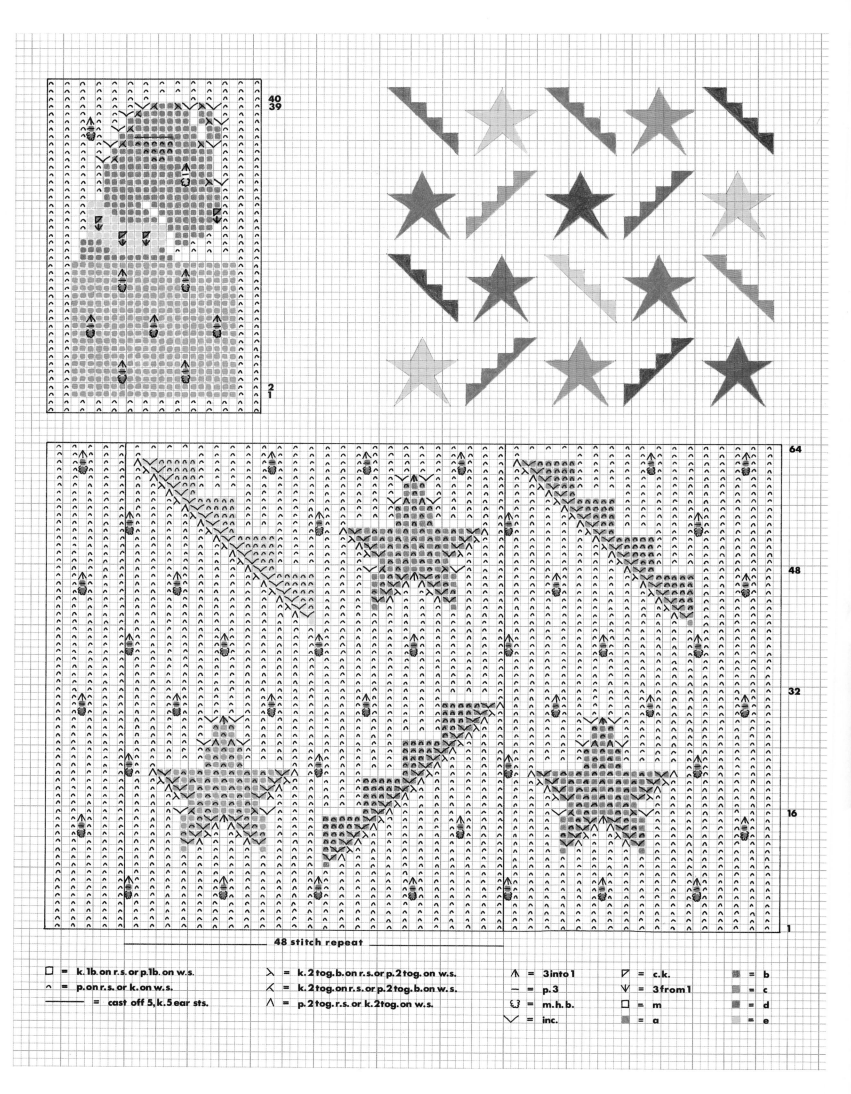

40
39

2
1

64

48

32

16

1

48 stitch repeat

□ = k.1b. on r.s. or p.1b. on w.s.
∧ = p. on r.s. or k. on w.s.
— = cast off 5, k. 5 ear sts.

⅄ = k. 2 tog. b. on r.s. or p. 2 tog. on w.s.
⋋ = k. 2 tog. on r.s. or p. 2 tog. b. on w.s.
∧ = p. 2 tog. r.s. or k. 2 tog. on w.s.

↑ = 3 into 1
— = p. 3
{} = m. h. b.
∨ = inc.

▽ = c. k.
∨ = 3 from 1
□ = m
■ = a

■ = b
■ = c
■ = d
■ = e

"Fleur" in a man's version
knitted in shetland tweed.
Subtle shades of marled
shetland are used for her
"Tinkerbell" outfit.

ZETA

MATERIALS Either 13 (14) 50 gram hanks of "Woollybear Shetland Fleck" or 20 (21) 50 gram balls of "Woollybear Cotton Crepe"● A medium sized cable needle●

For the woman's sweater a pair of each of size 3¾ mm and 3¼ mm Aero knitting needles●

For the man's sweater a pair each of size 4 mm and 3¼ mm Aero knitting needles●

TENSION For the woman's sweater: 18 stitches and 14 rows to 5 centimetres (2 inches) over the quilted rib pattern, using size 3¾ mm needles●

For the man's sweater: 17 stitches and 13 rows to 5 centimetres (2 inches) over the quilted rib pattern, using size 4 mm needles●

If you cannot obtain the correct tension using the size needles suggested, use larger or smaller ones accordingly●

ABBREVIATIONS K., knit● p., purl● st., stitch● tog., together● dec., decrease (by working 2 sts. tog.)● inc., increase (by working twice into same st.)● single rib is k.1 and p.1 alternately● cr.4lt., cross 4 left, slip next 2 sts. onto cable needle at front of work, p.2, then k.2 from cable needle● cr.4rt., cross 4 right, slip next 2 sts. onto cable needle at back of work, k.2, then p.2 from cable needle● cr.3lt., cross 3 left thus, p. into back of 3rd st. on left hand needle, then k. into front of 1st and 2nd sts., allowing all 3 loops to fall from left hand needle together● cr.3rt., cross 3 right, thus, k. into front of 2nd and 3rd sts. on left hand needle, then p. into front of first st., allowing all 3 loops to fall from left hand needle together● cr.2lt., cross 2 left, p. into back of 2nd st. on left hand needle, then k. into front of first st., dropping loops from left hand needle together● cr.2rt., cross 2 right, k. into front of second st. on left hand needle, then p. into front of first st., dropping both loops from left hand needle tog.● up 1, pick up the loop which lies between the needes, slip it onto left hand needle, then k. into back of it●

NOTE The instructions are given for the woman's sweater. Where they vary for the man's sweater, use the size needles given in [ ] square brackets.

Instructions in ordinary brackets ( ) are worked the number of times stated after the brackets.

MEASUREMENTS The measurements are given in centimetres followed by inches in brackets●

Underarms 100 (40) [105 (42)]● Length 61 (24½) [67.5 (27)]● Sleeve seam 45 (18) [49 (19½)]●

BACK With size 3¼ mm [size 3¾ mm] needles cast on 136 sts. and work 17 rows in single rib.

Now increase for main pattern and for easier working divide the sts. as follows: Next row: Rib 2, *up 1, rib 3; repeat from * 21 times more and leave these 90 sts. on a spare needle until required for left half back; *rib 3, up 1; repeat from * until 2 remain, rib 2 and continue on these 90 sts. for the right half back.

Right half back: Change to size 3¾ mm [No. 4 mm] needles and work in pattern as follows:

1st row: P.1, *k.2, p.2; repeat from * ending last repeat p.3.

2nd row: K.3, *p.2, k.2; repeat from * ending last repeat k.1.

3rd row: P.1, (k.2, p.2) 10 times, k.2, p.1, cr.3rt., p.2, (cr.3lt., p.1) 10 times, p.1.

4th row: (K.2, p.2) 10 times, k.1, p.1, k.2, p.2, k.1, (p.2, k.2) 10 times, p.2, k.1.

5th row: P.1, (cr.3lt., p.1) 10 times, cr.2lt., cr.3rt., p.1, cr.3rt., (cr.3lt., p.1) 10 times.

6th row: K.1, (p.2, k.2) 11 times, p.2, k.3,

"Zeta", sweatshirt to knit in our new thick "Shetland Fleck", available in black, brown, grey, cream, fuschia, orient blue or red.

Silk trousers, shirts and long Mohair coat all by Wendy Dagworthy, from Patricia Roberts, Covent Garden.

(p.2, k.2) 10 times.

7th row: (p.2, k.2) 10 times, p.2, cr.3rt., p.1, cr.3rt., p.2, (cr.3lt., p.1) 9 times, cr.2lt., p.1.

8th row: K.1, p.1, (k.2, p.2) 9 times, k.1, p.1, (k.2, p.2) 12 times, k.2.

9th row: P.2, (cr.3lt., p.1) 9 times, cr.3lt., (cr.3rt., p.1) twice, cr.3rt., (cr.3lt., p.1) 9 times, p.2 more.

10th row: K.3, (p.2, k.2) 11 times, p.4, (k.2 p.2) 9 times, k.1, p.1, k.1.

11th row: P.1, k.2, (cr.4lt.) 9 times, (p.1, cr.3rt.) 3 times, p.2, (cr.3lt., p.1) 9 times, p.1 more.

12th row: (k.2, p.2) 9 times, k.1, p.1, (k.2, p.2) 3 times, k.1, (p.2, k.2) 9 times, p.2, k.1.

13th row: P.1, k.2, p.2, (cr.4lt.) 8 times, p.2, (cr.3rt., p.1) 3 times, cr.3rt., (cr.3lt., p.1) 9 times.

14th row: K.1, *p.2, k.2; repeat from * until 5 remain, k.2 more, p.2, k.1.

15th row: P.1, cr.3lt., p.2, k.1, (cr.4lt.) 7 times, cr.2lt., (p.1, cr.3rt.) 4 times, p.2, (cr.3lt., p.1) 8 times, cr.2lt., p.1.

16th row: K.1, p.1, (k.2, p.2) 8 times, k.1, p.1, (k.2, p.2) 4 times, k.3, (p.2, k.2) 6 times, p.2, k.1, p.2, k.2, p.2.

17th row: (p.2, k.2) twice, p.1, (cr.4lt.) 7 times, (cr.3rt., p.1) 4 times, cr.3rt., (cr.3lt., p.1) 8 times, p.2 more.

18th row: K.3, (p.2, k.2) 12 times, p.4, (k.2, p.2) 6 times, k.3, p.2, k.2, p.2, k.2.

19th row: P.2, (k.2, p.2) twice, k.1, (cr.4lt.) 6 times, (p.1, cr.3rt.) 5 times, p.2, (cr.3lt., p.1) 8 times, p.1 more.

20th row: (K.2, p.2) 8 times, k.1, p.1, (k.2, p.2) 5 times, k.1, (p.2, k.2) 5 times, p.2, k.1, (p.2, k.2) 3 times.

21st row: P.2, (cr.3lt., p.1) twice, cr.3lt., (cr.4lt.) 5 times, p.2, (cr.3rt., p.1) 5 times, cr.3rt., (cr.3lt., p.1) 8 times.

22nd row: K.1, *p.2, k.2; repeat from * until 1 remains, k.1 more.

23rd row: P.3, (k.2, p.2) 3 times, (cr.4lt.) 4 times, (p.1, cr.4rt.) 6 times, k.2, (cr.4lt.) 7 times, cr.2lt., p.1.

24th row: K3, (p.2, k.2) 17 times, p.2, k.1., p.1, (k.2, p.2) 3 times, k.3.

25th row: P.3, (k.2, p.2) 3 times, k.2, (cr.4lt.) 3 times, cr.2 (cr.4rt.) 7 times, k.2, (cr.4lt.) 7 times, p.1.

26th row: K.1, *p.2, k.2; repeat from * until 1 remains, k.1 more.

27th row: P.3, (cr.3lt., p.1) 4 times, (cr.4lt.) twice, p.2, (cr.4lt.) 8 times, k.2, (cr.4lt.) 6 times, cr.2lt., p.1.

28th row: K.3, (p.2, k.2) 16 times, p.2, k.3, (p.2, k.2) 4 times, k.2 more.

29th row: P.4, (k.2, p.2) 4 times, k.1, cr.4lt., k.2, (cr.4rt.) 9 times, k.2, (cr.4lt.) 6 times, p.1.

30th row: K.1, (p.2, k.2) 16 times, p.2, k.1, (p.2, k.2) 5 times, k.2 more.

31st row: P.1, k.1, (p.2, k.2) 5 times, p.1, k.2, (cr.4lt.) 10 times, k.2, (cr.4lt.) 5 times, cr.2lt., p.1.

32nd row: K.3, (p.2, k.2) 15 times, p.3, (k.2, p.2) 5 times, k.2, p.1, k.1.

33rd row: P.1, k.2, (p.1, cr.3lt.) 6 times, (cr.4lt.) 10 times, k.2, (cr.4lt.) 5 times, p.1.

34th row: K.1, (p.2, k.2) 15 times, p.4, (k.2, p.2) 6 times, k.1.

35th row: P.1, (k.2, p.2) 7 times, (cr.4lt.) 10 times, p.1, k.1, (cr.4lt.) 4 times, cr.2lt., p.1.

36th row: K.3, (p.2, k.2) 3 times, p.2, k.1, p.2, k.3, (p.2, k.2) 16 times, p.2, k.1.

37th row: P.1, (k.2, p.2) 6 times, k.2, (cr.4rt.) 10 times, k.1, p.2, k.2, p.1, (cr.4lt.) 4 times, p.1.

38th row: K.1, (p.2, k.2) 3 times, p.2, k.3, p.2, k.2, p.2, k.1, (p.2, k.2) 9 times, p.4, (k.2, p.2) 6 times, k.1.

39th row: (p.1, cr.3lt.) 7 times, p.1, (cr.4lt.) 9 times, (p.1, cr.3lt.) twice, p.2, (cr.4lt.) 3 times, cr.2lt., p.1.

40th row: K.3, (p.2, k.2) twice, p.2, k.1, p.1,

---

k.2, (p.2, k.2) twice, p.1, k.1, (p.2, k.2) 8 times, p.2, k.1, (p.2, k.2) 7 times.

41st row: (P.2, k.2) 7 times, p.1, cr.2rt., (cr.4lt.) 8 times, (k.2, p.2) 3 times, k.2, (cr.4lt.) 3 times, p.1.

42nd row: K.1, (p.2, k.2) 14 times, p.2, k.3, (p.2, k.2) 7 times.

43rd row: P.2, (cr.3lt., p.1) 6 times, cr.3lt., (cr.4lt.) 8 times, k.1, p.1, (cr.3lt., p.1) 4 times, (cr.4lt.) twice, cr.2lt., p.1.

44th row: K.3, p.2, k.2, p.2, k.3, (p.2, k.2) 4 times, p.2, k.1, (p.2, k.2) 7 times, p.4, (k.2, p.2) 6 times, k.3.

Mark the beginning of the next row with a coloured thread.

45th row: P.3, (k.2, p.2) 7 times, (cr.4lt.) 7 times, p.1, (k.2, p.2) 5 times, k.1, (cr.4lt.) twice, p.1.

46th row: K.1, p.2, k.2, p.2, k.1, (p.2, k.2) 6 times, k.1 more, (p.2, k.2) 14 times, k.1 more.

47th row: P.3, (cr.3lt., p.1) 7 times, cr.2rt., (cr.4lt.) 6 times, k.2, (p.1, cr.3lt.) 6 times, cr.4lt., cr.2lt., p.1.

48th row: K.3, (p.2, k.2) 14 times, k.1 more, (p.2, k.2) 7 times, k.2 more.

49th row: P.1, k.1, (p.2, k.2) 7 times, p.1, (cr.4lt.) 6 times, (p.2, k.2) 7 times, p.2, cr.4lt., p.1.

50th row: K.1, p.2, k.4, (p.2, k.2) 7 times, p.1, k.1, (p.2, k.2) 5 times, p.2, k.1, (p.2, k.2) 7 times, p.1, k.1.

51st row: P.1, k.2, (p.1, cr.3lt.) 7 times, p.2, (cr.4rt.) 5 times, (cr.3lt., p.1) 8 times, p.1 more, k.1, cr.2lt., p.1.

52nd row: K.3, p.1, (k.2, p.2) 8 times, k.3, (p.2, k.2) 12 times, p.2, k.1.

53rd row: P.1, (cr.3lt., p.1) 8 times, cr.2rt., (cr.4rt.) 4 times, k.1, (p.2, k.2) 9 times, p.2.

54th row: (K.2, p.2) 10 times, k.1, (p.2, k.2) 4 times, k.1 more, (p.2, k.2) 8 times.

55th row: P.2, (cr.3lt., p.1) 7 times, cr.3lt., (cr.4rt.) 4 times, (p.1, cr.3lt.) 10 times, p.1.

56th row: K.1, (p.2, k.2) 10 times, p.1, k.1, (p.2, k.2) 3 times, p.4, (k.2, p.2) 7 times, k.1, p.1, k.1.

57th row: P.1, k.2, (cr.3lt., p.1) 8 times, (cr.4rt.) 3 times, (k.2, p.2) 10 times, k.2, p.1.

58th row: K.1, (p.2, k.2) 13 times, p.2, k.1, (p.2, k.2) 7 times, p.2, k.1, p.2, k.1.

59th row: P.1, k.2, (p.1, cr.3lt.) 8 times, p.2, (cr.4rt.) twice, (p.2, k.2) 11 times, p.1.

60th row: K.1, (p.2, k.2) 11 times, p.1, k.1, (p.2, k.2) 10 times, p.2, k.1.

61st row: P.1, k.2, p.2, (cr.3lt., p.1) 8 times, cr.2rt., cr.4rt., cr.2rt., (p.1, cr.3rt.) 11 times, p.1.

62nd row: (k.2, p.2) 12 times, k.1, p.2, k.3, (p.2, k.2) 8 times, k.1 more, p.2, k.1.

63rd row: P.1, k.2, p.2, k.1, (cr.3lt., p.1) 7 times, cr.3lt., cr.4rt., p.1, (k.2, p.2) 12 times.

64th row: (k.2, p.2) 12 times, k.3, p.4, (k.2, p.2) 7 times, k.1, p.1, k.2, p.2, k.1.

65th row: P.1, cr.2rt., p.1, cr.3rt., (cr.4lt.) 8 times, p.2, (cr.3rt., p.1) 12 times, p.1.

66th row: K.3, (p.2, k.2) 20 times, k.1 more, p.2, k.2, p.1, k.1.

67th row: P.1, k.1, p.2, k.2, p.2, k.1, (cr.4lt.) 8 times, (k.2, p.2) 12 times, p.1 more.

68th row: K.3, (p.2, k.2) 11 times, p.4, (k.2, p.2) 7 times, k.1, p.2, k.2, p.2, k.4.

69th row: P.3, (cr.3rt., p.1) twice, (cr.4lt.) 8 times, (p.1, cr.3rt.) 11 times, p.3.

70th row: K.4, (p.2, k.2) 10 times, p.2, k.1, (p.2, k.2) 7 times, p.2, k.1, p.1, (k.2, p.2) twice, k.3.

71st row: P.3, (k.2, p.2) twice, k.2, (cr.4rt.) 8 times, p.3, (k.2, p.2) 10 times, k.1, p.1.

72nd row: K.1, p.1, (k.2, p.2) 10 times, k.3, (p.2, k.2) 11 times, k.2 more.

73rd row: P.2, (cr.3rt., p.1) 3 times, k.1, (cr.4lt.) 8 times, (cr.3rt., p.1) 10 times, k.2, p.1.

74th row: K.1, (p.2, k.2) 10 times, p.4, (k.2, p.2) 7 times, k.1, (p.2, k.2) 4 times.

75th row: (P.2, k.2) 4 times, p.1, (cr.4lt.) 8 times, (p.2, k.2) 10 times, p.1.

76th row: K.1, (p.2, k.2) 18 times, k.1 more, (p.2, k.2) 4 times.

77th row: P.1, (cr.3rt., p.1) 4 times, k.2, (cr.4lt.) 8 times, cr.2rt., p.1, (cr.3rt., p.1) 9 times.

78th row: (K.2, p.2) 9 times, k.3, (p.2, k.2) 12 times, p.2, k.1.

79th row: P.1, (k.2, p.2) 5 times, (cr.4lt.) 8 times, (cr.3rt., p.1) 9 times, p.1 more.

80th row: K.3, (p.2, k.2) 8 times, p.1, k.1, (p.2, k.2) 7 times, p.2, k.1, p.1, (k.2, p.2) 5 times, k.1.

81st row: P.1, cr.2rt., (p.1, cr.3rt.) 5 times, (cr.4lt.) 8 times, (p.1, cr.3rt.) 8 times, p.3.

82nd row: K.4, (p.2, k.2) 7 times, p.2, k.1, (p.2, k.2) 8 times, k.1 more, (p.2, k.2) 5 times, p.1, k.1.

83rd row: P.1, k.1, (p.2, k.2) 5 times, p.2, k.1, (cr.4lt.) 8 times, p.2, (cr.3rt., p.1) 6 times, cr.3rt., k.1, p.3.

84th row: K.3, p.1, k.1, (p.2, k.2) 14 times, p.2, k.1, (p.2, k.2) 6 times, k.2 more.

85th row: P.3, (cr.3rt., p.1) 6 times, (cr.4lt.) 7 times, p.2, (cr.4rt.) 7 times, p.3.

86th row: K.3, (p.2, k.2) 14 times, p.2, p.1, k.1, (k.2, p.2) 6 times, k.3.

Mark the beginning of the next row with a coloured thread.

87th row: P.3, (k.2, p.2) 6 times, k.2, (cr.4lt.) 7 times, p.2, (cr.4rt.) 6 times, p.2, k.2, p.3.

88th row: K.3, p.2, k.2, p.1, k.1, (p.2, k.2) 20 times, k.1 more.

89th row: P.2, (cr.3rt., p.1) 7 times, k.1, (cr.4lt.) 6 times, p.2, (cr.4rt.) 6 times, k.2, p.2, k.2, p.3.

90th row: K.3, (p.2, k.2) 14 times, p.1, (k.2, p.2) 7 times, k.2.

91st row: (P.2, k.2) 8 times, p.1, (cr.4lt.) 6 times, p.2, (cr.4rt.) 5 times, (p.2, k.2) twice, p.3.

92nd row: K.3, (p.2, k.2) twice, p.1, k.1, (p.2, k.2) 10 times, p.2, k.1, p.1, k.1, (p.2, k.2) 8 times.

93rd row: P.1, (cr.3rt., p.1) 8 times, k.2, (cr.4lt.) 5 times, p.2, (cr.4rt.) 5 times, (k.2, p.2) 3 times, p.1 more.

94th row: K.3, (p.2, k.2) 21 times, p.2, k.1.

95th row: P.1, (k.2, p.2) 9 times, (cr.4lt.) 5 times, p.2, (cr.4rt.) 4 times, (p.2, k.2) 3 times, p.3.

96th row: K.3, *p.2, k.2; repeat from * ending last repeat k.1.

The last 96 rows form the pattern. Now work the first 60 rows again, but without marking the 45th pattern row with a coloured thread.

To slope the shoulder: Cast off 58 sts. in rib as set at the beginning of the next row.

On 32 sts. work 1 row, then cast off in rib.

Left half back● With right side of work facing rejoin yarn to the 90 sts. left on spare needle and work as given for right half back, but marking the end of the 45th and 87th rows instead of the beginning with coloured threads and working 1 extra row in pattern before sloping the shoulder.

FRONT Work as given for the back, reading left half front for right half back and right half front for left half back, until 100 rows have been worked in pattern on right half back.

**Left half front: To shape the neck: Dec. 1 st. at the neck edge – inner edge – on each of the next 2 rows. Work 1 row straight. Repeat the last 3 rows 8 times more, marking the neck edge on the last row with a coloured thread.

Dec. 1 st. at the neck edge on each of the next 14 rows. On 58 sts. pattern 15 rows.

To slope the shoulder: Cast off the remaining 58 sts. in rib pattern as set.

Right half front● With right side of work facing rejoin yarn to the 90 sts. left on spare needle and work as given for left half back until 101 rows have been worked in pattern as for left half back, but marking the end instead of the beginning of the 45th and 87th rows with coloured threads.

To shape the neck: Work as given for left half front to end.

Vee neck inset: With size 3¼ mm [3¾ mm] needles cast on 3 sts. and work 1 row in single rib. Continuing in single rib, inc. 1 st. at each end of the next row and the 15 following alternate rows. – 35 sts. Rib 1 row, then cast off in rib.

SLEEVES 4 halves alike● With right side of work facing rejoin yarn and using size 3¾ mm [4 mm] needles pick up and k. 68 sts. from the row ends between the marking thread at 87th pattern row and the shoulder. Work 6 rows in single rib.

Increase row: Rib 2, *up 1, rib 3; repeat from * to end. – 90 sts.

Work the first 20 pattern rows given for right half back – mark each end of the last row with coloured threads.

Continuing in pattern, dec. 1 st. at each end of the next row and the 19 following 4th rows. On 50 sts. work 7 rows.

Change to size 3¼ mm [3¾ mm] needles.

Decrease row: *P.2tog., k.2tog., p.1, k.2tog., p.1, k.2tog.; repeat from * to end. – 30 sts. Work 15 rows in single rib as set. Cast off loosely in rib.

NECKBAND Neatly join centre back seam, then centre front seam up to first neck decreases. Sew vee neck inset in place up to marking threads at neck edge. Join right shoulder seam, continuing seam down centre of right sleeve. With right side of work facing rejoin yarn at left front neck edge and using size 3¼ mm [3¾ mm] needles pick up and k. 30 sts. from left front neck edge, 26 sts. from top of vee neck inset, then 30 sts. from right front neck edge, then 46 sts. from back neck edge.

On 132 sts. work 5 rows in single rib, then cast off in rib.

INSETS Both alike● With size 3¼ mm [3¾ mm] needles cast on 3 sts. and work 1 row in single rib.

Continuing in rib. inc. 1 st. at each end of the next row and the 22 following alternate rows. – 49 sts. Work 1 row in single rib, marking each end of the row with coloured threads.

Dec. 1 st. at each end of the next 3 rows. Work 1 row straight. Repeat the last 4 rows 6 times more. – 7 sts.

Dec. 1 st. at each end of the next 2 rows. On 3 sts. rib 1 row, then slip 1, k.2tog., pass slip st. over and fasten off.

MAKING UP Join left shoulder seam, continuing seam down centre of left sleeve. Join underarm sleeve seam up to marking threads. Join side seams up to marking threads on 45th pattern row. Neatly sew insets in place, so that the row ends up to the marking threads are sewn to the free row ends at side seams and those above the marking threads are sewn to those on sleeves. ●

MATERIALS 21 25 gram balls of "Woollybear 100% Mohair" in main colour; 3 balls in first and third contrasts and 2 balls in each of the 4 other contrast colours● a pair each of size 3¼ mm and 2¾ mm Aero knitting needles● 3 buttons●

TENSION 11 stitches and 18 rows to 5 centimetres (2 inches) over the garter stitch using size 3¼ mm needles●

If you cannot obtain the correct tension using the size needles suggested, use larger or smaller ones accordingly●

ABBREVIATIONS K., knit● p., purl● st., stitch● tog., together● dec., decrease (by working 2 sts. tog.)● inc., increase (by working twice into same st.)● sl., slip● p.s.s.o., pass sl. st. over● y.r.n., yarn round needle● 3 from 1, k.1, p.1, k.1 all into next st.● s.s.k., sl.1, k.1, p.s.s.o.● m.b., make bobble thus, on a wrong side row, with appropriate contrast colour p.1, y.r.n., p.1 all into one st., turn, p.3, turn, k.3, turn, p.3, turn, pick up the loop in m., originally worked into, and slip it onto left hand needle, pass the 3 bobble sts. over this st.● m.k. this st.● garter st. is k. plain on every row● single rib is k.1 and p.1 alternately● m., main colour● a., first contrast● b., second contrast● c., third contrast● d., fourth contrast● e., fifth contrast● f., sixth contrast●

MEASUREMENTS The measurements are given in centimetres followed by inches in brackets●

Across back 55 (22)● Across fronts 36 (14.5)● Side seam 32.5 (13)● Length 57.5 (23)● Sleeve length 37.5 (15)●

BACK With size 3¼ mm needles cast on 122 sts. and work in pattern as follows: Use separate small balls of contrast colours for each leaf on each section of the roses and bobbles and separate balls of m. on each side of roses, so that colours not in use are not taken across the back of the work. When fastening off colours, take care to leave sufficiently long ends to darn in at completion of work. When counting sts., count the sts. for each leaf as one st.

1st to **5**th rows: With m. all k.

6th row: With m. k.1, *with a. m.b., with m. k.7; repeat from * ending last repeat with m. k.8.

7th row: With m. all k.

8th row: With m. k.1, *with b. p.1 for the leaf, with m. k.39; repeat from * ending last repeat with m. k.40.

9th row: With m. k.40, *with b. 3 from 1 for the leaf, with m. k.39; repeat from * ending last repeat with m. k.1

10th row: With m. k.1, *with b. p.3 for the leaf, with m. k.39; repeat from * ending last repeat with m. k.40.

11th row: With m. k.17, *with c. k.4, with m. k.1, with c. k.4, with m. k.14, with b. k.1, y.r.n., k.1, y.r.n., k.1 for the leaf, with m. k.16; repeat from * ending last repeat with m. k.1.

12th row: With m. k.1, *with b. p.5 for the leaf, with m. k.13, with c. p.1, k.4, p.1, k.4, p.1, with m. k.15; repeat from * ending last repeat k.16.

13th row: With m. k.15, *with c. k.12, with m. k.13, with b. k.2, y.r.n., k.1, y.r.n., k.2 for the leaf, with m. k.14; repeat from * ending last repeat k.1.

14th row: With m. k.1, *with b. p.7, with m. k.3, with b. m.b., with m. k.8, with c. p.1, k.12, p.1, with m. k.1, with b. m.b., with m. k.7, with b. m.b, with m. k.3; repeat from * ending last repeat k.4.

15th row: With m. k.14, *with c. k.14, with m. k.12, with b. k.3, y.r.n., k.1, y.r.n., k.3, with m. k.13; repeat from * ending last repeat k.1.

16th row: With m. k.1, *with b. p.9, with m. k.12, with c. k.14, with m. k.13; repeat from * ending last repeat k.14.

17th row: With m. k.14, *with c. k.14, with m. k.12, with b. k.3, sl.1, k.2tog., p.s.s.o., k.3, with m. k.13; repeat from * ending last repeat k.1.

18th row: With m. k.1, *with b. p.2, p.3tog., p.2, with m. k.12, with c. k.14, with m. k.13; repeat from * ending last repeat k.14.

19th row: With m. k.14, *with c. k.13, with b. k.1, sl.1, k.2tog., p.s.s.o., k.1, with m. k.13; repeat from * ending last repeat k.1.

20th row: With m. k.1, *with b. p.3tog., with m. k.14, with c. k.5, with m. p.4, with c. k.2, with m. k.14; repeat from * ending last repeat k.15.

21st row: With m. k.14, *with c. k.2, with m. k.2, p.1, k.1, p.1, k.2, with c. k.3, with m. k.1, with c. k.2, with m. k.25; repeat from * ending last repeat k.13.

The last 21 rows set the position of the pattern given in the chart. Work the **22**nd to

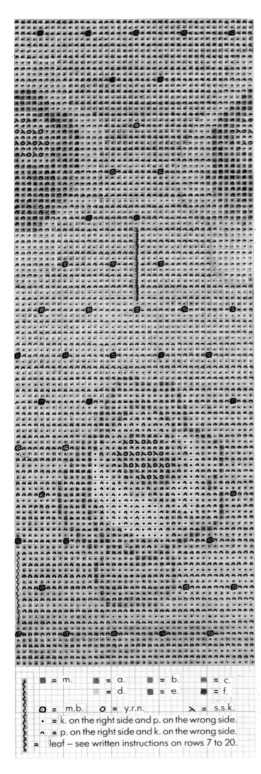

■ = m.	■ = a.	■ = b.	■ = c.
	□ = d.	■ = e.	■ = f.

O = m.b.   o = y.r.n.   ✕ = s.s.k.

• = k. on the right side and p. on the wrong side.

^ = p. on the right side and k. on the wrong side.

= leaf – see written instructions on rows 7 to 20.

"Poppy" jacket knitted in poppy red mohair. Black, fuschia or marine make good background colours.

Dress by "Gerard"; jewellery from "Butler and Wilson".

112th rows from the chart as set, then work the first 6 rows again. Mark each end of the last row with coloured threads to denote armholes.

Pattern 80 rows.

To slope the shoulders: Cast off 8 sts. at the beginning of the next 10 rows. Cast off the remaining 42 sts.

LEFT FRONT First work the pocket back: With size 3¼ mm needles and m. cast on 38 sts. and work 47 rows in stocking stitch.

Decrease row: P.3, *p.2tog., p.4; repeat from * ending last repeat p.3. — 32 sts.

Leave these sts. on a stitch-holder until required.

With size 3¼ mm needles and m. cast on 82 sts. and work 56 rows in pattern as given for back.

Pocket row: Pattern 25, slip next 32 sts. onto a stitch-holder at front of work and in their place, pattern across the 32 sts. of pocket back, pattern to end.

Work the **58**th to **112**th rows from the chart, then work the first 6 rows again. Work 1 extra row here when working right front.

To shape the armhole: Cast off 13 sts. at the beginning of the next row, marking the 7th of these sts. with a coloured thread. Work 1 row straight.

To slope the front edge. Continuing in pattern, dec. 1 st. at the end of the next row and the 28 following alternate rows.

On 40 sts. pattern 21 rows.

To slope the shoulder: Cast off 8 sts. at the beginning of the next row and the 3 following alternate rows. On 8 sts. work 1 row, then cast off.

Pocket top: With right side of work facing rejoin m. to the 32 sts. left on stitch-holder and using size 3¼ mm needles k.12 rows, then cast off loosely.

Left front band and collar: With size 2¾ mm needles and m. cast on 20 sts. and work 94 rows in single rib.

**Next row: Rib 4, 3 from 1, rib to end.

Rib 3 rows.

Repeat the last 4 rows 13 times, then work the increase row again. On 50 sts. rib 67 rows, then cast off.

RIGHT FRONT Work as given for left front until the pocket top has been worked, but note the variation in rows, before shaping armhole.

Right front band and collar: With size 2¾ mm needles and m. cast on 20 sts. and work 16 rows in single rib.

1st Buttonhole row: Rib 7, cast off 6, rib to end.

2nd Buttonhole row: Rib 7, turn, cast on 6, turn, rib to end.

Rib 36 rows.

Repeat the last 38 rows once more, then work the 2 buttonhole rows again.

Work as given for left front band and collar from ** to end

SLEEVES Both alike● With size 3¼ mm needles and m. cast on 63 sts. and k.7 rows. Work in pattern as follows: **6**th pattern row: With m. k.3, *with a. m.b., with m. k.7; repeat from * ending last repeat with m. k.3.

7th row: With m. all k.

8th row: With m. k.11, with b. p.1 for leaf, with m. k.39, with b. p.1 for leaf, with m. k.11.

9th row: With m. k.11, with b. 3 from 1, with m. k.39, with b. 3 from 1, with m. k.11.

10th row: With m. k.11, with b. p.3, with m. k.39, with b. p.3, with m. k.11.

11th row: With m. k.11, with b. k.1, y.r.n., k.1. y.r.n., k.1, with m. k.16, with c. k.4, with m. k.1, with c. k.4, with m. k.14, with b. k.1, y.r.n., k.1, y.r.n., k.1, with m. k.11.

12th row: With m. k.11, with b. p.5, with m. k.13, with c. p.1, k.4, p.1, k.4, p,1, with m.

Continued on page 48●

MATERIALS Either 9 (22) (24) 50 gram balls of "Patricia Roberts Cotton No. 2" in main colour plus 1 25 gram ball of "Patricia Roberts Fine Cotton" in the same colour and 1 in a contrasting colour.

Or 7 (18) (19) 50 gram balls of "Patricia Roberts Lambswool No. 2" in main colour plus 1 25 gram ball of "Lambswool No. 1" in the same colour and 1 in a contrasting colour.

Or 7 (18) (19) 50 gram hanks of "Patricia Roberts Shetland No. 2" in plain, flecked or marled colours in main colour plus 1 28 gram hank of "Shetland" in the same colour and 1 in a contrasting colour.

Or 17 (38) (40) 25 gram balls of "Patricia Roberts 100% Mohair" in main colour, plus 1 25 gram ball of "Patricia Roberts Kid Mohair" in the same colour and 1 in a contrasting colour●

A pair each of size 3mm and 2¼mm Aero knitting needles● 4 (5) (5) buttons●

TENSION 11 stitches and 24 rows – 12 rows to view – over the fisherman's rib to 5 centimetres (2 inches) using size 3mm needles and main yarn●

If you cannot obtain the correct tension using the size needles suggested, use larger or smaller ones accordingly●

ABBREVIATIONS K., knit● p., purl● st., stitch● tog., together● dec., decrease (by working 2 sts. tog.)● inc., increase (by working twice into same st.)● single rib is k.1 and p.1 alternately● k.1 down, k. into st. one row below next st. on left hand needle● cable 6, slip next 3 sts. onto cable needle and leave at front of work, k.3, then k.3 from cable needle● up 1, pick up the loop which lies between the needles, slip it onto left hand needle, then k. into back of it● m., main colour● up 2, pick up the loop which lies between the needles, slip it onto left hand needle and k. into back and front of it●

NOTE The instructions are given for the child's size. Where they vary work the figures in the first brackets for the woman's size and those in the second brackets for the man's size●

MEASUREMENTS The measurements are given in centimetres followed by inches in square brackets● Underarms – excluding bands: 84 [33½] (125 [50]) (125 [50])● Side seam 25 [10] (49 [19½]) (49 [19½])● Length 40 [16] (74 [29½]) (74 [29½])● Sleeve seam 25 [10] (44 [17½]) (49 [19½])●

BACK With size 3mm needles and m. cast on 89 (133) (133) sts. and work 21 (27) (27) rows in single rib.

Increase row: Rib 11, *up 1, rib 22; repeat from * ending last repeat rib 12. – 93 (139) (139) sts.

Now work in pattern as follows:

1st row: P.1, *(k.1 down, p.1) 4 times, k.6, (p.1, k.1 down) 4 times, p.1; repeat from * to end.

2nd row: K.1 down, *(p.1, k.1 down) 4 times, p.6, (k.1 down, p.1) 4 times, k.1 down; repeat from * to end.

3rd and **4**th rows: As 1st and 2nd rows.

5th row: P.1, *(k.1 down) 4 times, cable 6, (p.1, k.1 down) 4 times, p.1; repeat from * to end.

6th row: As 2nd row.

7th and **8**th rows: As 1st and 2nd rows.

The last 8 rows form the pattern; repeat them 10 (23) (23) times more.

To shape the armholes: **1**st row: P.1, k.1 down, p.3tog., pattern as set until 5 remain, p.3tog., k.1 down, p.1.

2nd row: K.1 down, p.1, k.1, work as set until 3 remain, k.1., p.1, k.1 down.

3rd row: P.1, k.1 down, p.1, pattern until 3

remain, p.1, k.1 down, p.1.

4th row: As 2nd row.

Repeat the last 4 rows 6 (8) (8) times more. – 65 (103) (103) sts.

Pattern 38 (72) (72) rows as set.

To slope the shoulders: Cast off 5 sts. at the beginning of the next 6 rows, then on the 2 adult sizes only 6 sts. on the following 6 rows. Cast off the remaining 35 (37) (37) sts.

LEFT FRONT With size 3mm needles and m. cast on 45 (67) (67) sts. and work 21 (27) (27) rows in single rib.

Work the increase row given for back. – 47 (70) (70) sts.

Work the 17 (41) (41) rows in pattern given for back.

Now divide the sts. for the 1st pocket opening: **N**ext row: Pattern 36 (55) (55), turn and continue on these 36 (55) (55) sts., leaving the remaining 11 (15) (15) sts. on a spare needle until required.

1st row: P.1, k.1 down, p.3tog., pattern to end.

2nd row: Pattern until 3 remain, k.1, p.1, k.1 down.

3rd row: P.1, k.1 down, p.1, pattern to end.

4th row: As 2nd row.

Repeat the last 4 rows 11 (15) (15) times more, then leave these 12 (23) (23) sts. on a spare needle until required. Rejoin m. to inner edge of the 11 (15) (15) sts. left on spare needle, inc. in first st., and work to end of row. Work as follows working the extra sts. into cable pattern.

****1**st row: Pattern until 3 remain, up 2 – see abbreviations, p.1, k.1 down, p.1.

2nd row: K.1 down, p.1, k.1 down, p.1, k.1, pattern to end.

3rd row: Pattern until 3 remain, p.1, k.1 down, p.1.

4th row: K.1 down, p.1, k.1 down, pattern to end.**

Repeat the last 4 rows 11 (15) (15) times more. – 36 (48) (48) sts.

Next row: Pattern 34 (46) (46), k.2tog., then onto same needle pattern across the 12 (23) (23) sts. left on spare needle. – 47 (70) (70) sts.

Pattern 9 (73) (73) rows.

***T**o slope the front edge: Dec. 1 st. at the end of the next row and the 2 following 4th rows.

On 44 (67) (67) sts. pattern 2 rows. Now divide the sts. for the 2nd pocket opening.

Next row: Pattern 8 (19) (19), inc. and leave these 10 (21) (21) sts. on a spare needle until required, pattern to end and continue on these 35 (47) (47) sts. Work 1 extra row here when working right front.

To shape the armhole and to slope the pocket: Repeat the 4 armhole shaping rows given for back 7 (9) (9) times.***

On 7 (11) (11) sts. work 1 row straight, then leave these sts. on a spare needle.

Rejoin yarn to inner edge of 10 (21) (21) sts. on spare needle. Continuing to dec. at front edge on every 4th row as before, shape pocket edge as follows:

*1st row: P.1, k.1 down, p.1, up 2, pattern to end.

2nd row: Pattern until 5 remain, k.1, p.1, k.1 down, p.1, k.1 down.

3rd row: P.1, k.1 down, p.1, pattern to end.

4th row: Pattern until 3 remain, k.1 down, p.1, k.1 down.*

Repeat the last 4 rows 6 (8) (8) times more. – 17 (30) (30) sts.

Onto the needle holding 7 (11) (11) sts. from before, work across these 17 (30) (30) sts. as follows: K.2tog., pattern until 2 remain – k.2tog. – for front edge dec. – 22 (39) (39) sts.

Pattern 3 (5) (5) rows.

****D**ec. 1 st. at the front edge on the next row and the 6 (5) (5) following 4th (6th) (6th) rows. – 15 (33) (33) sts.

Pattern 9 (35) (35) rows.

To slope the shoulder: Cast off 5 sts. at the beginning of the next row and the 2 following alternate rows. On the 2 adult sizes only, cast off 6 sts. on the 3 following alternate rows. Fasten off.

RIGHT FRONT Work as given for left front until 17 (41) (41) rows have been worked in pattern.

Now divide the sts. for the first pocket opening: Next row: Pattern 10 (14) (14), inc. and leave these 12 (16) (16) sts. on a spare needle until required, work to end and continue on these 36 (55) (55) sts

1st row: Pattern until 5 remain, p.3tog., k.1 down, p.1.

2nd row: K.1 down, p.1, k.1, pattern to end.

3rd row: Pattern until 3 remain, p.1, k.1 down, p.1.

4th row: As 2nd row.

Repeat the last 4 rows 11 (15) (15) times more. On 12 (23) (23) sts. work 1 row straight, then leave on a spare needle.

Rejoin yarn to inner edge of the 12 (16) (16) sts. on spare needle and work the 4 rows given for second pocket between * and * on left front 12 (16) (16) times. – 36 (48) (48) sts.

Now onto the needle holding 12 (23) (23) sts. work across these sts. as follows, dec., pattern to end. – 47 (70) (70) sts.

Pattern 10 (74) (74) rows.

Now work as given for left front from *** to ***.

Rejoin yarn to inner edge of 10 (21) (21) sts. on spare needle and work to end of row, decreasing 1st at front edge.

Continuing to dec. at front edge on every 4th row as before, repeat the 4 rows given between ** and ** on first pocket on left front 7 (9) (9) times.

Next row: Pattern until 2 remain, dec., then onto the same needle, pattern across the 7 (11) (11) sts. on spare needle. – 22 (39) (39) sts.

Pattern 2 (4) (4) rows.

Work as given for left front from **** to end.

SLEEVES: Both alike: With size 3mm needles and m. cast on 43 (64) (64) sts. and work 21 (27) (27) rows in single rib.

Increase row: Rib 1, *up 1, rib 10, up 1, rib 11; repeat from * to end. – 47 (70) (70) sts.

Work the 8 pattern rows given for back 2 (5) (8) times.

Working the extra sts. into the pattern as they occur, inc. 1 st. at each end of the next row and the 8 (15) (15) following 8th rows.

On 65 (102) (102) sts. pattern 7 rows.

To shape the sleevetop: Work the 4 armhole shaping rows given for back 7 (9) (9) times, then cast off the remaining 37 (66) (66) sts.

FRONTBANDS and half collar. Left front: With right side of work facing rejoin yarn and using size 3mm needles pick up and k. 70 (126) (126) sts. from left front edge up to first dec., pick up a further 56 (82) (82) sts. up to shoulder, then turn and cast on 22 (24) (24) sts. for back collar. – 148 (232) (232) sts.

Work 2 rows in single rib.

*Now work turning rows as follows:

1st and **2**nd rows: Rib 38 (52) (52), turn, rib to end.

3rd and **4**th rows: Rib 41 (55) (55), turn, rib to end.

5th and **6**th rows: Rib 44 (58) (58), turn, rib to end.

Thus working 3 sts. more on each successive repeat, work the 2 turning rows 10 (16) (16) times more.*

Now on all 148 (232) (232) sts. rib 9 (11) (11)

rows, then cast off very loosely, using a size larger needle.

Right front: With size 3 mm needles cast on 22 (24) (24) sts., then onto same needle from right front edge pick up and k. 55 (82) (82) sts. between shoulder and first front edge dec., then a further 63 (126) (126) sts. down to cast on edge. – 148 (232) (232) sts.
Work 1 row in single rib.
Work as given for left front collar from * to *, then on 148 (232) (232) sts. rib 2 rows.
1st Buttonhole row: Rib 80 (111) (111), * cast off 3 (4) (4), rib next 16 (23) (23); repeat from * ending last repeat rib next 4 sts.
2nd Buttonhole row: Rib 5, *turn, cast on 3 (4) (4) over those cast off, turn, rib 17 (24) (24); repeat from * ending rib 80 (111) (111).
Rib 4 (6) (6) rows, then cast off very loosely using a size larger needle.
POCKETS Large (two alike): With size 2¼ mm needles and m. in fine yarn cast on 37 (49) (49) sts. and work as follows:
1st and **2**nd rows: With m. all k.
3rd and **4**th rows: With contrast colour fine yarn k.1 row and p.1 row.
Repeat these 4 rows 24 (35) (35) times, then cast off.
Small (two alike): With size 2¼ mm needles and m. in fine yarn cast on 22 (25) (25) sts. and work the 4 stripe pattern rows given for large pocket 16 (23) (23) times, then cast off.
MAKING UP Do not press. Join shoulder seams. Set in sleeves, so that the dec. rows on sleevetops are sewn to the dec. rows on back and fronts. Join sleeve and side seams. Join row ends of collar at centre back neck. Then sew cast on edge at back neck in place. Fold pocket backs in half and join row end edges, then neatly sew cast on and cast off edges of pockets to the sloped pocket openings. Sew on buttons.

COCO Continued from page 53
Next row: Pattern across these 24 (28) sts., marking the last st. with a coloured thread, then onto the same needle pattern across the 16 sts. on spare needle. 40 (44) sts.
Now work as given for left sleeve from *** to end, then work the slit edging.
MAKING UP Do not press. Set in sleeves. Join sleeve and side seams. Neatly join mitred corners of edgings. Sew buttons in place on frontband. Neatly sew straight row end edge of sleeve slit edging in place, then secure this edging with 2 buttons on each sleeve. Catch shoulder pads in place.

SKIRT Back and Front Alike: With size 3¾ mm needles and m. cast on 84 (88) (92) sts. by the thumb method and k. 4 rows. Change to size 4 mm needles and p. 1 row, then work the 6 pattern rows given for back of jacket 17 times.
1st Decrease row: Pattern 20, sl.1, k.2tog., p.s.s.o., sl.1, k.2tog., p.s.s.o., pattern 32 (36) (40), sl.1, k.2tog., p.s.s.o., sl.1, k.2tog., p.s.s.o., pattern 20.
Pattern 11 rows.
2nd Decrease row: Pattern 18, sl.1, k.2tog., p.s.s.o., sl.1, k.2tog., p.s.s.o., pattern 28 (32) (36). sl.1, k.2tog., p.s.s.o., sl.1, k.2tog., p.s.s.o., pattern 18.
Pattern 5 rows.
Working 2 sts. less before, 4 sts. less between and 2 sts. less after the decreases on each successive repeat of the decrease row, repeat the last 6 rows twice more – 52 (56) (60) sts.
Change to size 3¾ mm needles and k.9 rows, then cast off loosely k.wise.
MAKING UP: Do not press. Join side seams. Join ends of elastic and catch in place with a herring bone casing.

"Fleur" the big cotton cardi to wrap yourself up in.

Isolda, right, with lifebelt
and sailors' hat motifs,
may be knitted for adults
too, in Shetland or cotton.
Fleur, left.

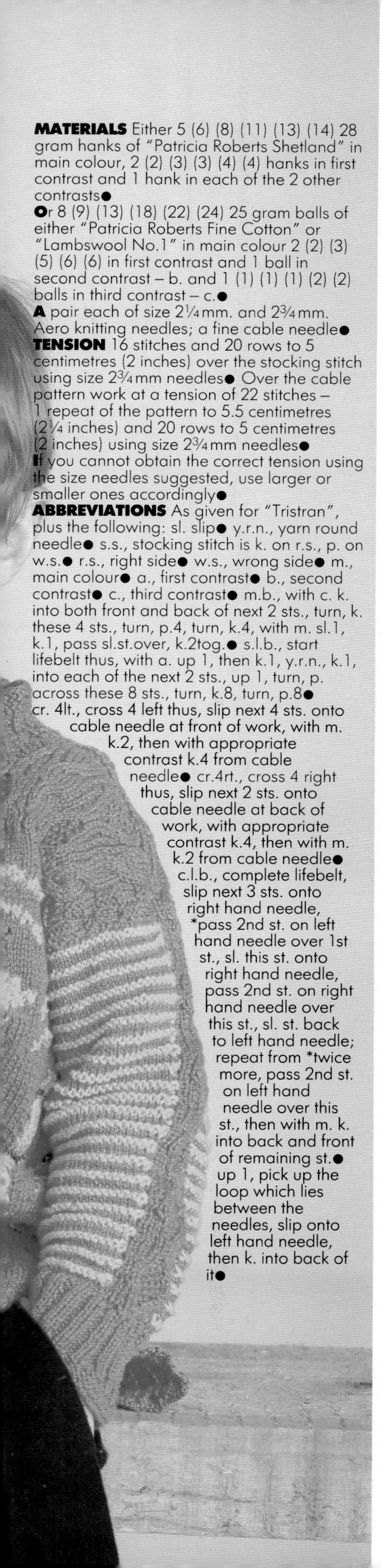

MATERIALS Either 5 (6) (8) (11) (13) (14) 28 gram hanks of "Patricia Roberts Shetland" in main colour, 2 (2) (3) (3) (4) (4) hanks in first contrast and 1 hank in each of the 2 other contrasts●
Or 8 (9) (13) (18) (22) (24) 25 gram balls of either "Patricia Roberts Fine Cotton" or "Lambswool No.1" in main colour 2 (2) (3) (5) (6) (6) in first contrast and 1 ball in second contrast – b. and 1 (1) (1) (1) (2) (2) balls in third contrast – c.●
A pair each of size 2¼mm. and 2¾mm. Aero knitting needles; a fine cable needle●
TENSION 16 stitches and 20 rows to 5 centimetres (2 inches) over the stocking stitch using size 2¾mm needles● Over the cable pattern work at a tension of 22 stitches – 1 repeat of the pattern to 5.5 centimetres (2¼ inches) and 20 rows to 5 centimetres (2 inches) using size 2¾mm needles●
If you cannot obtain the correct tension using the size needles suggested, use larger or smaller ones accordingly●
ABBREVIATIONS As given for "Tristran", plus the following: sl. slip● y.r.n., yarn round needle● s.s., stocking stitch k. on r.s., p. on w.s.● r.s., right side● w.s., wrong side● m., main colour● a., first contrast● b., second contrast● c., third contrast● m.b., with c. k. into both front and back of next 2 sts., turn, k. these 4 sts., turn, p.4, turn, k.4, with m. sl.1, k.1, pass sl.st.over, k.2tog.● s.l.b. start lifebelt thus, with a. up 1, then k.1, y.r.n., k.1, into each of the next 2 sts., up 1, turn, p. across these 8 sts., turn, k.8, turn, p.8●
cr. 4lt., cross 4 left thus, slip next 4 sts. onto cable needle at front of work, with m. k.2, then with appropriate contrast k.4 from cable needle● cr.4rt., cross 4 right thus, slip next 2 sts. onto cable needle at back of work, with appropriate contrast k.4, then with m. k.2 from cable needle● c.l.b., complete lifebelt, slip next 3 sts. onto right hand needle, *pass 2nd st. on left hand needle over 1st st., sl. this st. onto right hand needle, pass 2nd st. on right hand needle over this st., sl. st. back to left hand needle; repeat from *twice more, pass 2nd st. on left hand needle over this st., then with m. k. into back and front of remaining st.● up 1, pick up the loop which lies between the needles, slip onto left hand needle, then k. into back of it●

NOTE The instructions are given for the 2 year size. Where they vary work the figures in the first brackets for the 5 year size; those in the second brackets for the 8 year size; those in the third brackets for the 10 year size; those in the fourth bracket for the woman's size and those in the fifth brackets for the man's size●
Special note: For easier working, before commencing work read through the pattern and underline the number of sts. or rows to be worked for the relevant size.

MEASUREMENTS The measurements are given in centimetres followed by inches in square brackets●
Sizes: 2 yrs (5 yrs) (8 yrs) (10 yrs) (woman's) (man's)● Underarms: 60 [24] (75 [30]) (90 [36]) (105 [42]) (120 [48]) (120 [48])● Side seam: 23 [9¼] (27.5 [11]) (33.5 [13½]) (35.5 [14¼]) (39.5 [15¾]) (42.5 [17])● Length: 33.5 [13½] (39 [15½]) (46 [18½]) (59 [23½]) (62.5 [25]) (68 [27¼])● Sleeve seam: 20.5 [8¼] (25 [10]) (37 [14¾]) (40.5 [16¼]) (43 [17¼]) (47.5 [19])●

BACK With size 2¾mm needles and m. cast on 130 (152) (174) (218) (240) (240) sts. and work the 16 cable pattern rows given for "Tristran" 3 (3) (4) (5) (5) (5) times, then work the first 2 rows again.
Decrease row: K.2 (2) (5) (14) (7) (7), *k.2 tog., k.2 (3) (4) (2) (3) (3); repeat from * ending last repeat k.2 (3) (5) (14) (6) (6). – 98 (122) (146) (170) (194) (194) sts.
With m. p.1 row.
Now work in pattern as follows: Use separate balls of colour, whenever it is necessary to take colours not in use across back of more than 6 sts. at one time. Do not weave in the colours.
For 1st, 3rd, 5th and 6th sizes: 1st row: With m.k.23, * with a.k.1, with m.k.5, with a.k.16, with m.k.26; repeat from * ending last repeat k.5.
For 2nd and 4th sizes: 1st row: With m.k.23,* With a.k.1, with m.k.5, with a.k.16, with m.k.26; repeat from * until 3 remain, with a.k.1, with m.k.2.
The last row sets the position of the repeat pattern given in the chart. Continue in pattern from chart until 54 (76) (76) (76) (92) (114) rows have been worked, but marking

each end of the 40th (58th) (66th) (58th) (76th) (86th) rows with coloured threads to denote armholes.
Increase row: With m.k.2 (2) (5) (14) (7) (7), *up 1, k.3 (4) (5) (3) (4) (4); repeat from * ending last repeat k.3 (4) (6) (15) (7) (7).
On 130 (152) (174) (218) (240) (240) sts. with m. p.1 row ***
With m. work 26 (26) (40) (72) (72) (72) rows in cable pattern as given at beginning.
To slope the shoulders: Cast off 40 (48) (56) (72) (81) (81) sts. at the beginning of the next 2 rows. Cast off the remaining 50 (56) (62) (74) (78) (78) sts.

FRONT Work as given for back until *** is reached.
With m. work 21 (21) (31) (55) (55) (73) rows in cable pattern as given for back.
Now divide the sts. for the neck: Next row: Pattern 42 (50) (62) (86) (95) (95) and leave these sts. on a spare needle until required, cast off 46 (52) (50) (46) (50) (50), pattern to end and continue on these 42 (50) (62) (86) (95) (95) sts. for the left front shoulder.
Left front shoulder: Continuing in pattern as set, dec. 1 st. at the neck edge on each of the next 2 (6) (14) (14) (14) (14) rows.
On 40 (48) (56) (72) (81) (81) sts. work 2 rows, then cast off.
Right front shoulder: With right side of work facing rejoin yarn to inner edge of sts. left on spare needle and work to end of row, then work as given for left front shoulder to end.

SLEEVES Both alike: Work as given for 1st (2nd) (4th) (5th) (6th) (7th) size given for "Tristran" until *** is reached.
On 16 sts. work 40 (48) (56) (72) (80) (80) rows with m. in cable pattern, then cast off in pattern.

NECKBAND AND MAKING UP Set in right sleeve so that the row ends above the marking threads on back and front are sewn to the sts. cast off at top of sleeves, and so that the cable rows at the top of the sleeve are sewn to the shoulders and the 16 sts., cast off, form part of the neck edge. In the same way sew the left sleeve in place at front only.
Neckband and completion: Work as given for 1st (2nd) (4th) (5th) (6th) (7th) size given for "Tristran". ●

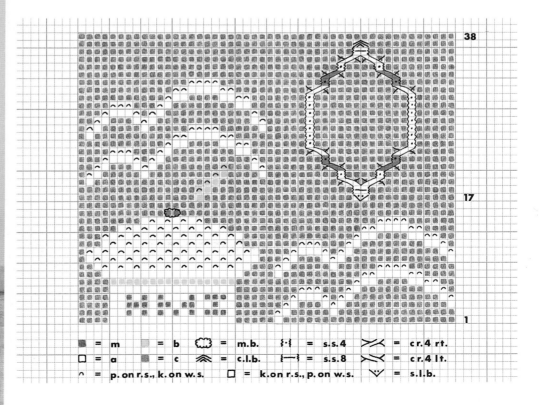

▨ = m		▨ = b	☁ = m.b.	⊢⊣ = s.s.4	⧅ = cr.4 rt.
□ = a		▨ = c	≋ = c.l.b.	⊢—⊣ = s.s.8	⧄ = cr.4 lt.
∧ = p. on r.s., k. on w.s.			□ = k. on r.s., p. on w.s.	⋁ = s.l.b.	

"Tristan", a stylish adaptation of the traditional fisherman's ganzy. Note the fluted edges to the collar and cuffs. Can also be knitted in one colour.

MATERIALS Either 6 (8) (10) (14) (18 (22) (23) balls of "Patricia Roberts Fine Cotton" in main colour plus 2 (3) (4) (5) (6) (7) (7) balls in contrast colour●

Or 4 (6) (8) (11) (13) (15) (16) 28 gram hanks of "Patricia Roberts Shetland" in main colour plus 2 (2) (3) (4) (4) (5) (5) hanks in contrast colour●

A pair each of size 2¼mm and 2¾mm Aero knitting needles; a fine cable needle●

TENSION 16 stitches to 5 centimetres (2 inches) and 28 rows to 6 centimetres (2½ inches) over the stripe pattern using size 2¾mm needles. Over the cable pattern work at a tension of 22 stitches — 1 repeat to 5.5 centimetres (2¼ inches) and 20 rows to 5 centimetres (2 inches) using size 2¾mm needles●

If you cannot obtain the correct tension using the size needles suggested, use larger or smaller ones accordingly●

ABBREVIATIONS K., knit● p., purl● st., stitch● tog., together● dec., decrease (by working 2 sts. tog.)● inc., increase (by working twice into same st.)● cable 6, slip next 3 sts. onto cable needle and leave at front of work, k.3, then k.3 from cable needle● cr.3rt., cross 3 right thus, slip next st. onto cable needle at back of work, k.2, then k.1 from cable needle● cr.3lt., cross 3 left thus, k. into back of 3rd st. on left hand needle, then k. into front of 1st and 2nd sts.● m., main colour● c., contrast colour● double rib is k.2 and p.2 alternately● up 1, pick up the loop which lies between the needles, slip it onto left hand needle, then k. into back of it●

NOTE The instructions are given for the 2 year size. Where they vary work the figures in the first brackets for the 4 year size; those in the second bracket for the 6 year size; those in the third brackets for the 9 year size; those in the fourth brackets for the 12 year size; those in the fifth brackets for the woman's size and those in the sixth brackets for the man's size●

Special Note: For easier working, before commencing work read through the pattern and underline the number of sts. or rows to be worked for the relevant size●

MEASUREMENTS The measurements are given in centimetres followed by inches in square brackets.

Sizes: 2 yrs (4 yrs) (6 yrs) (9 yrs) (12 yrs) (woman's) (man's)● Underarms: 61 [24½] (72 [28¾]) (82.5 [33]) (93 [37¼]) [104 [41½]) [114 [45¾]) Side seam: 22.5 [9] (25 [10]) (29 [11½]) (30 [12]) (34 [13½]) (42.5 [17]) (42.5 [17]) Length: 33 [13¼] (36 [14½]) (42.5 [17]) (50 [20]) (60 [24]) (68 [27¼]) (68 [27¼]) Sleeve seam: 20.5 [8¼] (25 [10]) (30.5 [12¼]) (37 [14¾]) (40.5 [16¼]) (43 [17¼]) (47.5 [19])

BACK With size 2¾mm needles and m. cast on 130(152) (174) (196) (218) (240) (240) sts. and work in cable pattern as follows:

1st row: K.3, p.4, k.6, *p.1, k.1, p.1, k.1, p.2, k.4, p.2, k.1, p.1, k.1, p.1 **, k.6; repeat from * until 7 remain, p.1, k.3, p.3.

2nd row: K.3, p.3, k.1, p.6, *k.1, p.1, p.1, k.2, p.4, k.2, p.1, k.1, p.1, k.1 **, p.6; repeat from * until 7 remain, k.4, p.3.

3rd row: P.3, k.3, p.1, k.6, *p.1, k.1, p.1, k.1, p.1, cr.3rt., cr.3lt., p.1, k.1, p.1, k.1, p.1 **, k.6; repeat from * until 7 remain, p.4, k.3.

4th row: P.3, k.4, p.6, *k.1, p.1, p.1, k.1, p.2, k.1, p.3, k.4, p.3, k.1, p.2, k.1, p.1, k.1 **, p.6; repeat from * until 7 remain, k.1, p.3, k.3.

5th row: P.3, k.3, p.1, cable 6, *p.1, k.1, p.1, k.1, cr.3rt., p.1, k.1, cr.3lt., k.1, p.1, k.1, p.1 **, cable 6; repeat from * until 7 remain, p.4, k.3.

6th row: P.3, k.4, p.6, *k.1, p.1, k.1, p.4, k.1, p.1, k.1, p.3, k.1, p.1 **, p.6; repeat from

* until 7 remain, k.1, p.3, k.3.

7th row: K.3, p.4, k.6, *p.1, k.1, p.1, cr.3rt., k.1, p.1, k.1, p.1, cr.3lt., p.1, k.1, p.1 **, k.6; repeat from * until 7 remain, p.1, k.3, p.3.

8th row: K.3, p.3, k.1, p.6, *k.1, p.1, p.2, k.1, p.1, k.1, p.1, p.3, k.1, p.1, k.1 **, p.6; repeat from * until 7 remain, k.4, p.3

9th row: K.3, p.4, k.6, *p.1, k.1, p.1, k.2, p.1, k.1, p.1, p.1, p.3, k.1, p.1, k.1 **, k.6; repeat from * until 7 remain, p.1, k.3, p.3..

10th to **14**th wrong side rows: Work as for 8th back to 4th wrong side rows.

11th row: P.3, k.3, p.1, k.6, *p.1, k.1, p.1, cr.3lt., k.1, p.1, k.1, p.1, cr.3rt., p.1, k.1, p.1 **, k.6; repeat from * until 7 remain, p.4, k.3.

13th row: P.3, k.3, p.1, cable 6, *p.1, k.1, p.1, k.1, cr.3lt., p.1, k.1, cr.3rt., k.1, p.1, p.1 **, cable 6; repeat from * until 7 remain, p.4, k.3.

15th row: K.3, p.4, k.6, *p.1, k.1, p.1, k.1, p.1, cr.3lt., cr.3rt., p.1, k.1, p.1, k.1, p.1 **, k.6; repeat from * until 7 remain, p.1, k.3, p.3.

16th row: As 2nd row.

The last 16 rows form the cable pattern.

Repeat them 2 (2) (3) (3) (4) (4) (4) times, then work the first 2 rows again.

Decrease row: K.6 (7) (8) (9) (10) (11) (11), *k.2tog, repeat from * ending last repeat k.6 (7) (8) (9) (10) (11) (11). — 100 (117) (134) (151) (168) (185) (185) sts. With m. p.1 row.

Now work in stripe pattern as follows:

1st row: With c. all k.

2nd row: With c. all p.

3rd and **4**th rows: With m. all k.

Repeat the last 4 rows 10 (13) (12) (14) (13) (23) (23) times more.

To shape the armholes: Continuing in stripe pattern, cast off 6 sts. at the beginning of the next 2 rows.

On 88 (105) (122) (139) (156) (173) (173) sts. work 13 (17) (13) (11) (17) (13) (13) rows in stripe pattern.

Increase row: With m. k. 3 (1) (2) (3) (4) (5) (5), *up 1, k.3; repeat from * ending last repeat up 1, inc. for first size, but for other sizes, k. (2) (3) (4) (5) (6) (6).-118 (140) (162) (184) (206) (228) (228) sts.

Now work in cable pattern as follows:

1st row: P.1, k.6, work from * on 1st cable pattern row until 1 remains, p.1.

2nd row: K.1, p.6, work from * on 2nd cable pattern row until 1 remains, k.1.

The last 2 rows set the position of the cable pattern given before***.

Work 24 (24) (40) (64) (84) (84) (84) rows in cable pattern as set.

To slope the shoulders: Cast off 34 (42) (50) (58) (66) (75) (75) sts. at the beginning of the next 2 rows.

Cast off the remaining 50 (56) (62) (68) (74) (78) (78) sts.

FRONT Work as given for back until *** is reached.

Work 19 (19) (31) (55) (67) (67) (67) rows in cable pattern as set.

Now divide the sts. for the neck: Next row: Pattern 36 (44) (56) (64) (80) (89) (89) and leave these sts. on a spare needle until required, cast off 46 (52) (50) (56) (46) (50) (50), pattern to end and continue on these 36 (44) (56) (64) (80) (89) (89) sts. for the left front shoulder

Left front shoulder: Continuing in pattern as set, dec. 1 st. at the neck edge on each of the next 2 (2) (6) (6) (14) (14) (14) rows.

On 34 (42) (50) (58) (66) (75) (75) sts. work 2 row, then cast off.

Right front shoulder: With right side of work facing rejoin yarn to inner edge of sts. left on spare needle and work to end of row, then work as given for left to front shoulder to end.

SLEEVES Both alike: With size 2¼mm needles and m. cast on 58 (62) (66) (70) (74) (78) (82) sts. and k.4 rows, then work 12 (16) (20) (24) (28) (28) (30) rows in double rib.

Change to size 2¾mm needles and work in stripe pattern with centre cable pattern as follows:

1st row: With m. k.21 (23) (25) (27) (29) (31) (33), then work from * to ** on 1st cable pattern row given for back, with m. k. to end.

2nd row: With m. k.21 (23) (25) (27) (29) (31) (33), work from * to ** on 2nd cable row given for back, pattern to end.

3rd row: With c. k. up to centre panel, with m. work from * to ** on 3rd cable row, with c. k. to end.

4th row: With c. p. up to centre panel, with m, work from * to ** on 4th cable row, with c. p. to end.

Continuing to work in stripes with centre panel in m. as given between * and ** on the 16 row pattern given for back, with m. k. 1 st. at each end of the next row and the 10 (12) (14) (17) (21) (25) (25) following 6th rows.

On 80 (88) (96) (106) (118) (130) (134) sts. work 9 (13) (23) (27) (15) (3) (19) rows.

Cast off 32 (36) (40) (45) (51) (57) (59) sts. at the beginning of the next 2 rows. Break off c.***

On 16 sts, with m. work 32 (36) (40) (44) (50) (56) (58) rows in cable pattern. Cast off.

Continued on page 118●

Hearts, bows and
vegetables adorn these
"Carmen" cotton knits.
Shirt, pants and dress by
'Frappe' from Patricia
Roberts Covent Garden.

CARMEN

MATERIALS For the longer sweater: Either 18 25 gram balls of "Patricia Roberts Fine Cotton " or 17 20 gram balls of "Patricia Roberts Angora" or 18 25 gram balls of "Patricia Roberts Kid Mohair" in main colour plus in any of these yarns, 5 balls in a., 3 balls in b. and 2 balls in each of the 3 other contrast colours●
For the short sweater: 11 balls of any of the yarns given above in main colour plus 3 balls in a., 2 balls in b and 1 ball in each of the 3 other contrast colours●
For the cardigan: 14 balls of any of the yarns given above in main colour, 4 balls in a., 2 balls in b. and c. and 1 ball in d. and e.; 5 buttons●
For any of these garments: A pair each of size 3¼mm, 2¾mm and 2¼mm Aero knitting needles●

TENSION 18 stitches and 24 rows worked (12 rows to view) to 5 centimetres (2 inches) over slipped stocking stitch, using size 3¼mm needles●
If you cannot obtain the correct tension using the size needles suggested, use larger or smaller ones accordingly●

ABBREVIATIONS K., knit● p., purl● st., stitch● tog., together● dec., decrease (by working 2 sts. tog)● inc., increase (by working twice into same st.) ● sl., slip● up 1, pick up the loop which lies between the needles, slip it onto left hand needle, then k. into back of it● y.r.n., yarn round needle● p.s.s.o., pass slip st. over● s.s.k., sl.1, k.1, p.s.s.o.● m.k., make knot: with appropriate colour, p., then k. into next st., turn, p.2, turn, with a. or e. as appropriate, p.2tog.● m.b., with m. p.1, y.r.n., p.1, turn, k.3, turn, p.3, pick up the loop originally worked into and slip it onto right hand needle, then pass the 3 sts. over this loop● r.s., right side● w.s., wrong side● bow – make thus, *with a. k.1, y.r.n., k.1 into next st., (turn, k.3, turn, k.1, with m. k.1, with a. k.1, turn, with a. k.1, with m. m.k., with a. k.1, turn, k.3) 4 times, turn with a. k.3, then turn and k. these 3 sts. tog.*, k. next st., then working into the following st., repeat from * to *● leaf – make thus, with b. working into next st. cast on 2 sts., then across these 3 sts. work as follows: K.1, y.r.n., k.1, y.r.n., k.1, (turn, cast off 1, y.r.n., k.1, y.r.n., k.2tog.) 3 times, turn, cast off 4● st.r., start radish thus, with m. k.1, y.r.n., k.1, y.r.n., k.1 all into next st., turn, p.5, turn, inc., k.1, then make tail, working into the next st., cast on 1 st., (then working into the st. just made k.1 and sl. this st. onto left hand needle) 11 times, then k.2tog. the last st. and original st., now k.1, inc.● c.r., complete radish thus, with e. k.2tog., k.3, k.2tog., turn, p.2tog., p.1, p.2tog., with m. sl.1, k.2tog., p.s.s.o.● m., main colour● a., first contrast● b., second contrast● c., third contrast● d., fourth contrast● e., fifth contrast● single rib is k.1 and p.1 alternately● s.s. stocking stitch is k. on the r.s. and p. on the w.s.● sl.s.s., slipped stocking stitch is sl.1 and k.1 alternately on r.s. and sl.1 p.wise p.1 alternately on w.s.●

NOTE Instructions in brackets are worked the number of times stated after the brackets. Special Note: When working radishes count the sts. of each radish as one st.●

MEASUREMENTS The measurements are given in centimetres followed by inches in brackets. The measurements for the cardigan are the same as for those for the short sweater●
Underarms – 110 (44)●Side seam: short: 22.5 (9) long: 42 (17)● Length: short: 41 (16½) long: 61 (24½)● Sleeve seam: short: 15 (6) long: 42.5 (17).●

SWEATERS

BACK With size 2¼mm needles and m. cast on 148 sts. and work 17 rows for the short sweater or 35 rows for the long one, in single rib. Now divide the sts. for the panels.
Next row: Rib 4, (up 1, rib 6) 11 times, leave these 81 sts. on a spare needle until required for left half back, rib 8 and leave these sts. on a spare needle until required for centre panel, (rib 6, up 1) 11 times, rib 4 and continue on these 81 sts. for the right half back.
Right half back: Change to size 3¼mm needles and work in pattern as follows: Use separate balls of m. at each side of the hearts, mushroom and turnip motifs and separate balls of a. for the 2 ribbon bands. When joining in and breaking off colours leave ends of approximately 8 centimetres (3 inches). On completion of each motif, thread the end into a bodkin and darn in the end, neatly finishing with a back st.
1st row: With m. (sl.1, k.1) 7 times, up 1, k.1, with a. k.3, with m. k.2tog., (sl.1, k.1) 17 times, up 1, k.1, with another ball of a. k.3, with m. k.2tog., (sl.1, k.1) 10 times, sl.1.
2nd row: With m. (p.1, sl.1 p.wise) 11 times, with a. k.3, with m. (sl.1 p. wise p.1) 11 times, with b. p.1, with another ball of m. (p.1, sl.1 p.wise) 7 times, with a. k.3, with m. (sl.1 p.wise, p.1) 8 times.
3rd row: With m. (sl.1, k.1) 7 times, sl.1, up 1, k.1, with a. k.1, with m. k.1, with a. k.1, with m. k.2tog., k.1, (sl.1, k.1) 5 times, with b. k.3, with m. (k.1, sl.1) 10 times, up 1, sl.1, with a. k.1, with m. k.1, with a. k.1, with m. k.2tog., with m. (k.1, sl.1) 10 times.
4th row: With m. (sl.s.s.7, m.b.) twice, sl.s.s.5, with a. k.1, with m. m.k., with a. k.1, (with m sl.s.s.7, m.b.) twice, sl.s.s.5, with b. p.5, with m. sl.s.s.5, m.b., sl.s.s.5, with a. k.1, with m. m.k., with a. k.1, with m. sl.s.s.17.
The last 4 rows set the position of the pattern given in the chart. Now work the **5th** to **90th** pattern rows for the short sweater or **166**th rows for the long one, from the chart. Work 1 extra row here when working left half back or right half front. Mark the end of the last row with a coloured thread.
To shape the armhole: Maintaining the continuity of the pattern as set, cast off 4 sts. at the beginning of the next row, then dec. 1 st. at the same edge on each of the next 11 rows.
On 66 sts. pattern 70 rows.
To slope the shoulder: Cast off 10 sts. at the beginning of the next row and the 3 following alternate rows. On 26 sts. work 1 row, then cast off.
Left half back: Work as given for right half back, noting the variation in the rows before shaping the armhole.
Centre panel: With right side of work facing rejoin yarn to the 8 sts. on stitch-holder for centre panel and using size 2¾mm needles work as follows:
1st row: *With m. k.4, with a. k.4.
2nd row: *With a. k.4, with m. p.4.
3rd row: *With m. k.4, with a. p.4.
4th row: *With a. k.4, with m. p.4.
5th row: *With a. k.4, with m. k.4.
6th row: *With m. p.4, with a. k.4.
7th row: *With m. p.4, with a. k.4.
8th row: *With m. p.4, with a. k.4.
These 8 rows form the pattern; repeat these 8 rows 18 times more for the short sweater or 26 times more for the long one, then cast off. Neatly sew the centre panel in position – by the invisible seam method.

Neckband: With right side of work facing rejoin m. and using size 2¼mm needles pick up and k. 50 sts. from back neck edge. Work 11 rows in single rib, then cast off in rib.

FRONT Work as given for the back until the armhole shaping has been worked on the right half back – reading left half front for right half back and right half front for left half back.
**Left half front continued: On 66 sts. pattern 41 rows.
Neck shaping: Continuing in pattern, cast off 10 sts. at the beginning of the next row, then dec. 1 st. at the same edge on each of the next 16 rows.
On 40 sts. pattern 12 rows.
To slope the shoulder: Cast off 10 sts. at the beginning of the next row and the 2 following alternate rows.
On 10 sts. work 1 row, then cast off.
Right half front: Work as given for left half front noting the variation in the number of rows, before shaping the armhole.
Centre panel: Work the 8 pattern rows given for back 15 times for the short sweater or 23 times for the long one, then cast off. Neatly sew centre panel in position by the invisible seam method.
Neckband: With right side of work facing rejoin m. and using size 2¼mm needles pick up and k. 23 sts. from left front neck edge, 22 sts. from centre front and 23 sts. from right front neck edge. – 68 sts. Work 11 rows in single rib, then cast off in rib.
Pocket backs: 2 alike: For the longer sweater: With size 2¾mm needles and a. cast on 40 sts. and work 50 rows in s.s., then cast off.

SLEEVES Both alike: With size 2¼mm needles and m. cast on 55 sts. and work 11 rows for short sleeves or 23 rows for long ones in single rib.
Increase row: Rib 3, *up 1, rib 2;repeat from * to end. – 81 sts.
Change to size 3¼mm needles and work 60 rows for short sleeves or 180 rows for long ones in pattern as given in chart. Mark each end of the last row with coloured threads.
To shape the sleevetop: Continuing in pattern as set, dec. 1 st. at each end of next row and the 19 following alternate rows.
On 41 sts. work 1 row.
Cast off 3 sts. at the beginning of the next 10 rows. Cast off the remaining 11 sts.
Gussets Both alike: With size 2¼mm needles and m. cast on 24 sts. and work 18 rows in single rib for short sweater or 36 rows for long sweater.
Change to size 2¾mm needles, join in a. and work in pattern as follows:
1st row: *With m. k.4, with a. k.4; repeat from * to end.
2nd to 8th rows: Repeating from * on each row, work as given for centre panel on back.
Repeat the last 8 rows 8 times more for short sweater or 16 times for long one, then work the first 4 rows again. Mark each end of the last row with coloured threads.**
Pattern 50 rows for short sleeves or 150 rows for long ones as set.
For long sleeves only: Next row: With m. *k.2tog., k.1; repeat from * to end. – 16 sts.
With size 2¼mm needles and m. work 12 rows for short sleeves or 23 rows for long ones in single rib, then cast off.

MAKING UP Do not press. Join shoulder seams. Set in sleevetops, matching the marking threads on back and front with those on sleeves. Sew gussets in place at side seams and underarms so that the marking threads align with those at underarms. For longer sweater, inset pockets in seam, above ribbing, between front and gussets. ●

CARDIGAN

BACK As given for short sweater.

LEFT FRONT With size 2¼mm needles and m. cast on 72 sts. and work 17 rows in single rib.

Increase row: (Rib 4, up 1, rib 4) 9 times. – 81 sts.

Now work as given for right half back of short sweater until the armhole shaping has been worked. Then work as given for the left half front of sweater from ** to end.

Neckband: With right side of work facing rejoin m. and using size 2¼mm needles pick and k. 44 sts. from neck edge. Work 11 rows in single rib, then cast off in rib.

Buttonband: With side 2¼mm needles and m. cast on 10 sts. and work 2 rows in single rib. Join in a.

1st row: With a. k.4, with m. (k.1, p.1) 3 times.

2nd row: With m. (k.1, p.1) 3 times, with a. p.4.

3rd and **4**th rows: As 1st and 2nd rows.

5th row: With m. (k.1, p.1) 5 times.

6th to **8**th rows: As 5th row.

Repeat the last 8 rows 17 times more then with m. rib 2 rows. Cast off in rib.

RIGHT FRONT Work as given for left front until the inc. row has been worked. Then work as given for right half back of short sweater, until the armhole shaping has been worked, noting the variation in the number of rows, then work as given for left half front of sweater from ** to end.

Neckband: As given for left front neckband.

Buttonhole band: With size 2¼mm needles and m. cast on 10 sts. and work 2 rows in single rib, then as follows:

1st row: With m. (k.1, p.1) 5 times.

2nd to **4**th rows: As 1st row.

5th row: With m. (k.1, p.1) 3 times, with a. k.4.

6th row: With a. p.4, with m. (k.1, p.1) 3 times.

7th and **8**th rows: As 5th and 6th rows.

4 Buttonhole rows: With m. rib 5, turn, rib 5, turn, rib 5, break off m., rejoin it to the other set of 5 sts. and rib across these 5 sts., turn, rib 5, turn, rib 5, turn and rib across all 10 sts.

Now beginning with the 5th pattern row above pattern 28 rows, then work the 4 buttonhole rows again.

Repeat the last 32 rows 3 times more. Work the 5th to 8th pattern rows, then with m. rib 2 rows. Cast off in rib.

SLEEVES Work long sleeves given for the sweater.

MAKING UP Do not press. Join shoulder seams. Join side seams. Sew row ends of gussets to row ends of sleeves up to marking threads. Neatly sew sleeves in place. Sew frontbands in place. Sew on buttons. ●

■ =	**m**
■ =	**a**
■ =	**b**
☐ =	**c**
■ =	**d**
■ =	**e**
I =	**sl.**
V =	**up1**
⋏ =	**k.2 tog.**
λ =	**s.s.k.**
◊ =	**m.b.**
o =	**m.k.**
^ =	**p. on r.s. k. on w.s.**
ε =	**st. r.**
→ =	**p.7**
← =	**k.7**
Ω =	**c.r.**
X =	**leaf**
⋈ =	**bow**

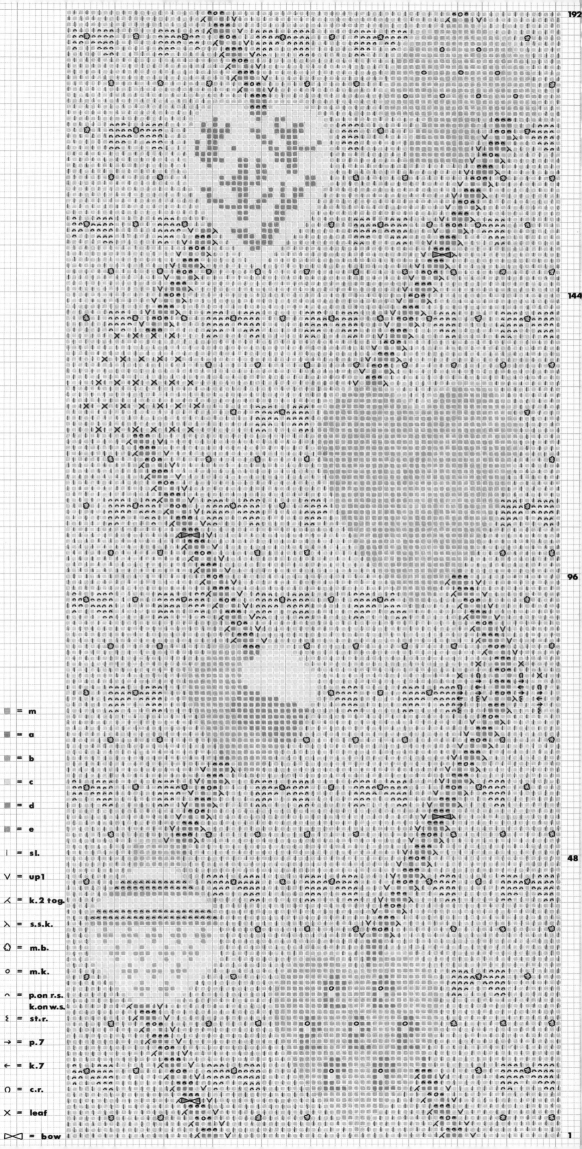

"Mikado" waisted cardigans and "Carmen" sweater knitted in fluffy angora. Wear them with glamorous 'Catherine Walker' evening skirts and 'Butler and Wilson' jewellery.

MIKADO

MATERIALS Either 13 20 gram balls of "Patricia Roberts Angora" in main colour plus 3 balls in contrast a. and 1 ball in each of the 4 other contrast colours; the kits include special ½ balls of c, d and e.●
Or 14 25 gram balls of "Patricia Roberts Kid Mohair" in main colour, 4 balls in contrast a. and 1 ball in each of the 4 other contrast colours●

A pair each of size 3¼mm and 3¾mm Aero knitting needles; 3 buttons; shoulder pads●

TENSION The tension is based on a stocking stitch tension of 12 stitches and 16 rows to 5 centimetres (2 inches) using size 3¾mm needles●

If you cannot obtain the correct tension using the size needles suggested, use larger or smaller ones accordingly●

ABBREVIATIONS K., knit● p., purl● st., stitch● tog., together● dec., decrease (by working 2 sts. tog.)● inc., increase (by working twice into same st.)● s.s., stocking stitch is k. on the right side and p. on the wrong side● single rib is k.1 and p.1 alternately● y.r.n., yarn round needle● sl., slip● p.s.s.o., pass sl.st. over● up 1, pick up the loop which lies between the needles, slip it onto left hand needle, then k. into the back of it● m.b., make bobble, thus, with a k.1, y.r.n., k.1, turn, k.3, turn, p.3, pick up the loop originally worked into and slip it onto right hand needle, then pass the 3 sts. just knitted over this loop● cable 8, slip next 4 sts. onto cable needle and leave at front of work. k.4, then k.4 from cable needle● s.s.k., sl.1, k.1, p.s.s.o.● r.s., right side● w.s., wrong side● bow — make thus, *with b. k.1, y.r.n., k.1 into next st., (turn, k.3, turn, k.1, with m. k.1, with b. k.1, turn, with b. k.1, with m. m.k., with b. k.1, turn, k.3) 4 times, with b. k.3, turn and k. these 3 sts. tog.*, k. next st., then working into the following st., repeat from * to *● m.k., make knot, p. into front then back of next st., turn, k.2, turn with b. p. 2tog.● m., main colour ● a., first contrast● b., second contrast● c., third contrast● d., fourth contrast● e., fifth contrast●

MEASUREMENTS The measurements are given in centimetres followed by inches in brackets●
Underarms — fastened 105 (42)● Side seam 44 (17½)● Length 64 (25½)● Sleeve seam 44 (17) long● Short — 15 (6)●

BACK With size 3¼mm needles and m. cast on 134 sts. and work 11 rows in single rib.
Change to size 3¾mm needles and divide the sts. for the back as follows:
Next row: Rib 61 and leave these sts. on a spare needle until required for left half back, rib 12 and leave these sts. on a stitch-holder until required for cente back panel, rib to end and continue on these 61 sts. for the right half back.
Right half back: Now work in pattern as follows. Do not weave in the contrast colour, but do twist the colours over and under each other on the 4th st. after each bobble to avoid long floats.
1st row: With m. all k.
2nd row: with m. all p.
3rd row: With m. k.2, *with first ball of a. m.b., with m. k.7; repeat from * ending last repeat with m.k.2. Leave a. hanging for use on 15th pattern row.
4th row: With m. all p.
5th row: With m. all k.
6th row: with m. p.2, *k.2, p.5, k.2, p.7; repeat from * ending last repeat p.2.
7th row: With m. k.2, *p.3, k.3, p.3, k.7; repeat from * ending last repeat k.2.
8th row: With m. p.2, *k.4, p.1, k.4, p.7; repeat from * ending last repeat p.2.

9th row: With m. k.2, p.4, with second ball of a. m.b., *with m. p.4, k.3, with a. m.b., with m. k.3, p.4, with a. m.b.; repeat from * until 6 remain, with m. p.4, k.2. Leave a. hanging for use on 21st pattern row.
10th row: With m. p.2, *k.3, p.3, k.3, p.7; repeat from * ending last repeat p.2.
11th and **12**th rows: As 1st and 2nd rows.
13th to **17**th rows: As 1st to 5th rows.
18th row: With m. p.1, *k.2, p.7, k.2, p.5; repeat from * ending last repeat p.1.
19th row: With m. p.3, k.7, p.3, *k.3, p.3, k.7; p.3; repeat from * to end.
20th row: With m. k.3, p.7, *k.4, p.1, k.4, p.7; repeat from * until 3 remain, k.3.
21st row: With m. p.3, k.3, with second ball of a. m.b., with m. k.3, p.4, *with a. m.b., with m. p.4, k.3, with a. m.b., with m. k.3, p.4; repeat from * ending last repeat p.3.
22nd row: With m. k.3, p.7, k.3, *p.3, k.3, p.7, k.3; repeat from * to end.
23rd and **24**th rows: With m. k.1 row and p.1 row.
The last 24 rows form the pattern; repeat them once more, then work the first 12 rows again.
**Work the waist ribbing as follows: Next row: With m. *k.2tog., p.1, k.1, p.1; repeat from * 5 times more, k.2tog., pattern to end as set. — 54 sts.
Next row: Pattern 29 as set, then with m. p.1, *k.1, p.1; repeat from * to end.
Next row: Rib 25, then pattern to end as set.
Repeat these 2 rows 6 times more.
Next row: Pattern 29, then with m. *p.1, up 1, k.1, p.1, k.1; repeat from * until 1 remains, up 1, p.1. — 61 sts.******
Continuing in pattern on all 61 sts., pattern 56 rows.
To shape the armhole: Continuing in pattern as set, cast off 6 sts. at the beginning of the next row, then dec. 1 st. at the armhole edge on the 6 following alternate rows. On 49 sts. pattern 43 rows.
To slope the shoulder: Cast off 8 sts. at the beginning of the next row and the 3 following alternate rows. On 17 sts. work 1 row, then cast off.
Centre panel: With right side of work facing rejoin m. to the 12 sts. at centre back and using size 3¼mm needles work as follows:
1st row: K.1, p.1, k.8, p.1, k.1.
2nd row: P.1, k.1, p.8, k.1, p.1.
3rd to **6**th rows: Repeat 1st and 2nd rows twice.
7th row: K.1, p.1, cable 8, p.1, k.1.
8th row: As 2nd row.
9th to **12**th rows: Repeat 1st and 2nd rows twice.
Repeat these 12 rows 16 times more. Then cast off.
Left half back: With right side of work facing rejoin m. to inner edge of 61 sts. left on spare needle and work as follows: Use separate balls of m. and a. at each side of the heart motifs. When joining in and breaking off colours leave ends of approximately 8 centimetres (3 inches). On completion of each motif thread the end into a bodkin and darn in the end, neatly finishing with a couple of back sts.
1st row: With m. k.26, s.s.k., with b. k.1, with m. k.1, with b. k.1, with m. k.1, up 1, k. to end.
2nd row: With m. p.31, with b. k.1, with m. m.k., with b. k.1, with m. p.27.
3rd row: With m. k.2, (with a. m.b., with m. k.7) twice, with a. m.b., with m. k.4, with d. k.1, with m. k.1, s.s.k., with b. k.3, with m. k.1, up 1, k.3, (with a. m.b., with m. k.7) 3 times, with a. m.b., with m. k.2.
4th row: With m. p.32, with b. k.3, with m. p.1, with d. p.3, with another ball of m. p. to end.

The last 4 rows set the position of the pattern given in the chart. Now work the 5th to 60th rows from the chart. Continuing in pattern from the chart work as follows:
**For the waist ribbing . Next row: Pattern 29, with m. k.2tog., *p.1, k.1, p.1, k.2tog.; repeat from * to end. — 54 sts.
Next row: With m. rib 25 as set, then pattern to end from chart as set.
Next row: Pattern 29, with m. rib to end.
Repeat the last 2 rows 6 times more.
Next row: P.1, up 1, *k.1, p.1, k.1, p.1, up 1; repeat from * 5 times more, pattern to end as set. — 61 sts.******
On all 61 sts. pattern 57 rows.
To shape the armhole: Work as given for right half back armhole shaping to end.
Neatly sew cabled panel in place at centre back, using the invisible seam method.
LEFT FRONT First work the pocket back: With size 3¾mm needles and a. cast on 32 sts. and work 55 rows in single rib, then leave these sts. on a spare needle until required.
With size 3¼mm needles and m. cast on 61 sts. and work 12 rows in single rib.
Change to size 3¾mm needles and work 34 rows in pattern from chart as given for left half back.
For the pocket edge: Continuing in pattern as set, cast off 12 sts. at the beginning of the next row, then dec. 1 st. at the same edge on each of the next 20 rows.
On 29 sts. work 4 rows.
Next row: Pattern as set across these 29 sts., then onto the same needle, with m. p. across the 32 sts. of pocket back. — 61 sts.
Work as given for right half back from ** to **.
On all 61 sts. pattern 36 rows.
***To slope the front edge: Continuing in pattern as set, dec. 1 st. at the end — front edge — on the next row and the 4 following 4th rows. On 56 sts. pattern 3 rows.
To shape the armhole and to slope the front edge: Continuing to dec. at front edge on every 4th row as set, cast off 6 sts. at the beginning — armhole edge — on the next row, then dec. 1 st. at the same edge on the 6 following alternate rows.
Pattern 32 rows, decreasing at neck edge as before. On 32 sts. pattern 11 rows.
To slope the shoulder: Cast off 8 sts. at the beginning of the next row and the 2 following alternate rows. On 8 sts. work 1 row, then cast off.
Pocket top: With right side of work facing rejoin m. and using size 3¼mm needles pick up and and k. 36 sts. from pocket edge. Work 5 rows in single rib, cast off in rib.
RIGHT FRONT First work the pocket back: With size 3¾mm needles and a. cast on 32 sts. and work 56 rows in single rib, then leave these sts. on a spare needle until required.
With size 3¼mm needles and m. cast on 61 sts. and work 12 rows in single rib.
Change to size 3¾mm needles and work 35 rows in pattern as given for right half back.
For the pocket: Continuing in pattern as set, cast off 12 sts. at the beginning of the next row, then dec. 1 st. at the same edge on each of the next 20 rows.
On 29 sts. work 3 rows.
Next row: With m. p. across the 32 sts. of pocket back, then onto the same needle, pattern across the 29 sts. — 61 sts.
Work as given for left half back from ** to ** On 61sts. pattern 37 rows.
Now work as given for left front from *** to end, including the pocket top.
Frontbands: With size 3¼mm needles and m. cast on 12 sts. and work 52 rows in single rib.

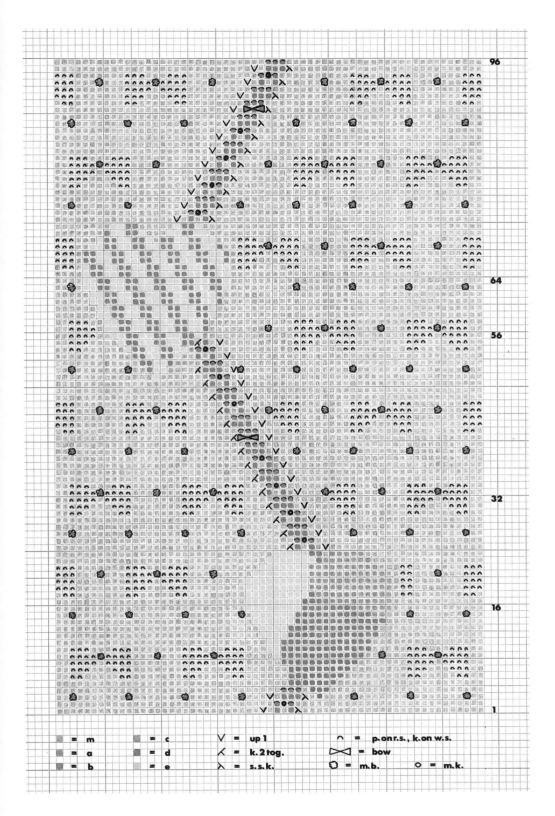

= m	= c	V = up 1	∩ = p. on r.s., k. on w.s.
= a	= d	⟋ = k. 2 tog.	⋈ = bow
= b	= e	⟍ = s.s.k.	⊕ = m.b. ○ = m.k.

MATERIALS 11 50 gram balls of "Patricia Roberts Cotton No. 2" in main colour, plus 3 25 gram balls of "Patricia Roberts Fine Cotton" in contrast a. and 1 ball in each of the 4 other contrast colours● A pair each of size 3mm, 3¼mm and 3¾mm Aero knitting needles; 3 buttons; shoulder pads●

TO WORK As given for main pattern, until the sleeves are reached.

SHORT SLEEVES Both alike: With size 3¼mm needles and m. cast on 70 sts. and work 15 rows in single rib.

Increase row: Rib 2, * up1, rib 3; repeat from * ending last repeat rib 2. —93sts.

Work 34 rows in spot pattern given for right half back.

To shape the sleeve top: Work as given for long sleeves to end, when 21 sts. will remain.

Next row: With m., * sl.1, k.2tog., p.s.s.o.; repeat from * to end. —7 sts. Cast off.

TO COMPLETE Work as given for main pattern to end.   ●

1st Buttonhole row: Rib 4, cast off 4, rib to end.

2nd Buttonhole row: Rib 4, turn, cast on 4, turn, rib to end.

Rib 22 rows.

Repeat the last 24 rows once more, then work the 2 buttonhole rows again.

Rib 320 rows.

Join shoulder seams. Neatly sew frontbands in place so that the last buttonhole is in line with last front edge dec. on right front edge. Correct length of band, casting off when correct length is assured.

SLEEVES: Both alike: With size 3¼mm needles and m. cast on 53 and work 32 rows in single rib.

Change to size 3¾mm needles and work 12 rows in pattern as given for right half back.

Continuing in pattern as set and working the extra sts. into the pattern as they occur, inc. 1 st. at each end of the next row and the 15 following 6th rows. On 85 sts. pattern 5 rows.

To shape the sleeve top: Cast off 6 sts. at the beginning of the next 2 rows, then dec. 1 st. at each end of the next row and the 6 following 4th rows, then at each end of the 11 following alternate rows.

Work 1 row.

Cast off 3 sts. at the beginning of the next 8 rows. Cast off the remaining 13 sts.

MAKING UP Join side seams so that the last 24 rows of pocket backs form part of side seam. Sew erest of pocket backs and row ends of pocket tops in position. Join sleeve seams. Set in sleeves. Sew on buttons. Catch shoulder pads in place.   ●

For glitzy evenings, wear
"Tinsel" with its flattering
waist and peplum, with
'Butler and Wilson'
jewellery.

"Rita", right, glamorous
and boldly patterned has
an open neck and choice of
neckband or collar. May
also be worked in
lambswool or shetland.
"Jane", left, knitted in
lurex is just "Plain"
stylish.

TINSEL

MATERIALS 13 25 gram balls of either "Patricia Roberts Lurex No.2" or "Fine Cotton" in main colour and 2 balls of the same yarn in each of the 4 contrast colours● A pair each of size 2¼mm. and 2¾mm. Aero knitting needles● shoulder pads optional●

TENSION 32 stitches and 52 rows to 10 centimetres (4 inches) over the stripe pattern and 32 stitches and 44 rows to 10 centimetres (4 inches) over the checker pattern using size 2¾mm. needles and 2 strands of lurex or 1 strand of cotton●
If you cannot obtain the correct tensions using the size needles suggested, use larger or smaller ones accordingly●

ABBREVIATIONS K., knit● p., purl● st., stitch● tog., together● dec., decrease (by working 2 sts. tog)● inc., increase (by working twice into same st.)● single rib is k.1 and p.1 alternately● double rib is k.2 and p.2 alternately● m., main colour● a., first contrast● b., second contrast● c., third contrast● d., fourth contrast●

NOTES Instructions in brackets are worked the number of times stated after the brackets●
When using lurex the yarn is used double throughout ie. 2 strands together●

MEASUREMENTS The measurements are given in centimetres followed by inches in brackets.
Underarms 110 (44)● Side seam 34 (13½)● Length 51 (20¼)● Sleeve seam 34 (13½)●

BACK With size 2¾mm needles and m. noting that 'Lurex' is used double throughout – cast on 242 sts. and work in checker pattern as follows:
1st row: K.3, *p.4, k.4; repeat from * ending last repeat k.3.
2nd row: P.3, *k.4, p.4; repeat from * ending last repeat p..3.
3rd and **4**th rows: As 1st and 2nd rows.
5th row: As 1st row.
6th row: K.3, *p.4, k.4; repeat from * ending last repeat k.3.
7th row: P.3, *k.4, p.4; repeat from * ending last repeat p.3.
8th and **9**th rows: As 6th row and 7th row.
10th row: As 6th row.
Repeat the last 10 rows 4 times more.
Decrease row: K.2, *k.2tog., k.1; repeat from * to end. – 162 sts. K.1 row.
Change to size 2¼mm needles and work as follows:
1st row: With m. (k.2, p.2) 17 times, k.1, join in a., with a. k.24, with another ball of m. k.1, (p.2, k.2) 17 times.
2nd row: with m. (p.2, k.2) 17 times, p.1, with a. p.24, with m. p.1, (k.2, p.2) 17 times.
3rd row: With m. (k.2, p.2) 17 times, still with m. k.26, (p.2, k.2) 17 times.
4th row: With m. (p.2, k.2) 17 times, p.1, still with m. k.24, p.1, (k.2, p.2) 17 times.
5th to **8**th rows: As 1st to 4th rows, but using b. instead of a.
9th to **12**th rows: As 1st to 4th rows, but using c. instead of a.
13th to **16**th rows: As 1st to 4th rows, but using d. instead of a.
These 16 rows form the stripe sequence.
Next row: With m. rib 67 as set, with a. k.28, with m. rib 67 as set.
Next row: With m. rib 67, with a. p.28, with m. rib 67.
Next row: With m. rib 65, k.32, rib 65.
Next row: With m. rib 65, k.32, rib 65.
Thus continuing in stripe sequence as set, pattern 38 rows, working 2 sts. less in rib at each side and 4sts. more in stripe pattern at centre on every alternate row. This

completes the ribbed side panels.
Change to size 2¾mm needles. Now continuing on all 162 sts. in stripe pattern only work 16 rows straight.
Inc. 1st. at each end of the next row and the 7 following 6th rows. – 178 sts. Mark each end of the last row with coloured threads to denote armhole.**
Work 85 rows in stripe pattern.
To slope the shoulders: Cast off 56 sts. at the beginning of the next 2 rows. Cast off the remaining 66 sts.

FRONT Work as given for back until ** is reached.
Work 58 rows in stripe pattern.
Now divide the sts. for the neck: Next row: Pattern 81, and leave these sts. on a spare needle until required for right front shoulder, cast off 16 sts., work to end and continue on these 81 sts. for the left front shoulder.
Left front shoulder: To shape the neck: Dec. 1 st. at the neck edge on each of the next 25 rows. On 56 sts. work 1 row.
To slope the shoulder: Cast off.
Right front shoulder: With right side of work facing rejoin yarn to inner edge of sts. left on spare needle and work to end of row, then work as given for left front shoulder to end.
Neckband: First join right shoulder seam. With right side of work facing rejoin m. to left front shoulder and using size 2¼mm needles pick up and k. 29 sts. from left front neck edge, 16 sts. from centre front and 29 sts. from right front neck edge and 66 sts. from back neck edge. – 140 sts.
K. 5 rows, then cast off loosely.

SLEEVES Both alike: First join left shoulder seam. With right side of work facing rejoin m. and using size 2¾mm needles pick up and k. 106 sts. between the marking threads on back and front.
With m. k.1 row.
Join in a. and work 30 rows in stripe pattern only as for back.
Continuing in stripe pattern, dec. 1 st. at each end of the next row and the 15 following 4th rows.
On 74 sts. work 3 rows, ending with a contrast colour stripe.
Now work in stripe and rib pattern as follows: Change to size 2¼mm needles.
1st row: With m. all k.
2nd row: With m. k.36, p.2, k.36.
3rd row: With contrast, k.36, join in a separate ball of m., with m. k.2, with contrast k.36.
4th row: With contrast p.36, with m. p.2, with contrast p.36.
5th and **6**th rows: As 1st and 2nd rows.
7th row: With contrast k.34, with m. p.2, k.2, p.2, with contrast k.34.
8th row: With contrast p.34, with m. rib 6, with contrast p.34.
9th row: With m. k.34, p.2, k.2, p.2, k.34.
10th row: With m. k.32, p.2, k.2, p.2, k.2, p.2, k.32.
11th row: With contrast k.32, with m. rib 10, with contrast rib 32.
12th row: With contrast p.32, with m. rib 10, with contrast rib 32.
Thus working 2 sts. less in stripe pattern at each side and 4 extra sts. in rib at centre on each successive 4th row, as set, work a further 40 rows.
On all 74 sts. with m. k.2 rows.
With m. work 20 rows in single rib, then cast off.
To complete: Do not press. Join side and sleeve seams. Catch shoulder pads in place if required. ●

ZEE-ZEE

MATERIALS 20 25 gram balls of either "Patricia Roberts Fine Cotton", "Lambswool No. 1" or "Lurex No. 2"●
A pair each of size 2¼mm and 2¾ mm Aero knitting needles●
TENSION As for "Tinsel" ●
ABBREVIATIONS As for "Tinsel"●
NOTES AND MEASUREMENTS As for "Tinsel"●
TO WORK Work exactly as given for "Tinsel" but all in one colour. ●

TRISTAN Continued from page 107
NECKBAND AND MAKING UP Set in right sleeve, so that the 6 sts. cast off at underarms are sewn to the row ends of the last 6 rows in stripe pattern on sleeves, so that the cable rows at the top of the sleeve are sewn to the shoulders and the 16 sts. cast off form part of neck edge. In the same way, sew the left sleeve in place at front only.
Neckband: With right side of work facing rejoin m. to sts. cast off at top of left sleeve, and using size 2¼mm needles, pick up and k. 18 (18) (22) (22) (28) (28) (28) sts. from left front neck edge – including sleeve panel, then 46 (52) (50) (56) (46) (50) (50) sts. from centre front, 18 (18) (22) (22) (28) (28) (28) sts. from right front neck edge and 50 (56) (62) (68) (74) (78) (78) sts. from back neck edge.
On 132 (144) (156) (168) (176) (184) (184) sts. work 7 (7) (11) (11) (15) (15) (19) rows in double rib. K.4 rows, then p.1 row and cast off loosely.
Completion: Join left back sleeve and shoulder seam continuing along neckband. Join sleeve seams. Join side seams, beginning 4 (5) (6) (7) (8) (9) (9) centimetres 1½ (2) (2¼) (2¾) (3) (3½) (3½) inches above cast on edges of back and front. Do not press. ●

SAILOR HAT

MATERIALS Either 2 25 gram balls of "Patricia Roberts Fine Cotton" or 2 28 gram hanks of "Patricia Roberts Shetland" in main colour, plus 2 balls or hanks in contrast colour c. and 1 ball or hank in contrast a. for the pom-pom●
A pair each of size 2¼mm and 2¾mm Aero knitting needles
●**TENSION** 16 stitches and 24 rows to 5 centimetres over the stripe pattern using size 2¾mm needles●
ABBREVIATIONS K., knit● p., purl● st., stitch● tog., together● double rib is k.2 and p.2 alternately● up 1, pick up the loop which lies between the needles, slip it onto left hand needle and k. into back of it● p.s.s.o., pass slip st. over● sl., slip● m., main colour● c., contrast colour● a. colour for pom-pom● inc., increase (by working twice into same st.)●
NOTE AND SIZES The instructions are given for the 2 years size followed by instructions in the first brackets for the 4 years size and instructions in the second brackets for both older children and adults●
TO WORK With size 2¼mm needles and m. cast on 112 (120) (128) sts. by the thumb method and k. 4 rows, then work 16 (20) (24) rows in double rib.
Increase row: Inc. in first st. * up 1, k.1 repeat from * to end – 224 (240) (256) sts. k. 1 row.

Change to size 2¾mm needles and work as follows:
With c. k.1 row, then p.1 row.
With m. k. 2 rows.
The last 4 rows form the pattern; repeat them 5 (6) (7) times more.
Continuing in stripe pattern as set, work the decrease rows as follows;
1st decrease row: With c. * k. 2 tog., k. 24 (26) (28) sl. 1, k.1, p.s.s.o.; repeat from * to end – 208 (224) (240) sts.
Pattern 3 rows.
2nd decrease row: With c. * k.2 tog., k. 22 (24) (26), sl.1 k.1, p.s.s.o.; repeat from * to end. – 192 (208) (224) sts.
Thus working 2 sts. less between the decreases on each successive repeat of the decrease row; repeat the last 4 rows 11 (12) (13) times – 16 sts.
With appropriate colour p.1 row
Next row: With m. * k.2 tog.; repeat from * to end – 8 sts.
Break off yarn leaving a long end; thread through the remaining sts. and draw up firmly, then using this end join row end edges. With a. make a pom-pom – 7.5 centimetres (3 inches) in diameter and sew in place. ●

RAOUL Continued from page 31
75th row: With a. h.b., *with e. p.1, s.s.k., p.1, k.1, with m. and a. c.4b., with m. k.1, with m. and a. c.4f., with e. k.1, p.1, s.s.k., p.1, with a. h.b.; repeat from * to end.
76th row: With a. k.2, *with e. rib 4, with a. k.2, with m. k.1, p.1, k.1, p.1, k.1, with a. k.2, with e. rib 4, with a. k.2; repeat from * to end.
77th row: With e. s.s.k., *still with e. rib 2, with m. and a. c.4b., with m. k.1, p.1, k.1, p.1, k.1, with m. and a. c.4f., with e. rib 2, s.s.k; repeat from * to end.
78th row: With e. rib 3, *with a. k.2, with m. k.1, (p.1, k.1) 4 times, with a. k.2, with e. rib 5; repeat from * ending rib 3.
79th row: With e. k.1, *with m. and a. c.4b., with m. m.st.9, with m. and a. c.4f., with e. k.1; repeat from * to end.
80th row: With a. k.3, *with m. m.st.13, with a. k.5; repeat from * ending last repeat with a. k.3.
81st row: With m. 2 onto 1, *with m. p.1, up 1, p.1, k.1, with a. h.b., with m. m.st.5, with a. h.b., with m. k.1, p.1, up 1, p.1, 4 onto 1; repeat from * ending last repeat 2 onto 1.
82nd row: With m. m.st.5, *with a. k.2, with m. m.st.5, with a. k.2, with m. m.st.9; repeat from * ending m.st.5.
83rd row: With a. inc., *up 1, with m. s.s.k., p.1, k.1, cr.3f., with m. m.st.3, cr. 3b., with m. k.1, p.1, k.2tog., with a. up 1, 1 into 3; repeat from * ending last repeat inc. instead of 1 into 3.
84th row: With a. k.3, *with m. (k.1, p.1) twice, with a. k.2, with m. p.1, k.1, p.1, with a. k.2, with m. (p.1, k.1) twice, with a. k.5; repeat from * ending k.3.
85th row: With m. k.1, *with m. and a. c.4f., with m. k.1, p.1, c.3f., with m. k.1, c.3b., with m. p.1, k.1, with m. and a. c.4b., with m. k.1; repeat from * to end.
86th row: With m. k.1, *p.1, k.1, with a. k.2, with m. k.1, p.1, k.1, with a. k.5, with m. k.1, p.1, k.1, with a. k.2, with m. k.1, p.1, k.1; repeat from * to end.
87th row: With m. k.1, *p.1, k.1, s.s.k., k.1, p.1, up 1, p.1, 4 onto 1, p.1, up 1, p.1, k.1, s.s.k., k.1, p.1, k.1; repeat from * to end.
88th row: With m. k.1, *p.1, k.1; repeat from * to end.

(vertical text left margin: RAOUL)

The last 88 rows form the pattern.
Work the first 4 (16) (30) (46) (46) rows again. Mark each end of the last row with coloured threads to denote armholes.
Pattern 40 (50) (60) (86) (86) rows more.
To slope the shoulders: Cast off 42 (49) (56) (71) (70) sts. at the beginning of the next 2 rows. Slip the remaining 45 (47) (49) (51) (53) sts. onto a stitch-holder until required.
Pocket backs 2 alike: With size 3mm needles and b. cast on 28 (32) (36) (40) (40) sts. and work 70 (80) (90) (100) (100) rows in stocking stitch. Cast off in rib.
FRONT Work as given for back until 111 (133) (143) (189) (189) rows have been worked in pattern.
Now divide the sts. for the neck: Next row: Pattern 57 (64) (71) (86) (85) and leave these sts. on a spare needle for right front shoulder, cast off 15 (17) (19) (21) (23), pattern to end and continue on these 57 (64) (71) (86) (85) sts. for the left front shoulder.
Left front shoulder: To shape the neck: Dec. 1 st. at the neck edge on each of the next 15 rows.
On 42 (49) (56) (71) (70) sts. pattern 5 (5) (19) (15) (15) rows. Cast off.
Right front shoulder: With right side of work facing rejoin yarn to inner edge of sts. on spare needle and work to end of row. Then work as given for left front shoulder to end.
Neckband: First join right shoulder seam. With right side of work facing rejoin m. and using size 2¼mm needles pick up and k. 20 (20) (34) (40) (40) sts. from left front neck edge, 15 (17) (19) (21) (23) sts. from centre front, 20 (20) (34) (40) (40) sts. from right front neck edge, then 45 (47) (49) (51) (53) sts. from back neck edge.
On 100 (104) (136) (152) (156) sts. work 9 (11) (11) (13) (13) rows in single rib, then cast off loosely in rib.
SLEEVES Both alike: With size 2¼mm needles and m. cast on 41 (49) (57) (65) (73) sts. and work 17 (21) (25) (29) (29) rows in single rib.
Increase row: Rib 3 (2) (5) (2) (6), *up 1, rib 5 (3) (2) (2) (2); repeat from * ending last repeat rib 3 (2) (6) (1) (5). – 49 (65) (81) (97) (105) sts.
Change to size 3mm needles and work 6 (6) (6) (12) (14) rows in pattern as given for back.
Continuing in pattern as set and working the extra sts. into the pattern as they occur, inc. 1 st. at each end of the next row and the 7 (11) (15) (23) (27) following 6th (6th) (6th) (4th) (4th) rows. On 65 (89) (113) (145) (161) sts. work 5 (5) (5) (23) (25) rows, then cast off.
MAKING UP Do not press. Join shoulder seams. Set in sleeves between marking threads on back and front. Join sleeve seams. Fold pocket backs in half and join row end edges. Join side seams inserting pocket backs above ribbing. ●

MATERIALS As given for "Raoul" on page 15, but adding one extra ball or hank in the colour chosen for the front bands and collar● 3 buttons●
TENSION As given for "Raoul" ●
ABBREVIATIONS As given for "Raoul"●
NOTE AND MEASUREMENTS As given for "Raoul"●
BACK As given for "Raoul", including pocket backs.
FRONT Work as given for back until 45 (53) (53) (91) (101) rows have been worked in pattern.
Now divide the sts. for the front opening. Next row: Pattern 59 (67) (75) (90) (90) and leave these sts. on a spare needle until required for right half front, cast off 11 (11) (11) (13) (13), pattern to end and continue on these 59 (67) (75) (90) (90) sts. for the left half front.
Left half front: Pattern 46 (50) (64) (42) (32) rows. Mark the end of the last row to mark armhole.
Pattern 19 (29) (25) (45) (55) rows.
To shape the neck: Continuing in pattern as set, cast off 2 (3) (4) (4) (5) sts. at the beginning of the next row. Then dec. 1 st. at the neck edge on each of the next 15 rows.
On 42 (49) (56) (71) (70) sts. pattern 5 (5) (19) (25) (15) rows, then cast off.
Right half front: With right side of work facing rejoin yarn to inner edge of sts. left on spare needle and work to end of row, then work as given for left front shoulder to end.
Buttonband: With size 2¼mm needles and b. cast on 12 (12) (12) (14) (14) sts. and work 66 (80) (90) (88) (88) rows in single rib, then leave these sts. until required.
Buttonhole band: With size 2¼mm needles and b. cast on 12 (12) (12) (14) (14) sts. and work 18 (24) (26) (28) (28) rows in single rib.
1st Buttonhole row: Rib 4 (4) (4) (5) (5), cast off 4, rib to end.
2nd Buttonhole row: Rib 4 (4) (4) (5) (5), turn, cast on 4, turn, rib to end.
Rib 20 (24) (28) (26) (26).
Repeat the last 22 (26) (30) (28) (28) rows once more, work the 2 buttonhole rows again, then rib 2 rows. Continue on these sts. for the neckband or the collar as required.
Neckband (optional): neatly sew button and buttonhole bands in place. Then rib across the 12 (12) (12) (14) (14) sts. of button or buttonhole band as appropriate for male or female, then onto same needle pick up and k. 22 (23) (38) (44) (36) sts. from right front neck edge, 44 (46) (48) (50) (52) sts. from back neck edge and 22 (23) (38) (44) (36) sts. from left front neck edge, then rib across the 12 (12) (12) (14) (14) sts. of buttonhole band.
On 112 (116) (148) (166) (152) sts. work 3 rows in single rib.**
Decrease row: Rib 2, sl.1, k.2 tog., p.s.s.o, rib until 5 remain, sl.1, k.2 tog., p.s.s.o., rib 2.
Rib 1 row.
Repeat the last 2 rows 3 (3) (3) (4) (4) times.
On 96 (100) (112) (146) (132) sts. work 1 row, then cast off loosely in rib using a size larger needle.
Collar (optional): Work as given for neckband until ** is reached.
Increase row: Rib 2, 1 into 3, rib until 3 remain, 1 into 3, rib 2.
Rib 3 rows.
Repeat the last 4 rows 2 (2) (2) (3) (3) times.
Cast off loosely, using a size larger needle the 124 (128) (160) (182) (168) remaining sts.
SLEEVES As for "Raoul".
MAKING UP As for "Raoul", then sew buttons in position ●

"Tinkerbell Too", for small children is very practical knitted in Shetland. Centre, "Rita" sweaters knitted in shetland left or lambswool right. For summer both designs work well in cotton.

TINKERBELL-TOO

MATERIALS For the sweater: Either 6 (7) 28 gram hanks of "Patricia Roberts Shetland" or 10 (11) 25 gram balls of "Patricia Roberts Fine Cotton" in main colour; plus 2 hanks or balls in first contrast a. and 1 in each of the 4 other contrast colours.●
For the skirt: Either 4 (5) 28 gram hanks of "Patricia Roberts Shetland" or 6 (7) 25 gram balls of "Patricia Roberts Fine Cotton" in main colour; plus 2 hanks or balls in first contrast and oddments left over from the sweater in the 4 other contrast colours●
A pair each of size 2¼mm and 2¾mm Aero knitting needles for the first size or size 2¾mm and 3mm needles for the second size●
TENSION Either 20 stitches and 20 rows to 5 centimetres (2 inches) over the twisted rib pattern using size 2¾mm needles for the first size or 18 stitches and 18 rows to 5 centimetres (2 inches) over the twisted rib using size 3mm needles for the second size. If you cannot obtain the correct tension using

the size needles suggested, use larger or smaller ones accordingly●
ABBREVIATIONS As given for "Tinkerbell"●
NOTE The instructions are given for the first size. Where they vary work the instructions in the brackets for the second size●
MEASUREMENTS The measurements are given in centimetres followed by inches in square brackets. Sizes 4 years (6 years)●
Sweater: Underarms 70 [28] (78 [31]) Side seam 22.5 [9] (26 [10½]) Length 40 [16] [45 [18]) Sleeve seam 22 [8¾] (29.5 [11¾])
Skirt: All round 70 [28] (78 [31])
Length 29 [11½] (31 [12½]).

BACK With size 2¼mm (2¾mm) needles and m. cast on 121 sts. and work 15 rows in single rib.
Work the increase row given for the back of adult version "Tinkerbell" – 141 sts.
Change to size 2¾mm (3mm) needles and work as given for back of adult version.

FRONT Commencing as given for back above work as given for adult version.

Neckband: As given for adult version but using size 2¼mm (2¾mm) needles instead of size 3¼mm.

SLEEVES Both alike: Using size 2¾mm (3mm) needles instead of size 4mm, work as given for adult version until the first 16 pattern rows have been worked.
Maintaining the continuity of the pattern and working the extra sts. into the pattern as they occur, inc. 1 st. at each end of the next row and the 15 following 4th (6th) rows.
On 85 sts. pattern 11 rows marking each end of the last row with coloured threads.
To shape the sleevetop: Work as given for adult version.

MAKING UP As for adult version.

SKIRT Back and front alike: With size 2¾mm (3mm) needles and m. cast on 141 sts. and work 104 rows in pattern as given for back of sweater.
Change to size 2¼mm (2¾mm) needles and work the decrease row and complete as for adults skirt.●